The Real Cheese Companion

Sarah Freeman's first job was with Penguin Books; she then worked on *Harper's Bazaar* (as it then was), *Wine and Food* (now defunct), and on *Harpers and Queen* as arts editor. She left to write a biography of Mrs Beeton (*Isabella and Sam: The Story of Mrs Beeton*), which she followed up some years later with *Mutton and Oysters: The Victorians and their Food*. In the course of writing and researching both these books, she tried out a huge number of recipes, not only traditional ones but her own, since devising new recipes is the aspect of cooking which she most enjoys. In recent years, she has compiled a series of best-selling cookery books for students and written *The Best of Modern British Cookery*, published in 1995.

The Real Cheese Companion

A GUIDE TO THE BEST HANDMADE CHEESES OF BRITAIN AND IRELAND

Sarah Freeman

LITTLE, BROWN AND COMPANY

BOSTON NEW YORK TORONTO LONDON

A LITTLE, BROWN BOOK

First published in Great Britain in 1998
by Little, Brown and Company (UK)

The photographs in this book are copyright © The Anthony Blake Photo Library,
with the following exceptions: Bruce Coleman Ltd/Fritz Prenzel (Anglo-Nubian
kids), John Sims (Toggenburg goat), Gerd Seeber (Friesians, Ardrahan), Peter
O'Toole (Leon Downey and Llangloffan), Travel Ink/Abbie Enock (Keen's,
Waterloo, Spenwood), and Robert Harding Picture Library (Blue Vinny).

A CIP catalogue record for this book
is available from the British Library

ISBN 0-316-88322-0

10 9 8 7 6 5 4 3 2 1

Little, Brown and Company (UK)
Brettenham House
Lancaster Place
London WC2E 7EN

CONTENTS

Acknowledgements

This book is a co-operative effort: I could not have written it without the help of the cheesemakers included, who not only offered me hospitality and gave me their time but also made the research more fun than anything I have ever attempted. I thank them all most warmly and sincerely. I also owe particular thanks to James Aldridge, Piers Feilden, Matthew Organ, Iain Meliss, and Polly Freeman for help of various kinds; to Eurwen Richards for technical advice; to David Natt for his contribution on wine; to Randolph Hodgson and Gerd Seeber for supplying photographs which show that cheese has a visual interest at least equal to its gastronomic appeal; to Vivien Bowler, Julia Charles, and Arianne Burnette at Little, Brown for their patience, humour, and – well, for being just wonderful; and finally to my husband, who came with me on some of my visits and ultimately made the whole project possible.

Introduction

The past two decades have seen a wonderful, if overdue revival of British handmade cheeses. I was brought up on post-war mousetrap and loved it, never having tasted anything better. Then came the revelation of Brie, Camembert and other imported French cheeses, followed by Mary Holbrook's rich goats' and sheep's cheeses, Veronica Steele's Milleens, the Curtises' Bonchester, flowing and creamy, from Scotland, and a little later Anne Wigmore's hard and semi-soft sheep's cheeses. Meanwhile, Patrick Rance launched a campaign for Real Cheese with *The Great British Cheese Book*, which Randolph Hodgson of Neal's Yard Dairy, James Aldridge at Beckenham, and others took up, scouring the country for traditionally made, unpasteurized cheeses. During the period of wartime rationing, only seven varieties, all hard and all pasteurized, were permitted: recovery did not begin for another generation, but now hundreds are made, ranging from fresh or mould-ripened soft, washed-rind, and blue to hard and semi-hard.

I set out to write this book in the spirit of discovery – not so much to discover the cheeses themselves, most of which I already knew, but to find out where and how they were made and what makes each different, in the belief that knowing a little about them enhances enjoyment. The result has turned out to be longer than I anticipated because every cheesemaker's method is individual and all have something particular to contribute. For reasons of space, it has not been possible to include them all, and I apologize to those I have omitted; however, the majority, in all their diversity, are here. A few come from families who have made cheese for generations; some are dairy-farmers who became depressed by the milk lake or saw cheese as a way of adding value to their quota; and others, rejecting the nine-to-five routine, have adopted it as a creative form of downshifting – although, as all would confirm, the hours they work are far longer than the office day.

In the course of my visits, just about every conceivable subject connected with cheese was discussed, from the importance of hygiene to the problems of marketing. The standard of hygiene everywhere, in small and larger dairies alike, is truly impressive and indeed is one of the reasons for the long hours cheesemakers work: washing and disinfecting the floor, vat, and every implement used can take almost as long as the cheesemaking itself. One of many points which arose in relation to marketing was that because of short shelf-life and the need for refrigerated transport, many soft cheeses are not widely distributed, but are sold only from the farms or locally; another was that, in spite of the popularity of grilled goats' cheese in restaurants and pecorino (sheep's cheese) for sprinkling, strong prejudice still exists in favour of cows' cheese. Although the best known traditional cheeses are cows', sheep's cheeses have a much longer history in this country: cows did not overtake sheep for dairying until the sixteenth century, when they prevailed because of their higher yield and because their milk has larger fat globules and thus is easier to separate for butter.

After cows' cheeses became the norm, the cheese eaten by most people was made partly or entirely of skimmed milk: the whole-milk cheeses which we now take for granted were luxuries for the better-off. Good low-fat cheeses are difficult to make, because as well as contributing to texture fat plays a major part in the development of flavour. However, three very low-fat traditional varieties plus one or two others are included here and I hope will encourage further experiment, not perhaps with skimmed but low-fat milk: Thelma Adams's Caerphilly, Caws Cenarth, made with morning milk only, is relatively low in fat yet tastes deliciously full and buttery.

For reasons of gastronomy as well as health, we also need a wider range of organic cheeses. The difference between organically and conventionally raised animal foods of all kinds, including milk, is startling: organic milk has almost as much flavour again as unpasteurized compared to pasteurized. Until recently, because there were so few of them, makers of organic cheese tended to concentrate on the ever-popular, long-matured Cheddar types, hence the depressingly narrow selection in organic shops. This is slowly changing: we now have a number of organic soft cheeses, two pecorino-style sheep's cheeses, one from Staffordshire and one from Ireland, goats' and sheep's feta, halloumi and a new cheese made with Duchy of Cornwall milk. However, there are no organic blue cheeses and only one white mould-ripened cheese, although several others are almost organic, notably Mary Holbrook's (page 71).

In fact, while we need many more cheeses of every kind, the lack of the white mould-ripened type is one of the most obvious; even more acute is the shortage of washed-rind varieties, of which we have only half a dozen altogether. The lack of washed-rind cheeses is perhaps a matter of tradition, but competition from the creamery-made versions in the supermarkets has also discouraged makers from committing themselves to the popular traditional types. One of the saddest results is that the authentic, crumbly Lancashire made with a double curd has become a rarity, and at the time of writing no one was making unpasteurized Red Leicester, which in its pasteurized form tastes of little more than the orange colouring (annatto). Excellent Cheshire and Caerphilly are made, but not enough, and only two people are currently making Dunlop-style cheese (one of which, sweet-milk, is organic: page 243).

Since by definition handmade or farmhouse cheeses cannot be made on a large scale, more cheese means more cheesemakers. At this stage I should perhaps define what I mean by handmade or farmhouse cheesemakers, since neither term always applies literally. Whereas some small-scale makers do in truth carry out every operation, even milling, by hand, others use machinery for part of or occasionally almost the whole process. To some makers, the *sine qua non* of making cheese is using the milk from their own herd or flock; others buy it in, either for lack of labour or because they work with relatively large quantities. I have included several creameries, all small by commercial standards but larger than the term 'farmhouse' might be supposed to imply, because they share the artisan maker's aim – namely, first-class quality; profit, beyond the need for viability, is incidental. First-class cheese, as with any other product, demands first-class material: the taste and quality of milk depends on the soil, standards of hygiene and husbandry, and the breed of animal, which is why I have commented on the type of country, the farms, and the livestock, as well as the cheesemakers themselves and their craft.

This kind of cheesemaking demands experience and judgement which have to be exercised on a daily basis rather than relying simply on technical expertise. Until now, cheesemakers were taught at agricultural colleges, by their mothers, or by consultants, informal or otherwise; some have learnt simply by means of books and their own experiments with a bucket and ladle in the kitchen. However, because of the small number of applicants, courses adapted to hand- as opposed to larger-scale creamery cheesemaking at the colleges have become few and far between. The Specialist Cheesemakers' Association was formed in 1989, initially to give support to makers using unpasteurized milk: this year a long-gestated plan has come to fruition and the Association is moving its headquarters to Harper Adams College, Newport, Shropshire, where advice for artisan producers will be available and, when building work is complete, courses specifically designed for their needs will be organized. This should do more than perhaps anything else to encourage recruits into the business and ensure that cheeses in the future are made to as high or an even higher standard than has already been achieved. It is also hoped that the Association will liaise with retailers so that the cheeses become more widely available in Britain and the world at large.

MILK, CHEESE, AND MICROBES

One of the cheesemakers whom I visited remarked, 'Cheesemaking is almost farming bacteria'. In fact, this was an understatement: he might more accurately have missed out the 'almost' and (since he makes blue cheese) have added 'and moulds'. If this sounds unattractive, it is worth remembering that the world is densely populated with microbes of many kinds: as well as the fact that they may be in food and drink, they inhabit the soil, air, our own intestines, and the stomachs of ruminant animals, who are not nourished by protein directly derived from the herbage they eat but from bacteria which feed on it in their stomachs.

The milk of carefully fed, healthy animals is sterile in the udder but picks up bacteria on the teats, from the surrounding atmosphere after milking, and later from the vessels in which it is transported. Some of the bacteria, far from being undesirable, play a crucial part in the development of flavour in the cheese; others are pathogenic. Milk is tested regularly: routine tests do not discriminate between the different kinds of bacteria, but with due precautions the total number can be kept far below the level at which they represent any possible threat to human health. The Specialist Cheesemakers' Association recommends a count only a tenth as high as the authorized maximum: with milk of this standard, and provided that it is maintained at this standard before use, pasteurization is unnecessary. It is also unnecessary for long-matured cheeses in which bacterial activity is much reduced; in addition there is an argument to the effect that the favourable bacteria in untreated milk act as a natural control over pathogens. On the other hand, pasteurization is essential in places where there is any risk of tuberculosis, which cannot be detected by the usual means, or if there is doubt about hygiene during transport. Some artisan makers who buy rather than produce their own milk pasteurize simply because it has been transported; the creameries invariably do so because their milk is not only transported but also comes from different sources. It should be stressed, however, that it is by no means the guarantee of safety that it is often taken to be because undesirable bacteria may enter the milk during processing. Therefore, *pregnant women and others who are immuno-compromised should not eat any cheese, whether pasteurized or not, which has been matured for less than four months* if they wish to be sure of avoiding listeria.

The 'real' cheese lamented by Patrick Rance differs from pasteurized cheese in having 'depth', by which it is meant that the taste is complex rather than simple, i.e. made up of a variety of different flavours. These develop as a result of the wide variety of bacteria naturally present in untreated milk, which cannot be, or up until now have not been, precisely reproduced by artificial means. However, as well as Real Cheeses there are a number of extremely good, or even excellent pasteurized ones: these include blues and washed-rind cheeses, where mould contributes as much as bacteria, others in which local factors combined with consummate cheesemaking seem to override the effect of pasteurization, and several made with a starter preparation containing a larger number of bacterial strains than is usual at present. Starters of this kind are now used by some of the larger creameries, with noticeable results, and offer the prospect of considerable improvement in the overall standard of pasteurized cheeses in the future.

BSE, as is well known, is caused by a mutant protein rather than an organism. It dogged me throughout my research for this book; at the time of going to press, nothing new has been reported, but I feel that I should emphasize that no one has succeeded in finding the protein in milk. Several of the cheesemakers who were using traditional calves' rennet were considering alternatives; most of those milking their own cattle said that they will make up their own feed in future. (Anyone who asks why dairy cows cannot be fed entirely on grass or its equivalent must remember that an animal expected to give a high yield of milk over a long period needs extra protein.) We are still living with salmonella in hens; if as a result of this second, far worse episode, greater support is given to organic farming and less intensive methods of agriculture in general, some good will come of it in the end.

CHEESEMAKING

The basic ingredients of cheese are milk, rennet, and salt. Starter has also been almost universally used in the last fifty years; before that, makers relied on the natural bacteria in the milk. Similarly, blue mould (*Penicillium roqueforti*) for blue cheese and white penicillin mould, which produces a white rind, are now inoculated into cheeses but originally occurred naturally: the blue entered through cracks in the rind, as the odd thread of accidental green or blue mould sometimes invades non-blue cheeses; also, an orange mould, *B. linens*, is rubbed over the surface of several Irish cheeses.

The composition of *milk* varies enormously: sheep's, goats' and buffaloes' milk is more homogeneous than cows'; sheep's and buffaloes' are higher in fat and more concentrated. Milk at the beginning and end of lactation is creamier than in the middle. Fat content is also influenced by feeding: a cow's morning milk may contain substantially less cream than in the evening, after she has been grazing all day. Fat can also be reduced, the proportion of saturated fats reduced, or the proportion of protein increased with certain concentrates. Increased protein is clearly of interest to cheesemakers, but those whom I asked about feeds were certainly not manipulating their milk in this way.

Starter inoculates the milk with several strains of lactic acid-producing bacteria, which may be introduced directly into the milk or via a culture. Milk contains about five per cent milk-sugars called lactose (the lactose is the reason milk rises when it boils). The bacteria feed on the lactose and produce acid: as they reproduce, the acidity of the milk or curd rises. If left for twenty-four hours or more, the milk can be curdled by the acid alone, as for fresh, so-called 'lactic' cheeses such as Highland crowdie; with rennet, it sets more firmly in only thirty to fifty minutes.

Traditional *rennet*, called chymosin, is an enzyme derived from a suckling calf's stomach; alternatives are a genetically engineered copy (Chymosin), which is approved by the Vegetarian Society, or extracts from moulds or plants. Partly because of BSE and vegetarianism, most makers favour mould extract, although purists and those whose cheeses need long maturing still use the traditional version, and a few have adopted Chymosin.

Salt, the last ingredient to be added, is needed for flavour. It also has the effect of drawing out moisture and inhibiting bacterial action.

Broadly defined techniques for making the different types of cheeses have evolved over the centuries, but as every maker adapts them to suit his or her own circumstances, there are in effect as many methods as there are makers (although some may be similar). With any method, the art of making good cheese is to balance the rate of bacterial growth with the action of the setting enzyme on the curd. To reproduce, bacteria need food, water, warmth, and a particular level of pH (acidity): different conditions favour different kinds of bacteria. Once the starter bacteria are added, everything the cheesemaker does will affect their behaviour: depending on the type of starter used, their activity will rise faster or more steadily and then drop towards the end of the make. At this stage, the cheesemaker will texture the curd for hard or semi-hard cheeses by cutting, breaking, or piling it in blocks; for soft cheeses, in contrast, it will be transferred to moulds with as little disturbance as possible. Salt will be added or the cheeses brined after moulding, or both; finally, depending on the type of cheese and the maker's method, the curd may be milled before moulding and pressing.

During ripening or maturing, a series of complex chemical reactions takes place. The bodies of the dead bacteria release enzymes which act as catalysts to give flavour. Fats and proteins break down, which also adds to the flavour, and further contributions to both flavour and texture are made by yeasts and moulds, either from the atmosphere or deliberately introduced. Mould-ripened cheeses soften because enzymes produced by the mould contribute to the breakdown of proteins and to the increase in pH, which draws calcium from the body of the cheese to the surface.

Temperature and humidity throughout the maturing period, and for the rest of a cheese's life, are as important to its eventual quality as the skill of the maker at an earlier stage. The moisture balance within the cheese affects the reactions taking place, which in turn, again, affect both texture and flavour. Cheeses exude moisture through the rind: a humid atmosphere or covering them with lard or wax are ways of preventing them from dehydrating. The reason for the traditional practice of wrapping cheeses in cloths is that the cloth absorbs and to some extent regulates moisture loss.

In most cases, I have described the individual cheesemakers' procedures with the entries, sometimes briefly, sometimes in more detail: the following, however, is a summary of the main basic methods.

The simplest method is that used for soft or unpressed cheese, which includes *fresh and white-rind varieties*; for convenience, I have referred to it as the *Coulommiers* method, although similar methods are just as traditional to Britain. The aim is to keep as much moisture as possible in the curd, which is therefore not cut at all, or only slightly. Rather than whey (the liquid part of the milk) being drawn off before moulding, the cheeses are left to drain in the moulds, with no pressure other than their own weight; this is called 'free-draining'. Fresh cheeses, as a general rule, should be eaten as soon as possible. For the white mould-ripened type, the penicillin which forms the rind is added, usually at the beginning with the starter or rennet, and the cheeses are packaged when the rind has developed, usually after ten to sixteen days; a further maturing period, varying from two to six weeks, is needed before the cheeses are ripe.

A moist curd is also needed for *semi-soft cheeses*, which are sometimes lightly pressed, and as a rule are matured for two to three months. This category includes *washed-rind cheeses*, which may be washed with cider or perry, wine, or brine, and those smeared with *B. linens* mould. Smearing or washing encourages micro-organisms to reproduce on the surface, thus giving rise to a second ripening process, which takes place from the outside inwards: water is not used because of its impurities, but the kind of liquid is relatively unimportant except insofar as it influences the species of microbe involved (salt, although discouraging to many, is tolerated by others). Washed-rind cheeses are the kind which proverbially smell of old socks; however, while the point of them is that they should be distinctive, the smell may be stronger and quite different from the taste.

Blue cheeses, most of which are also semi-soft, are not only inoculated with the mould but are also pierced to introduce extra air into the cheese as a way of controlling maturing. Stilton is matured for five to six weeks before piercing and allowed to develop a rind, whereas cheeses made by the Roquefort method are pierced at two to five days old and air excluded by wrapping them in foil when the blue has developed sufficiently. As mould flourishes in a high-acid environment, the curd is drained naturally and sometimes left with the whey for an extended period.

For *Cheddar*, the curd is cut very small and heated, or 'scalded', to about 40–41°C/104–106°F, both of which help to expel moisture and give the cheese a firm, hard texture; during scalding, the curd is stirred continuously to ensure even distribution of heat. It is then drained and textured by being cut into blocks and piled at the sides of the vat. Traditionally, the cheeses are finished by rubbing them with lard and wrapping them in cloth; maturing may be for as long as one to two years. Double Gloucester is made similarly but scalded to a lower temperature and matured more quickly.

Caerphilly is scalded, textured by cutting rather than blocking and piling, and brined; traditionally, it is eaten after only a few weeks, but Neal's Yard Dairy mature Duckett's for up to three months and Patrice Savage-Onstwedder (page 157) keeps hers for eight or longer.

North of England cheeses, such as Cheshire, Lancashire, and white Wensleydale, have a light, flaky, or crumbly texture and are often classified as *semi-hard*. The curd is cut, broken, or crumbled instead of being blocked and piled, as for Cheddar; the curd for Lancashire, the crumbliest, is made with a mixture of fresh and the previous day's, plus sometimes two-day-old curd. Maturing times vary from a few weeks to six months.

BUYING, KEEPING, AND SERVING CHEESES

Most of the cheeses included in this book are sold only at specialist shops or cheese-counters, where they will be freshly sliced to your order. Several people whose judgement I respect will say that pre-slicing makes no difference to the taste, and I would agree that the effect is less noticeable with some than others: some in fact are made with pre-slicing and supermarket sales in mind. Similarly, many cheesemakers welcome vacuum-packing because it increases shelf-life and helps the cheese to survive the wrong storage conditions. However, I maintain that unpasteurized cheese with a range of flavours will start to lose its subtlety and aroma from the moment of cutting, and that to be enjoyed at its best it should not be sliced until purchase. For the same reason, you should eat it as soon as possible: buy only as much as you think you will need and use any left over for cooking.

If a cheese has to be kept after it is purchased, or sent by post, a small whole one is a good idea; however, for immediate eating a slice from a large one is almost always a better choice because it will have been matured for longer and consequently have developed deeper flavours.

Most cheese-shops will encourage you to taste before buying. This not only enables you to try new cheeses but is also useful because one of the attractions of artisan products is that results vary. Apart from maturity, cheeses will differ according to the time of year or weather when they were made, or even the field in which the animals grazed, so the one that you thought you wanted may not in fact be as good as another on this particular occasion. As with fruit and vegetables, be flexible: buy according to judgement rather than plan.

Just as there are not enough cheeses or makers, so there is a lack of good cheese-shops. A few of the makers included here sell to supermarkets: according to one school of thought, there should be many more, but an opposing faction feels that this would be undesirable because it would threaten specialist cheese-shops. The fate of other independent shops gives substance to this fear; on the other hand, as Eurwen Richards points out, supermarkets can and do offer sales outlets in places where specialist shops would be out of the question. In general, various considerations, including care of the cheeses and the issue of pre-packing, small output, and the variable nature of specialist cheeses, make it questionable whether supermarkets will want to compete seriously in this area. As Eurwen says, 'Selling is possibly a greater problem with small-scale manufacturing than the making!'

Some cheeses from the north of England and Scotland are at present almost or completely unobtainable in the south; similarly, one of the Irish cheeses included cannot be bought in Britain. In cool weather, however, most cheeses can be sent by rail or post: contact the makers, but leave plenty of time, since small producers do not always have matured spare cheeses immediately available.

If cheese has to be kept, the best conditions for it are those in which it has been matured: for hard, semi-hard, and most semi-soft cheeses, these are 8–13°C/46–55°F, with eighty-five per cent or higher humidity. For most people, with no cellar and only a centrally heated house or refrigerator to choose from, this presents a problem. Both central heating and refrigeration are drying: keep the cheese wrapped in the waxed paper in which it was (or should have been) sold and, to increase humidity but maintain the circulation of air, place it in a loose-fitting, unsealed food-bag. It also helps to cover the cut surfaces of whole cheeses with clingfilm if you can make it stick without covering the rind. Then put it in a cool room or the boot of the car (this is Neal's Yard Dairy's suggestion); in hot weather, you will probably have to resort to the refrigerator. The garden or windowsill is not a good idea, since animals like cheese too. Soft cheeses should be wrapped similarly and kept chilled.

Most makers recommend chilling blue cheeses. Be particularly careful to wrap blue cheeses all over as mould spores spread readily not only to other cheeses but also to anything else near. If other cheeses develop mould on cut surfaces, just trim it off: the rest of the cheese will be unaffected.

I do not recommend freezing for preference, but many small, fresh sheep's and goats' cheeses and some white mould-ripened and blue cheeses, including Stilton, do in fact freeze satisfactorily. Defrost the cheese in the refrigerator and then leave it at room temperature for one to two hours before serving. Eat mould-ripened cheeses promptly, as ripening will be quicker than usual thereafter. It is, however, a mistake to try to ripen immature ones by this means: they must be ready to eat before freezing.

A large number of cheeses is not needed to make up a cheeseboard: what matters are quality and the relation of the cheeses to each other. A selection of three is quite enough: four gives an opportunity to include one which is particularly good just then but does not balance the rest quite as effectively as another. Generally speaking, cheeses which contrast in strength, taste and texture, preferably from different types of animal, will set each other off to advantage and create a satisfying whole. For example, you might choose Beenleigh Blue (sheep's), Ragstone or St Francis (white-rind goats'), and Lincolnshire Poacher or Staffordshire Organic (Cheddar-type); a fourth could be Wigmore (semi-soft sheep's), Wrydwell (semi-soft Jersey), or Lancashire (crumbly). A wonderful selection of Irish cheeses would be Mine-Gabhar (effectually organic white-rind goats'), Cashel Blue (cows'), and

Gabriel (hard cows') or Orla (organic hard sheep's), with Milleens (soft cows', rind smeared with *B. linens*) as a fourth. Another approach might be to choose at least two cheeses of different types and strengths but with background tastes in common, thus creating an underlying harmony against which their other characteristics can be better appreciated. This is often achieved with cheeses from the same area, or even the same farm: a very successful cheeseboard along these lines could be made up with St Cuthbert's Cave (mild but distinctive semi-soft cows'), mature Berwick Edge (hard and as strong as a blue), both from North Doddington Farm in Northumberland, with Innes Button (light, fresh goats') as a contrast. A similar example, this time of cheeses from different farms but adjacent areas, might be Bonnet (hard goats'), Lanark or Dunsyre Blue, and Bonchester. The better you know the cheeses, the more interesting and subtle the effects you can achieve: the possibilities are endless.

If you do not want to buy three cheeses, two, or even just one really good cheese is sufficient. A well balanced board of three or four does not need additions, but with only one or two contrast can be supplied or flavours followed through with fruit, nuts, or salad vegetables. Where applicable, I have given particular suggestions, sometimes from the makers themselves, with the entries: more general ones include apples, notably crisp, sharp/sweet James Grieve or Falstaff, with Cheddar or Cheddar-style cheeses; pears, grapes, or figs with blues or hard sheep's cheeses; strawberries with mild, soft goats' cheeses, and plum or cherry tomatoes and/or olives with almost any goats' cheese. An alternative to fresh fruit is fruit 'cheese', which is boiled down to a solid consistency and made with half as much sugar as jam. Walnuts are often served with blue cheeses; pecans are delicious with salty ones such as Isle of Mull; hazelnuts bring out sweet, earthy, nutty or mushroom-like tones. Mellow or earthy-tasting cheeses are also excellent with asparagus; an ideal accompaniment to every kind of cheese is organic celery, which is as different from the conventionally grown version as handmade from creamery Lancashire. Salad leaves, whether as garnishes or part of a composed salad, should be bitter, or at least not sweet, e.g. chicory, endive, batavia, frisee, chard, sorrel, or any sort of red lettuce; celeriac tops are strong but interesting with mild Cheddars; the sharpness of watercress matches Stilton and other blue cheeses; mizuna or rocket contrasts pleasingly with mild sheep's or goats' cheeses.

Cheese served before the sweet means that you can continue to drink the main course wine and do not have to adapt from a sweet to savoury taste:

three or more cheeses served at this stage are not only better without extras such as fruit but can probably also be eaten without bread or biscuits. Otherwise, I favour bread rather than biscuits partly because most of the biscuits around are so disappointing. The ideal bread for most cheeses is sourdough, but rye, wholemeal, and rough, gritty Irish soda bread go especially well with soft and semi-soft cheeses; so, in a different way, does very crisp, light French bread. Like other accompaniments to particular cheeses, flavoured breads are mentioned in the text. The only biscuits that I have come across which seem to me worthy of good cheese are: Clarke's thin wholemeal biscuits, handmade and a true luxury; Cottage Delight's Oval Alberts; similar biscuits from Highland Fine Celtic Foods (run by Susannah Stone, who also makes Highland Crowdie: page 245); Miller Damzel's oat and wheat biscuits; and the rather more substantial Duchy Originals. Carr's plain water biscuits make a crisp, light foil to soft cheeses; Marks & Spencer's cheese digestives work particularly well with mellow cheeses.

Whether with bread or biscuits, butter should be unsalted, or only very lightly salted: salty butter clashes with the flavour of cheese. Several of the cheesemakers make either ordinary or whey-butter, including the Keens, Applebys, and Bill Hogan: whey-butter is deliciously sweet and especially good with cheese because it has a more delicate, slightly less rich texture than usual, but melts at a relatively low temperature and therefore should not be left in a hot room for long or used for pastry.

Cheeses which have been kept chilled should be taken out of the refrigerator one and a half to two hours before serving, since, as with red wine, cold deadens flavour; it also hardens soft cheeses so that white mould-ripened types will not flow. The only rinds meant to be eaten, and treated accordingly, are the white mould kind; others should be washed. Divide cheese so that everybody has an equal share of the inside and outside: with round cheeses, this means cutting them in wedges, like a cake; cheese bought in slices should be cut lengthwise rather than across. Tall truckles are easier to serve if sliced horizontally before serving (some cheesemakers sell half-cheeses sliced in this way); the cut surface must then be covered with clingfilm or closely wrapped with cheese-paper.

COOKING WITH CHEESE

When cheese is heated to a certain point, it coagulates in the same way as meat and forms lumps as dense and resilient, and reputedly indigestible, as chewing-gum: it is therefore essential to avoid overcooking. If it does not melt sufficiently, you can always return it to the heat, but once coagulated it is beyond rescue. Apart from this, its behaviour when heated depends on the structure of the milk and the way the cheese was made. Cows' milk, with relatively large fat globules, will spread and may leach some of the fat; goats' and sheep's milk, which is more homogeneous, will break down less easily. This is one of the reasons for the popularity of goats' cheeses for grilling; it also means that sheep's cheeses in sauces and fillings need more heat than cows' before they will melt and amalgamate. Cheeses heated to a high temperature when they are made, which shrinks and hardens the curd particles, may similarly remain firm: an extreme example is halloumi, which can be fried without a protective coating.

Just as the taste of cheese is deadened by cold, it also changes when hot; however, whereas the effect of cold is consistent, that of heat is very variable. Goats' cheeses generally become sweeter; skim-milk or very low-fat cheeses tend to lose their flavour. Otherwise, no easily defined rule applies: some cheeses become bland, some taste more intense. When you have a cheese which you have not used for cooking before, and for which no recipes are given here, toast a small piece before proceeding, but bear in mind that even if it seems to keep its flavour, the taste may not be strong enough to make itself felt in a sauce.

THE RECIPES

You may feel that cooking with expensive, handmade cheeses is extravagant, but the maxim holds: you cannot produce a first-class result without first-class ingredients. There is also the fact that left-over pieces of cheese will deteriorate. However, on the assumption that you will buy the cheeses primarily for eating rather than cooking, I have balanced the recipes in favour of quick, simple dishes; in choosing them, I have also tried to give an idea of the enormous scope of cheese cookery. Blue cheese in particular can be used to give zest to meat dishes; soft cheese adds a creamy consistency to soups, can be served with fruit as a healthier alternative to cream, and used as the basis of salad dressing instead of mayonnaise. As the fact that fruit goes well with cheese suggests, the options are not limited to savoury dishes: you can use cheeses to make delicious sweets and even excellent cakes.

Unless otherwise stated, large eggs the equivalent of size 2, olive oil (not extra virgin), unsalted butter, freshly ground black pepper, and Malden sea-salt should be used throughout. Full instructions have been given with every recipe except for the following, which occur repeatedly.

19

Short Pastry

Making pastry is actually very easy if you bear three points in mind: it must be kept cool, worked as little as possible, and mixed with as little water as possible. The fat should not be taken from the refrigerator until directly before use: if the dough becomes sticky, either because of a warm kitchen or through overworking, a lot of extra flour will be needed for rolling out. The same will apply if it is too wet; in either case, the proportion of fat will be reduced, with the result that the pastry will be tough. Overworking, besides generating heat, develops the gluten in the flour, which is desirable for bread or pasta but, again, will make for tough pastry.

The pastry can be kept in the refrigerator, rolled or unrolled, for three days before baking; it also freezes well. The quantity given is enough to line a 22-cm/8^1/$_2$-inch tart tin or dish.

> 200g/7oz plain flour, white, wholemeal, or a mixture, plus extra for rolling
> salt
> 50g/1^3/$_4$oz each butter and lard *or* 100g/3^1/$_2$oz butter (for vegetarians)

Blend the flour with a pinch of salt. Add and cut the fat into it as finely as possible with a sharp knife; then rub it with your fingertips until the mixture is like fine breadcrumbs. Make a well in the centre, add a scant 2 table-spoonsful of iced or very cold water, and draw the ingredients into a ball of dough, gradually adding just as much more water as is needed to take up all the flour. Leave the dough to rest for 15–20 minutes in the refrigerator. Dust the rolling-pin and board with flour and roll out the dough to 4–5mm/just under ^{1}/$_4$ inch thick. Place the dough over the tart tin or dish and press it loosely and gently into the edges: it should fit closely without being stretched. Trim it generously to allow for slight shrinkage; if you are using a dish, stamp it round the rim.

Baking blind, which partly cooks the pastry, will ensure that it stays crisp under a liquid filling. Cover the pastry closely, including the rim, with cooking foil; to prevent it from rising, weigh it down with baking beans if they are available. Bake in a pre-heated oven at 200°C/400°F/Gas 6, for 10–12 minutes; remove the foil and bake for a further 5 minutes or until the pastry starts to colour.

Puff Pastry

Puff pastry takes a little time to make because, in order to produce the layers which make it puff up, you have to chill it at intervals. The following is not the classic method but the one which I find quickest and easiest. Like short pastry, it can be kept chilled for up to three days and freezes well.

200g/7oz plain white flour plus extra for rolling
salt
200g/7oz butter straight from the refrigerator
a few drops of lemon juice
1 small free-range egg for glazing (optional)

Mix the flour with a little salt. Cut 150g/5^1/$_4$oz of the butter into thin slices and, unless the kitchen is very cool, return it to the refrigerator until needed. Cut the rest into the flour as for short pastry; then rub with your fingertips until it has disappeared. Make a well in the centre and add the lemon juice and 3 tablespoonful of iced or very cold water; mould the ingredients into a dough, adding more water as necessary. Sprinkle the rolling-pin and board with flour, set the sliced butter to hand, and roll the dough into an oblong 5mm/^{1}/$_4$ inch thick. Distribute half the butter over it, leaving a margin of at least 3cm/over 1 inch round the edges. Fold over the top third of the pastry and cover with the bottom third, as if folding writing-paper to fit into an envelope. Seal the edges all round and roll it out again. Add the rest of the butter, fold, and seal as before. Sprinkle the dough lightly with flour, cover it with clingfilm, and put it into the refrigerator for 30–45 minutes or until it becomes firm and cool but not hard. Re-roll and fold the pastry twice more. Return it to the refrigerator and repeat the process. To use the pastry, roll it out to 5–6mm/about ^{1}/$_4$ inch thick and follow the directions given with the recipe. If you are making a pie, trim it very generously to allow for shrinkage. Brush it with egg if you wish and bake it at 220°C/425°F/Gas 7.

 Stock

Making stock is perceived as taking a great deal of time; however, I have tested all the recipes in this book with chicken stock consisting simply of a free-range chicken carcass, 1.4–1.5 litres/2^1/$_2$–2^3/$_4$ pints of water, and 4 or 5 peppercorns (no salt), covered and simmered for 3^1/$_2$–4 hours. Often, the chicken was pot-roasted with herbs and garlic, and sometimes wine or a couple of teaspoonful of sherry vinegar, which help, but a plain roasted carcass will do perfectly well. The stock should be strained promptly and chilled before use so that you can skim off the fat. It will keep in the refrigerator for three days and for an extra day if reheated and simmered for 15 minutes.

Vegetarians may have their own preferences, but mushrooms are a good basis for a stock sympathetic to cheese. For flavour as well as convenience, I suggest dried porcini (but not chanterelles): any mushroom stalks or skins which may be available are a useful addition.

Vegetable Stock
10g/$\frac{1}{4}$oz porcini, soaked for 20 minutes in 300ml/$\frac{1}{2}$ pint hot water
2 medium onions (about 300g/10$\frac{1}{2}$oz together), peeled and sliced
2 medium carrots (about 200g/7oz together), peeled and sliced
mushroom stalks and skins if available, washed
a sprig of rosemary
5 peppercorns
2 tsp sherry vinegar
700ml/1$\frac{1}{4}$pints water

Put the ingredients, including the porcini liquid, into a large saucepan. Bring to the boil, cover, and simmer for 25 minutes. Strain and use the same day.

 ## Grilling Cheeses

Toast made in a toaster tends to be moist and leathery: for a really crisp base, the bread must be dried in the oven. This is less of a nuisance than it sounds because it can be prepared twenty-four hours or more in advance. Cut the crusts from the bread and bake it at 200°C/400°F/Gas 6 for 10–12 minutes or until it turns pale gold; if baked far ahead of time, store the toast in a tin or wrapped in foil.

Before adding the cheese, sprinkle the bread with a little oil for goats' or sheep's cheeses or butter it thinly for cows'; if the cheese is very mild, add just a few grains of salt and a little pepper. With goats' cheeses, you can also rub the bread with a clove of garlic. Even with cows' cheeses, which (unless made into rarebit) will spread, make sure that the cheese covers it completely: any exposed edges will burn. As goats' and sheep's cheeses will not release fat, moisten the top of the cheese with a little more oil. Place the bread under a fairly hot grill until the cheese bubbles slightly and begins to colour: do not let it become very brown. Serve the grilled cheese alone or with celery, tomatoes, or bitter leaves.

Frying Cheeses in Breadcrumbs

This is a rich but delicious way of serving soft mould-ripened cheeses; you can also roll fresh goats' cheeses into balls and fry them by the same method. It is essential that the cheese should be hardened in the refrigerator before being cut and coated; it is equally important that the oil should be hot enough to brown and crisp the outside before the cheese has had time to melt and escape. The oil should be sunflower or olive: olive is expensive and gives a slightly less crisp result but better flavour. Avoid groundnut oil, which sometimes produces a bitter taint. Serve the cheese with a salad of cherry tomatoes and bitter leaves.

For 3–4 as a first course

25g/1oz white flour
1 medium free-range egg, beaten
40–50g/1^1/$_2$–1^3/$_4$oz fresh fine brown or white breadcrumbs
salt and pepper
150–160g/5^1/$_4$–5^1/$_2$oz cheese
oil for frying
fat or sugar thermometer *or* a few small squares of stale bread

Sprinkle the flour over a large plate, pour the egg into a saucer or small bowl, and spread the breadcrumbs over another plate. Season the flour and egg moderately with salt and pepper. Take the cheese out of the refrigerator and cut it into 1.5-cm/^{1}/$_2$-inch squares (do not cut off the rind, which will add to the flavour). Coat the cheese, first with the flour, then with the egg, then the breadcrumbs: shake off any surplus but be particularly careful to ensure that the cheese is completely coated on all sides. Return the cheese to the refrigerator until you are ready to start frying.

Line a plate with absorbent paper to drain surplus fat from the cheese after it has cooked. Use a small, heavy pan for frying: pour in at least 3.5cm/1^1/$_4$inches of oil. Place over fairly high heat until the oil has reached 180°C/350°F. If you do not have a thermometer, slide in cubes of bread: the oil is hot enough when they turn golden in about 40 seconds. Reduce the heat slightly to maintain the temperature and gently lower in a few pieces of cheese. Do not drop them in, since they might splash (be careful: hot oil burns badly and ignites easily). Add only as many as will fit into the pan without touching. Cook the cheese until just golden, then remove it instantly; drain it on the paper. Serve the first batch before you fry the next.

Fruit Cheeses

Fruit cheese is so called because of its stiff consistency: people with fruit in their gardens used to make and eat it, not necessarily with but instead of cheese. This version goes particularly well with strong Cheddar and Single Gloucester.

Apple Cheese
1kg/2lb 4oz Bramley apples
5 cloves
5-cm/2-inch stick cinnamon
about 425g/15oz granulated or caster sugar

Wash and chop but do not peel the apples, and put them into a large saucepan with the cores, spices, and 450ml/16fl oz of water. Bring the water slowly to the boil, stir, skim, and simmer for 1 hour, until the apples are very soft. Sieve them and weigh the purée; return it to a heavy-bottomed pan, preferably non-stick, and add half the purée's weight of sugar. Set the pan over low heat, stir until the sugar has melted, and boil it gently for another hour or until stiff and jelly-like. Lightly butter a shallow mould; pour in the cheese and leave it to cool.

Using this basic recipe, you can also make Plum and Apple Cheese, which tones well with mellow cheeses, notably Double Gloucester and Cheshire, or Pear and Apple Cheese, which is especially recommended with hard goats' cheeses. For the Plum and Apple Cheese, use 500g/1lb 2oz each Bramley apples and red plums (washed and diced), the same quantities of cloves and cinnamon as for Apple Cheese, and about 300g/10$\frac{1}{2}$oz granulated or caster sugar. For the Pear and Apple Cheese, use 500g/1lb 2oz each Bramley apples and Conference pears (chopped fairly small) and about 375g/13oz pectin sugar.

Cheese with Wine

By David Natt

The combination of cheese with wine has changed from 1960s cliché to 1990s conundrum. Successful matching requires a little careful thought. To guide your choices, you will need to consider the ways in which both sides of the partnership are constituted in order to get the chemistry right.

In the brief examples given here, I am envisaging cheese being served before dessert as part of an evening meal. It is always worth seeing how the red wine you have been drinking carries through into the cheese course, but I would recommend serving a sweet white wine simultaneously – either a semi-sweet Riesling or Chenin Blanc to herald the dessert wine to come or bringing a suitable dessert wine with good acidity forward in the meal.

FRESH SOFT GOATS' OR SHEEP'S CHEESES

The light, chalky texture of goats' cheeses, such as Ragstone or Gedi Moillion, or a sheep's cheese such as Wigmore, suggests a lightish wine. Soft cheeses have fat which is 'free' or not bound into the structure of the cheese. This protects against tannins in the wine, but it also acts as a barrier against the perception of flavour. If a wine is to cut through, it must have enough acidity. Sauvignon Blanc is a classic partner but is out of place after a red wine. A degree of sweetness in the wine will not go amiss. Semi-sweet Vouvray or German Riesling Spatlese or Auslese work very well and provide a natural bridge into a sweeter dessert wine.

MOULD-RIPENED CHEESES

Mould-ripened cheeses, such as Bonchester or Milleens, coat the mouth and demand copious acidity (or alcohol) to cut through them. The persistent cabbage flavour of ripe examples plays havoc with the complex finish on mature red wines (though 'farmyardy' Burgandy is better than cedary claret). The clean apple flavours of Chenin Blanc blend much better, or the piercing acidity of a semi-sweet German Riesling also cuts through refreshingly and is capable of taking the overlay of cheese flavour on the finish. If red wine is essential, then a young, uncomplicated wine with bracing fruit and plenty of acidity works best.

WASHED-RIND CHEESES

Creamily textured, with pungent aromas and complex, persistent flavours, washed-rind cheeses such as Tornegus are a challenge to match. Red wines need to be very young and straightforward, and even then are likely to fade badly as tannins essential to their structure are stripped away. Young red Burgundy can become pleasantly rose-scented (if rather watery), but on the whole white wines have a better chance of success. The star turn here is good quality Alsace Gewurztraminer. Its weight of flavour and floral high notes seem well suited to such cheese, forming an interesting mixture of the slightly fetid and the scented. A semi-sweet Riesling with sufficient body can work similarly.

CHEDDAR AND CHEDDAR-STYLE

The high acidity of a mature farmhouse Cheddar or Cheddar-style cheese will eviscerate any wine where acidity is not a linchpin of its constitution. A mature claret becomes a pointless companion, despite the traditional association. Younger reds are rather cowed by the cheese but do co-exist better, provided they are not particularly tannic, since there will be little ameliorative free protein or fat in the cheese, but plenty of Umami or 'savour' to react adversely. A crisp, dry white will seem thin (as well as misplaced at this stage in a meal). The required weight needs to come from sugar. What you are looking for in many ways is the vinous equivalent of sweet pickle. Is it such a sacrilege to suggest a sweet Chenin Blanc – right in terms of acidity, sweetness, and body, and the wine world's flavour equivalent to cider, a traditionally British Cheddar accompaniment? Other rich sweet wines with good acidity can also work successfully.

BLUE CHEESES

You are not yet at the port stage of the meal, so that familiar companion is not available. A good Stilton will certainly finish off your red for you if that is what you are intent on: its combination of salt, acidity, savour, and crumbly/creamy texture simultaneously point up tannins, take out fruit acids and block flavours. A Sauternes, however, is as much at home in this environment as with blue Wensleydale or Roquefort. Other sweet wines with good acidity also work well, especially if they are already or can be botrytis-affected, when they seem to exhibit a particular affinity to the tang of blue mould. Sweet Chenin Blanc and Riesling seem good choices once more.

South-east England

Village Maid

ANNE AND ANDY WIGMORE, THE COTTAGE, BASINGSTOKE ROAD, RISELEY, READING, BERKSHIRE RG7 1QD. TEL: 0118 9884564

Anne Wigmore is unique among the cheesemakers in Britain in coming, not from a farming background but from the other, more modern arm of cheesemaking, the laboratory – and stands as proof of just how valuable an intimate knowledge of the relevant chemistry and microbiology can be. After studying the digestive processes of ruminants and spending several years making experimental cheeses for scientific purposes, she did not set out to revive an old recipe but aimed to create an entirely new cheese unlike any which at that time were produced in Britain. Even for her, however, perfecting it took time; perhaps because she had a very clear idea of what she wanted, she did not feel that she had completely mastered it (her word) for seven years. This was Spenwood, a hard, full-flavoured sheep's cheese: several other cheeses of this type are now made but, despite Olivia Mills and the British Sheep Dairying Association (page 32), still not nearly enough. Her next cheese was a hard Guernsey cheese, Wellington, so named because the milk originally came from the Duke of Wellington's estate, Stratfield Saye, which is just up the road; the cheeses were also matured in the Duke's cellar. The two hard cheeses were followed by Wigmore, a semi-soft sheep's cheese which remains unique in this country, and a soft Guernsey cheese, Waterloo. When I went to see them, they were still making Wellington, but they have now decided to discontinue it in favour of twice as much Waterloo. Particularly in view of the general lack of soft cheeses, this is excellent news with regard to Waterloo; however, I regret Wellington, which was distinguished for its clean, crisp tang and quite exceptional toasting properties.

When Anne started, Andy worked as a journalist, but as the cheese business gathered momentum he abandoned writing and joined her; they now work together, helped by three assistants who are employed on a part-time basis so that, like Anne herself, they can combine cheesemaking with looking after their children. The milk for the sheep's cheeses comes from four farms, one of which, in Dorset, also supplies the Blunts (page 46). The Stratfield Saye milk dried up, so to speak, when the estate was inherited by a new heir who decided to convert it entirely to arable land and sell the cows. However, Milk Marque now brings milk from two specific farms which suits the cheese; the arrangement also means that the Wigmores need only take it when they wish and so, unlike many cheesemakers, can go away for holidays.

It so happened that I visited them on the very first day of the new delivery: normally, although they have two vats, they make only one cheese at a time, but on this occasion, partly because they were anxious to test the new milk, they were making both Wellington and Waterloo. When I arrived, Andy was piling the blocks of curd for Wellington, which was a Cheddar-style cheese, while Anne was using a hose to wash the curds, i.e. replace some of the whey with water, for Waterloo. This is a process typically used for Gouda which reduces acidity and helps to give the cheese a mild, sweet flavour; she also uses it for her semi-soft sheep's cheese, Wigmore.

WATERLOO

Silver Medal, British Cheese Awards 1997
A semi-soft cows' cheese; full-fat, unpasteurized milk; vegetarian rennet. 900g/2lb rounds

Waterloo is luscious and creamy, with the sweetness of the rich milk and undertones of herbs and grass. If allowed to mature for an extended time (as on occasion at Neal's Yard), it becomes firm and buttery, rather like a milder version of Durrus or Gubbeen (pages 134 and 139). If you have any left over, fry it in egg and breadcrumbs (page 23) and serve with redcurrant jelly.

Waterloo is made according to the very simple Coulommiers method, by which the curds are ladled into moulds without prior draining, so that the whey, or in this case whey and water, pours out in a stream; no pressure is applied except by piling the moulds. Anne stacks them in piles of three for the first hour; they are then turned, remoulded, and stacked in sixes. A point about which she is especially particular, because of its effect not only on taste but also on moisture content and ripening, is salting: like a few but increasing number of other makers, she favours both a light dry salting and brining, which is partly why Waterloo is notable for a consistently creamy texture all the way through. It is matured for four weeks and remains creamy for a further two to two and a half; by ten, it will have become buttery.

WIGMORE

Gold Medal, British Cheese Awards 1996 and 1997
A semi-soft sheep's cheese; unpasteurized milk; vegetarian rennet. 450g/1lb or
1.4–1.8kg/3–4lb rounds

Wigmore is fairly firm when young but flows slightly when older (the Wigmores mature it for two to three months). Although creamy, the texture has the lightness characteristic of soft sheep's cheeses; the balance of flavours changes according to season but includes grass, herbs, and flowers. The overall impression is subtle, cool, and refreshing: the cheese does not clamour for attention, but once tried becomes compulsive. The two successive Gold Medals at the British Cheese Awards are absolutely justified.

SPENWOOD

A hard sheep's cheese; unpasteurized milk; vegetarian rennet. 2.3kg/5lb truckles

When matured for six months, Spenwood is relatively moist and mild, with a delicate but distinctive grassy tang; as is characteristic of all the Wigmores' cheeses, the flavour is precisely balanced between salty and sharp. At this age, it is ripe for the table: at eight to ten months, it becomes harder, drier, and stronger, not unlike a soft-tasting pecorino, and is ideal for sprinkling over risotto or pasta.

 ## Tagliatelle with Spenwood and Spring Vegetables

Use young beans: old ones have tough skins which it is preferable to remove after cooking. Similarly, as old peas can take a long time to cook, I recommend frozen (if you use fresh ones, boil them separately). Omit the egg yolk if the dish is for children or anyone at risk.

Cooking time: about 30 minutes
For 2–3

125g/4$^1/_2$oz frozen or young fresh broad beans, weighed after podding
salt
150g/5$^1/_4$oz frozen peas
100g/3$^1/_2$oz baby spinach, washed
250g/9oz fresh tagliatelle, plain or flavoured with garlic and herbs
25g/1oz butter
1 tbsp oil
200g/7oz baby or very young leeks, chopped into 1-cm/$^1/_2$-inch slices, washed, and left to dry
1 medium shallot (about 50g/1$^3/_4$oz), peeled and finely chopped
3 cloves garlic, peeled and finely chopped

2 tsp flour

2 tsp Dijon mustard

2 tsp white wine vinegar

pepper

1 large free-range egg yolk, beaten

2 tbsp double cream

140g/5oz Spenwood (8–10 months old), finely grated

Boil the beans in 600ml/1 pint slightly salted water for 9–10 minutes or until just tender. Add the peas and spinach, stirring to ensure that the spinach is submerged; bring the water back to the boil and cook for a bare 2 minutes (no longer). Drain the vegetables over a bowl; reserve the cooking liquor. Cover the vegetables to keep them warm.

Set a large pan of water to boil for the tagliatelle. Melt the butter in the oil over medium heat and fry the leeks and shallot for about $1^{1}/_{2}$ minutes. Add the garlic and continue to fry for another 2–3 minutes or until the leeks are soft and the shallot starts to change colour; turn constantly, since leeks burn easily. Stir in the flour off the heat. When it is thoroughly incorporated, pour in 300ml/$^{1}/_{2}$ pint of the vegetable liquor (do not throw away the rest), return the pan to the heat, and stir until the sauce thickens. Add the mustard, vinegar, and a moderate seasoning of salt and pepper; reduce the heat to low and simmer for 3–4 minutes, stirring constantly. Remove the pan from the heat.

While the sauce simmers, cook the tagliatelle. Check that the water is boiling: add a little salt and the pasta, bring the water back to the boil, stir, and boil briskly for 2–3 minutes or according to the instructions on the packet, until the pasta is *al dente*. Drain at once and return it to the hot pan.

While the pasta cooks, gradually add about a tablespoonful of the remaining vegetable liquor (which should still be fairly hot) to the egg yolk, beating continuously with a fork; continue beating until it is smooth and set it aside. Add the cream to the sauce and bring it to the boil. Stir in the peas, beans, and spinach, return the sauce to the boil, and add all but about 3 table-spoonsful of the cheese. Remove the pan from the heat and stir in the egg yolk. Continue stirring until the mixture thickens; if necessary, return the pan to low heat for a moment but do not allow it to boil or the egg may curdle. Toss the sauce with the tagliatelle and serve immediately with the rest of the cheese sprinkled on top.

Brebilait Products

OLIVIA MILLS, WIELD WOOD FARM, UPPER WIELD, ALRESFORD,
HANTS SO24 9RU. TEL: 01420 563151/564182

The revival of sheep dairy-farming in Britain is largely Olivia Mills'
achievement: with Robin Congdon (page 104), she led the way in raising
sheep for milking; she is also the founder and secretary of the British Sheep
Dairying Association and author of the remarkably downright but often
wryly funny *Practical Sheep Dairying*, which covers not only raising sheep but
also how to make it pay. Almost everyone planning to milk sheep, from the
Whites in Cornwall (page 110) to Allan Brown in Wigtownshire (page 233),
goes to her for advice. To stimulate new ideas in a field which she is striving
to turn into a profitable industry, she takes members of the Association
abroad every spring: last year, a group which included the Hardys and Mary
Holbrook (pages 41 and 71) went to Bulgaria.

Innovation in the dairy sector, as well as cheesemaking and her 200-ha/
500-acre farm near the perhaps rather too pretty village of Preston
Candover, are all part of her inheritance. The farm was bought by her father,
who, with Hosier (the inventor of the Hosier bale), pioneered machine-
milking for cows; her mother taught her to make cheese – and be mistress of
it. No cheesemaking routine, Olivia declares, should be onerous to the
maker: 'Never let your cheese rule you.' On the other hand, she agreed that
cheesemakers should take the trouble to learn about the chemistry involved
even if in practice they work by judgement and eye. A point which she was
especially anxious that I should emphasize was that, like Mark Hardy's or
Giovanni Irranca's (pages 41 and 145), any kind of sheep's cheese should be
accompanied by ricotta (which is made from the whey): 'Ricotta represents
profit.' These days her attention is turning away from products and towards
the sheep themselves. At present, she has a flock of over 200, mainly
Frieslands although other breeds have been included for assessment, but her
aim in future will be to breed a few choice Frieslands for sperm and embryos.

WALDA

*A hard or semi-hard sheep's cheese, according to maturity; thermized milk; vegetarian
rennet. 1–2kg/2lb 4oz–4lb 6oz*

The young cheese is moist and very mild, tasting gently of the Sussex grass
but with a slight peppery aftertaste; the more mature cheese is drier and

harder, with a distinctive tang and quite a strong aftertaste. It is sold plain or with caraway or green peppercorns: the latter is especially recommended.

The recipe for Walda is very simple. The milk is heated to 57–58°C/135–136°F, i.e. thermized, which does not kill all the bacteria present but reduces the likelihood of off-flavours, 'blowing' caused by gas-producing organisms, and destroys some pathogens; it is then cooled to 29°C/84°F before starter and rennet are added. When the curd has set, it is drained, cut, and left to rest for about another half-hour before being salted and moulded; salting (dry) follows after unmoulding the next day. The maturing time is three months to a year: if you want a mature cheese, which is especially suitable for cooking, it can be ordered from the farm.

Walda and Anchovy Salad

This is delicious but potent: serve it with rough, crusty bread. If possible, wash the salad leaves an hour or so before the meal to give them plenty of time to dry.

For 4

1 clove garlic, peeled and chopped
4 tbsp virgin olive oil
1 tbsp red wine vinegar
salt and pepper
175–225g/6–8oz mixed curly endive and non-sweet salad leaves, such as lamb's lettuce, baby spinach, red chard leaves, mizuna or rocket, washed and allowed to dry
175g/6oz Walda (plain)
12–16 anchovy fillets, rinsed
85g/3oz (20–24) black olives, pitted if you wish
about 16 basil leaves, washed and allowed to dry

Crush the garlic in a mortar. Add the oil, vinegar, a very little salt, and a moderate seasoning of pepper, and beat until homogeneous. Arrange the salad leaves on the serving plates. Thinly slice or (if very mature) crumble the Walda over the leaves, then add the anchovy fillets and olives. Tear the basil leaves into two or three pieces and scatter them over the top. Beat the dressing again with a fork and pour it over the salad directly before serving.

Old Scotland

PAT VIGOR, OLD SCOTLAND FARM, STAPLE LANE, SHERE,
GUILDFORD, SURREY. TEL: 01483 222526

Why the farm is called Old Scotland, nobody is quite sure, although Pat has been told that it may be because of an ancient Scots' tax. Neither she nor her cheese are in any way connected with Scotland; nor, until she married, had she any connection with farming. Possibly this explains her feelings for her animals – cows, sheep, ducks, and hens – all of whom she looks on as very much part of her family.

Since her husband died, she has managed the farm herself with the help of her son, Tim, who introduced their first French cow. Until two years ago, she made the cheese from a herd of 110 Friesians; soon after leaving college, however, Tim went to France and was so enthused by the Friesian–Holsteins he saw there that he invested all his savings in Jemima, a heifer from the champion Olympian herd. She is tall and elegant, and very conscious of her superior breeding, mooing to order and, as Pat puts it, 'insisting on her regular shampoo and set'. However, she is also such an exceptional milker that Tim finally induced Pat to make a decision which for her was particularly difficult but has proved to be the wisest of her career: to exchange her Friesians for Friesian–Holsteins. The new herd is fed on grass, home-produced, quickly fermented silage, and cake locally made to her own requirements, and give over twice as much milk as their predecessors, so that, with only fifty-five (she has recently added ten more), she can make an extra cheese a day. In terms of quality, the final seal of approval, at least so far as she and I are concerned, comes from the fact that when James Aldridge wants cows' milk, he buys it from her.

For several years before starting to make cheese professionally, she had experimented with it in her kitchen; then her sister, who was working for a cheesemaker called David Doble, gave her the recipe for his cheese, which at that time was known as Castle Hill. Eventually, David decided to join her at Old Scotland, where they now work side by side, using a row of handsome antique cheese-presses and a Victorian mill from the cheesemaking school in Somerset, Cannington. Each has his or her own vat and works separately to the same recipe. They thus afford an interesting example of two people who, except for vat size, are operating in identical conditions and yet produce different results. Pat's touch is lighter and her cheeses softer and 'rounder': the difference is slight but noticeable if you try hers and David's together.

OLD SCOTLAND

A hard Cheddar-style cows' cheese; full-fat, unpasteurized milk; vegetarian rennet.
1.8kg/4lb truckles or 3.6–4.5kg/8–10lb wheels

With its dryish, slightly grained texture, Old Scotland tends to become crumbly when mature; the taste is soft, subtle, and earthy, with a pronounced smoky tang. At three and a half to four months it is moderately strong and at six or more mellower but powerful. It retains its flavour well when heated: because of its smoky overtone, it can be used in much the same way as pecorino.

The recipe is in effect the same as for the old Castle Hill. Cheesemaking begins at about 6.20 a.m., following the morning milking at 5. Starter is added thirty minutes before the rennet and the curd left to set for about another thirty minutes; it is then cut very small with two fine cheese knives, one with vertical and the other with horizontal blades, and stirred by hand with a wooden rake for nearly an hour. This is followed by slight scalding, i.e. heating, from 30°C/86°F to 33°C/91°F, during which it is stirred continuously. After breakfast, the whey is run off and the curd is scooped to the side of the vat, cut into blocks, and drained. The blocks are repeatedly stacked and squeezed by means of a board and bowls weighted with sand. When the curd has drained completely, it is put through the mill and weighed to determine the amount of salt needed (even though the volume of milk may be the same, its solid content varies according to the time of year). After salting and moulding, the cheeses are lightly pressed, and in the evening turned and put under heavier pressure overnight. Next morning, they are turned again and pressed hard for twenty-four hours. Thereafter, they are turned and wiped every day for a fortnight and at less frequent intervals as they mature; the minimum maturing time is three and a half months, but I recommend six and according to Pat they are even better at nine.

Eastside Cheese Co.

JAMES AND PAT ALDRIDGE, EAST LODGE, TANDRIDGE HILL
LANE, GODSTONE, SURREY RH9 8DD. TEL: 01883 743617
WEBSITE: HTTP://WWW.USERS.GLOBALNET.CO.UK/~DAIRY

Whereas Randolph Hodgson has probably done more than anyone else in recent years to publicize British cheeses, James is the *éminence grise* behind the scenes: by maturing, experimenting, and instructing others, he has enlarged their range and contributed perhaps far more than he realizes to improving quality. He started out in the building trade, where he would probably have stayed if he had not been forced to change his occupation because of an injury. His first idea was to open a sandwich shop, but he was deflected by Pat, who was at that time working in a store selling cheap cheese and ham near Southampton. Although the cheese was by no means of the type that he has spent nearly twenty years promoting, it roused his curiosity: the first 'real' cheese he tasted, and still loves, was Duckett's Caerphilly.

He opened James's of Beckenham in 1981 and, along with the usual blocks of creamery-made Cheddar, sold the unpasteurized, farmhouse-made cheeses for which the shop became known. As Neal's Yard Dairy does now, he collected them himself, and to minimize travelling would take as many as the makers were prepared to sell, whether they were ripe or not, which led him into maturing. The expertise which this demands increasingly engrossed him; it also led him to develop his first washed-rind cheese, Tornegus, based on Duckett's Caerphilly. After eight years, having become far more interested in this side of his business than retailing, he gave up the shop to set up as a wholesaler-cum-maturer, in the style of French *affineurs*.

Since then, he has worked from his home maturing, rind-washing, and making his own cheeses in a dairy which is in effect a laboratory. Of numerous cheeses which he has produced at one time or another, the ones I particularly remember are a hard goats' cheese called Gruff, which was mild but at the same time powerful, sweet yet smoky, flowery yet cool and refreshing on the tongue, a combined sheep's and goats' cheese of extraordinary richness and subtlety, and a marvellously sweet sheep's Wensleydale, as well as Lord of the Hundreds (page 53) and St Francis (page 38). Sadly, I shall probably never taste the first three again. His attitude to cheesemaking is like that of the developmental chef: once a recipe is perfected, his interest in it recedes and he progresses to the next. Certainly when he started experimenting not all his ideas were successful, but for James learning is the whole point of the exercise: he does not mind if a recipe turns out less well than he expected so long as he is able to find out why.

The need for both instruction and recipe development is shown by the number of cheesemakers who apply to him when they have problems or want to extend their range. Usually, he goes to them, partly because they may not be able to leave their animals, but mainly in order to assess their working environment. All his services are given for love: he never charges, and says that he will gladly help anybody.

His definition of Real Cheese has not changed over the years: to him, the particular joy of it is the taste of the ripened milk unfolding in successive layers of flavour on the tongue. This cuts out pasteurization: if you argue that a few good pasteurized cheeses are nevertheless made, he will reply that they may perhaps be good, but never very good (though he does concede that blue cheeses are a little different). Multiple starters are therefore of no interest to him either; he feels that if you want to flavour a cheese, you might as well do so directly. He is also one of the few people I have met who states flatly that there is no substitute for animal rennet, which he uses for all his own cheeses (though his washed-rind ones, made by others, are vegetarian). One of his concerns about the present revival is that success may tempt makers to increase output at the expense of quality: in particular, he worries about hygiene, since the more people are involved in any operation, the harder it becomes to maintain impeccable standards.

In future, he intends to cut down on experimental cheesemaking; instead, he has begun to write, having already produced a paper on acidity which I have found singularly clear and helpful. However, he will continue to make St Francis in very limited quantities, and produce Tornegus and his second washed-rind cheese, Celtic Promise. He passed on the recipe for St Francis two or three years ago to Ruth Lawrence at Womerton Farm, Shropshire (page 176). Tornegus is washed with local Kentish wine, lemon verbena, and mint. Celtic Promise is John and Patrice Savage-Onstwedder's Teifi (page 155), washed with cider and water; they now produce it too.

TORNEGUS

A washed-rind cows' cheese; full-fat, unpasteurized milk; vegetarian rennet.
2kg/4lb 6oz drums

The name is derived from the Somerset word 'tor' (the original cheese is made in Somerset) and 'negus' to signify flavoured wine. The cheese has a silky feel and is soft enough to spread with a knife but not flow; when moderately ripe, it is sweet and spicy, with a spectrum of flavours including a slight reminder of alcohol. When riper, it becomes fruitier and more powerful, although not as pungent as the smell may suggest. Of all cheeses, it rewards care in choosing the right wine.

CELTIC PROMISE

A washed-rind cows' cheese; full-fat, unpasteurized milk; vegetarian rennet. 600g/1lb 5oz

The basic cheese is Gouda-style, with herbal and rich, spicy undertones; the rind-washed version is cool-tasting and brings out the herbal rather than spicy side of its character. Although distinctive, it is milder and more delicately flavoured than Tornegus.

ST FRANCIS

A soft, white mould-ripened goats' cheese; full-fat, unpasteurized milk; traditional rennet. 1kg/2lb 4oz log or round

The cheese is luxuriously soft and creamy, with the close, fine-textured feel characteristic of all James's cheeses; the taste is perfectly balanced between herbal and a fresh sweetness suggestive of strawberries or sweet/ sharp apples (Ruth Lawrence's version is milder and more flowery). I refuse to commit myself to a favourite cheese because of variations according to season and other factors which affect quality, but this one would certainly be at the top of the shortlist. In particular, it is wonderful with strawberries; it is also excellent baked in puff pastry (below).

St Francis Crescents

Cooking time: 12–14 minutes
Makes 6–8

100g/3$^{1}/_{2}$oz St Francis
2 tbsp double cream
pepper
1 tsp fresh sage, washed and finely chopped (optional)
1 quantity puff pastry (page 21)

Beat together the cheese, cream, a moderate grinding of pepper, and the sage. Roll out the pastry to 3–4mm/less than $\frac{1}{4}$ inch thick, and cut it into 6 or 8 squares. Put $\frac{1}{2}$ tablespoonful of the cheese on one side of each square; moisten the edges thoroughly with water, fold the square over the cheese to form a triangle, and make sure that the edges are securely sealed. Form the triangle into a croissant shape by twisting and turning the outside corners inwards and wrapping the remaining corner over the top. Make two or three small slashes for air-holes and bake in a pre-heated oven at 220°C/425°F/Gas 7 for 12–14 minutes, until golden. Serve hot with bitter leaves.

Old Plaw Hatch Organic
MICHAEL DUVEEN, OLD PLAW HATCH FARM, SHARPTHORNE,
EAST GRINSTEAD, WEST SUSSEX RH19 4JL. TEL: 01342 810857

Old Plaw Hatch Farm is an old, probably very old foundation: according to the former director, Andrew Carnegie, there has probably been a farm on the site since medieval times, when it marked one of the entrances to the Ashdown Forest ('Hatch' means gate: the forest used to be a royal hunting preserve). It is not merely organic but biodynamic: biodynamism, which was first propounded by Rudolf Steiner in 1924, extends the organic principle to self-sufficiency, or near self-sufficiency (a ten per cent margin to allow for temporary problems is permitted) in order to avoid exploitation of the environment and ensure infinite sustainability. Thus Old Plaw Hatch grows all its own hay, wheat, and oats for animal feed and the plants from which its own range of homeopathic medicines is made. Recently, it went into partnership with another biodynamic farm about 10km/6 miles away, and, to raise capital towards extending their activities, the two farms have turned themselves into a co-operative. As such, they sold shares during their first year to 120 people, mostly local residents, who include a merchant banker, a vice-president of an American bank, two managing directors, a lecturer in agriculture, and a journalist. All of them value the chance to play a part in producing their own food; they can visit the farms whenever they like, attend Open Days and other events, and the farms benefit from their financial and other expertise.

The second farm, Tablehurst, specializes in meat, has a flock of Friesland sheep, whose milk goes to Mark Hardy at Sussex High Weald Dairy (page

41), and grows field vegetables: the range of vegetables, however, is to be greatly increased and a vegetable-box scheme launched this year. Plaw Hatch already produces a wide selection of quite exceptionally excellent fruit and vegetables, eggs, and milk, cheese, yoghurt, and beef from a dual-purpose herd of dark red Dutch MRI (Meuse-Rhine-IJssel) cows, whose yield is lower than Friesian but the milk more concentrated and with smaller fat globules, which makes it especially suitable for cheese. As yet, only one cheese is produced, a hard Cheddar-type made to a recipe selected to suit the cows and conditions at the farm by the Dutch organic cheesemaker Cees Stötjn; however, new ones are planned, which in view of the present lack of organic cheeses are the more welcome.

OLD PLAW HATCH ORGANIC

A hard, Cheddar-style cows' cheese; full-fat, thermized milk; vegetarian rennet.
5kg/11lb truckles

The smooth, silky, slightly elastic texture of the cheese is slightly reminiscent of Gouda, although it is not made by the Gouda method; the taste is full and rounded, with grassy and herbal flavours and a well developed Cheddar-like tang. It comes in different strengths according to maturity: all go especially well with wholemeal bread and apples or apple cheese (page 24); the mature version is also excellent for cooking.

The cheese as described was made by cheesemaker Rachel Webb, who has now left; at the time of going to press, a successor had not yet been appointed. The milk is first heated to 63°C/145°F, i.e. thermized, to kill organisms likely to sour or give it off-flavours; it is then cooled to 35°C/95°F and starter added, followed by rennet thirty-five minutes later. When the curd has set, it is cut into 1-cm/$^1/_2$-inch squares, stirred for fifteen minutes, left to rest, and stirred and scalded to 38°C/100°F for another fifteen minutes. After a brief rest, the whey is run off and as much liquid as possible is drained from the curd by a repeated process of pressing in a cheesecloth, turning, and cutting. The next stage is milling and salting, followed by moulding in tall truckle moulds and pressing for thirty-six hours. Finally, the cheeses are brined and oiled with sunflower oil to inhibit the growth of mould on the surface. For the next two to three weeks they are turned and oiled every day, and thereafter once a week or fortnight, depending on their age and the weather, for three or five months.

Sussex High Weald Dairy Products
MARK HARDY, PUTLANDS FARM, DUDDLESWELL, UCKFIELD, EAST SUSSEX TN22 3BJ. TEL: 01825 712647

Putlands Farm is in an idyllic situation on the edge of a plateau in the middle of the Ashdown Forest, with views over a richly wooded valley and rolling hills; in the foreground is an artificial lake created for ornamental and conservation purposes by Mark's father. The Hardys senior, who bought the farm on their return from Kenya, did not originally envisage cheesemaking, but decided to rear sheep because they had limited acreage. At first, the success of the cheese prompted them to rent extra land and increase their flock until they were grazing and milking 300, but at this point they accepted that they could not keep up with Mark's needs and he began to buy in extra milk. They have now reduced their flock to forty and he buys milk from seven neighbouring farms – and still complains that there is never enough, especially in winter. The lack of sheep's milk was his main reason for enlarging his range with a cows' cheese, Ashdown Foresters, which in my view is the subtlest and most interesting of all his products.

His cheesemaking began as a result of an agreement to supply milk to a cheesemaker who planned to make halloumi for the Cypriot community in London but then withdrew: unwilling to abandon the idea, Mark went to Cyprus to learn how to make it and began to produce it himself. Initially, it sold well; after two or three years, however, the Cypriots in Cyprus started exporting a cheap cows' milk substitute which spoiled his market and forced him to diversify. First, he developed Duddleswell, a full-flavoured hard cheese which might be described as the sheep's equivalent to Cheddar; next came a soft cheese, Sussex Slipcote, made to a traditional local recipe. From the beginning, he had utilized the whey left over from cheese for ricotta; now, besides Ashdown Foresters, he makes feta, fromage frais, yoghurt, and small amounts of sheep's whey-butter and cream. He also makes a fresh, low-fat soft cows' cheese with a slight flavour of herbs and a texture like thick cream, which can be used as a base for dips, fillings, and stuffings or sweetened and served as an accompaniment to some soft fruits (not strawberries). As much of the sheep's milk as is available is organic; the cows' cheeses are made with organic Guernsey milk from Sir Julian Rose's estate in Oxfordshire. Between them, he and his cheesemaker, Colin Brinkhurst, plus assistants, process 400–900 litres/88–198 gallons a day; cheese is made five or six days a week, yoghurt on the sixth or seventh.

DUDDLESWELL

Silver Medal, British Cheese Awards 1995
A hard sheep's cheese; pasteurized milk, sometimes organic; vegetarian rennet.
2kg/4lb 6oz rounds

Duddleswell has a short, slightly fudgy texture and a rich, sweet, faintly caramel-like taste with undertones of butter and grass.

The milk is heated to 32°C/90°F, starter is added, and the milk left to ripen for an hour before renneting. When the curd has formed, after about fifty minutes, it is cut into 1-cm/$\frac{1}{2}$-inch cubes and scalded to 38°C/100°F over a further forty-five minutes. It is then drained and Cheddared twice, i.e. cut into blocks and piled at the sides of the vat. As soon as it has reached the correct acidity, probably after another forty-five minutes, it is milled, very lightly seasoned with sea-salt, moulded, and pressed for forty-eight hours, with turning after twenty-four; finally, it is brined for a further twenty-four and matured for a minimum of two months.

SUSSEX SLIPCOTE

Silver Medal, British Cheese Awards 1996
A fresh sheep's cheese; 19% fat, pasteurized milk; vegetarian rennet. 115g/4oz rounds
or 1kg/2lb 4oz rolls

Sussex Slipcote is made according to a recipe dating back to the sixteenth century (before sheep's cheese had been eclipsed by cows'). Originally, the name was used for cheeses which had been matured for at least two weeks, until they 'slipped' off their 'coats' because they became soft and runny under the rind. The Sussex High Weald version, however, is a soft cheese with the mousse-like texture typical of fresh sheep's cheese; the taste is mild and flowery, with a faint lemon-like tang. It comes plain, coated with crushed peppercorns, or flavoured with garlic and herbs.

The milk is heated to 32°C/90°F, starter and rennet are added together, and the curd is left in an incubator for twenty-four hours. The excess whey is skimmed from the top and the curd is salted and flavoured before being put into moulds to drain naturally for twenty-four to thirty hours. The cheeses can be eaten directly but will keep (chilled) for up to a month.

HALLOUMI

A semi-hard fresh sheep's cheese; organic milk; vegetarian rennet.
8-cm/3¹/₄-inch blocks

Halloumi has a dense, toffee-like texture: its particular characteristic is that, because it has already been cooking in boiling whey, it does not melt when heated and can be fried or grilled like tofu or meat. Chiefly because of heating to a high temperature, it is too bland to eat without accompaniments or some form of flavouring; as is traditional, Mark uses mint.

Partly because of its texture, proper halloumi must be made with sheep's milk, which is heated to 32°C/90°F. Rennet is added, and the curd is left to set for an hour (no starter is used). The curd is then cut, scalded slightly, pressed into shallow moulds, and stacked for another hour to extract the whey. When the whey has run off, it is heated to 85°C/185°F and the cheese cut into blocks which are thrown into the hot liquid and allowed to stew, literally in their own juice. Finally, the blocks are folded, brined for about an hour, and dusted with mint.

To serve, season the cheese with coarse pepper and just a grain or two of salt, dry-fry or grill it until golden on both sides (do not add oil), and drizzle very generously with lemon juice. For a simple but delicious salad, serve it on top of a mixture of hot and bitter salad leaves.

RICOTTA

A soft, fresh, cooked sheep's whey cheese; vegetarian rennet. Blocks of various weights

Ricotta is very mild and intended primarily for cooking with added flavouring; however, it can also be served on the cheeseboard or used as a spread. Most versions are of a creamy consistency, but Mark's is drained to a block for vacuum-packing: this means that it is ideal when a stiff filling is needed but may need moistening for other purposes. For the table, it combines the mousse-like quality characteristic of fresh sheep's-milk products with the nutty texture of the cooked curds. There are various ways of flavouring it, but two good ones are with chives and fromage frais or sage.

To make the ricotta, the whey is heated to 85°C/185°F, the acidity adjusted if necessary, and the cheese scooped out as soon as it floats to the surface; it is then lightly salted and drained in shallow moulds.

FETA

A hard Greek-style sheep's cheese preserved in brine; pasteurized milk, sometimes organic; vegetarian rennet. Blocks of various weights

Although feta, like halloumi and ricotta, is now often made with cows' milk, it was originally a sheep's cheese. It is salty, as the brine suggests, but also sharp and fresh-tasting: to modify the saltiness, soak the cheese for a couple of hours in cold water. There is no better way of eating it than simply to toast it, when it melts as smoothly as cream and needs no addition except perhaps a few drops of lemon juice.

Starter and rennet are added to the milk simultaneously, as for Sussex Slipcote; when the curd has set, it is lightly scalded, scooped into moulds, and left to drain, with turning at intervals, for two or three days. It is then immersed in brine for a minimum of two months.

FROMAGE FRAIS

A soft fresh sheep's cheese; 9% fat, unpasteurized milk; vegetarian rennet. 175g/6oz cartons (plain) or 90g/3^1/$_4$oz tubs (flavoured)

The unflavoured version is fairly sharp and is intended for cooking, when its sharpness comes into its own: I have found no other cheese which gives the same tang and intensity of flavour. For eating *per se*, it is flavoured with fruit, including orange, lemon, and raspberry.

Although simple enough now, the recipe for the cheese took Mark and Colin over a year and a half to develop. The milk is heated to 82–85°C/180–185°F, and then cooled to 45°C/113°F before starter is added. After renneting, the curds (which are not drained) are kept at 45°C/113°F for twenty-four hours.

 ## Putlands Farm Sticky Lemon Pudding

In this recipe, the cheese is used instead of eggs, which gives a much more concentrated flavour: by replacing it with three medium-sized eggs, you can turn it into an excellent moist cake. To accompany the pudding, serve either the lemon or raspberry fromage frais or the plain cheese flavoured to taste.

Cooking time: 35–40 minutes
For 6

200g/7oz butter
250g/9oz caster sugar
175g/6oz Sussex High Weald Dairy sheep's fromage frais
1 small lemon, preferably organic
1 tbsp brandy
125g/4¹/₂oz finely ground self-raising wholemeal flour
¹/₂ tsp bicarbonate of soda
50g/1³/₄oz ground almonds

Set the oven to 180°C/350°F/Gas 4; grease a 22-cm/8¹/₂-inch soufflé dish. Beat the butter and sugar to a cream; add the fromage frais and beat until smooth. Wash and finely grate the lemon zest into the mixture; squeeze and stir in 2 tablespoonsful of the juice and the brandy. Sift together the flour, bicarbonate of soda, and almonds; add to the mixture and stir thoroughly. Turn it into the dish and bake for 35–40 minutes, until the pudding has risen and turned golden brown. Serve hot.

ASHDOWN FORESTERS (ORGANIC)

Bronze Medal, British Cheese Awards 1996 and 1997; Winner of the Organic Food Awards 1997
A hard cows' cheese; full-fat, pasteurized milk; vegetarian rennet. 1.5kg/3lb 5oz and 3.5kg/7lb 11oz truckles

The cheese has a wonderfully smooth, creamy feel and, although pasteurized, a spectrum of gentle flavours: in particular, a freshness reminiscent of tart apples is offset by the rich taste of the Guernsey milk. Altogether, it is subtle and delicious.

Starter is added and the milk left to ripen for an hour, after which it is heated to 32°C/90°F, rennet is added, and the curd is left to set for another hour. It is then scalded slowly to 40°C/104°F, scooped into basket moulds, kept at 20°C/68°F for twenty-four hours, and turned at intervals. Finally, the cheeses are brined for a further twenty-four hours and matured for six to eight weeks.

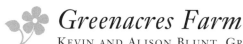

Greenacres Farm

KEVIN AND ALISON BLUNT, GREENACRES FARM, WHITESMITH, EAST SUSSEX BN8 6JA. TEL: 01825 872380

Rather than setting out to make cheese, the Blunts were handed it on a plate, so to speak. Their original ambition was simply to farm: when they bought Greenacres, which has only 2.4ha/6 acres, they planned to specialize in free-range hens, but bought a bonus of four goats for Kevin, who up until then had worked chiefly with cows. However, as in the case of the Jenners (page 49), the goats completely captivated them, and now (including kids) they have 180, as well as 1,000 hens. At first, they sold only eggs and milk, but as the milk yield rose, they began, almost inevitably, to experiment with cheese. An expatriate French neighbour, Regis Dussatre, who also kept goats and made two cheeses, Chabis and Dussatre, decided to sell up and return to France. As a result, they were not only able to buy his milking parlour and some of his goats and equipment, but they also inherited his recipes and out-lets, including Neal's Yard Dairy and James Aldridge's shop at Beckenham. Since then, they have continued Chabis, turned Dussatre into Golden Cross (named after the nearest village), and added a third, triumphant cheese to their range, Flower Marie, made to a recipe devised for them by James.

Lacking the space to raise sheep themselves, they buy in the milk for Flower Marie from Dorset (when they started making it, none was available locally, perhaps partly because of Mark Hardy: page 41). The goats, who are mainly Saanens but with a few British Alpines and Toggenburgs, produce between 250 and 450 litres/55 and 99 gallons a day; milking takes five hours. The Blunts acknowledge that if they settled for fewer goats and bought in extra milk, they could make more cheese, which would almost certainly pay, but their love of the goats is overriding, so instead they have reduced the number of hens (which peaked a few years ago at 2,000). They have two herds, divided into spring and autumn kidding, so that the supply of milk, although uneven, is continuous.

I visited them in the spring kidding season and watched a mother giving birth as easily and calmly as if she did it every morning. At that time of year Kevin keeps them in, but they are let out during the day in summer; how-ever, he says that if there is the slightest nip in the air they never stay out for more than half an hour, and they always return at the first drop of rain or at dusk. During very hot weather, he has tried to induce them to go out in the evenings instead of the heat of the day, but without success.

On the other side of the yard is the dairy, which has a hot-room or incubator as well as a drying room equipped on the same principle as the Jenners' but with an ordinary freezer unit and fan. In the cheesemaking room, my attention was caught by the Blunts' French moulds, which are fitted with trays above for the surplus curd as a way to save the labour of refilling: some came from Dussatre but the rest they had to buy from France, since, like other items of cheesemaking equipment, they are not made in this country.

CHABIS

Bronze Medal, British Cheese Awards 1997
An unpressed goats' cheese with a white mould rind; full-fat, unpasteurized milk;
vegetarian rennet. 90–100g/3$^1/_4$–3$^1/_2$oz rounds

The Blunts sell Chabis when it is one week old, but some cheese-shops mature it on for a further three to four weeks. When young, it is mild, but at four weeks it has developed a gentle but distinctive tang.

To make Chabis, the morning and evening milk are mixed, heated to 20°C/68°F, and starter, rennet, and penicillin for the rind added simultaneously. The curd is left in the incubator for twenty-four hours before being ladled into the moulds, with the surplus in the trays. The cheeses are turned after ten to twelve hours, and after another twelve hours are moved to the drying room. They are salted the next day, kept for a further one to two days, and then transferred to the maturing room for five to six days while the rind starts to develop. From this point, they can be eaten or left to mature for longer according to taste.

GOLDEN CROSS AND LAUGHTON LOG

Bronze Medal, British Cheese Awards 1996 and 1997 (Golden Cross)
An unpressed goats' cheese log with a white mould rind; full-fat, unpasteurized milk;
vegetarian rennet. Golden Cross: 225g/8oz; Laughton Log: 1kg/2lb 4oz

The two cheeses differ only in size. On both, the white penicillin rind is grown over a charcoal (as opposed to ash) coating: the charcoal adds considerably to the taste. In particular, they are notable for their fine, silky texture and in being among the very few British goats' cheeses which are moderately strong: partly for this reason, they are outstanding for grilling.

47

Golden Cross and Laughton Log are made in a similar way to Chabis, but are dusted with charcoal and packaged to prevent the rind from becoming crusty after it dries. The maturing time at the Blunts' is three to four weeks, but Neal's Yard Dairy mature them on for another four to six: when I tried to buy one directly after it had been delivered, I was firmly told to come back after a month.

FLOWER MARIE

Bronze Medal, British Cheese Awards 1996
An unpressed white mould rind sheep's cheese; unpasteurized milk; vegetarian rennet.
200g/7oz or 600g/1lb 5oz squares

The name is appropriate since the cheese has a blossom-like lightness and sweetness; as well as flowers, the flavours include herbs, summer grass, and cream. The texture is soft, sometimes molten under the rind, but the longer the cheese is matured, the firmer it becomes, with a correspondingly deeper, richer taste. The only other white mould-ripened sheep's cheeses made in the UK or Ireland are Mary Holbrook's Emlett and Little Ryding (pages 73 and 74): all three show how wonderful this type of sheep's cheese can be.

The milk, which all comes from the same farm, is delivered frozen. After defrosting, it is heated to 20°C/68°F and starter, rennet, and penicillin added together, as for the other cheeses. The curd is ladled into square moulds and left to drain for one to one and a half hours; it is then turned at intervals for the rest of the day, i.e. for the next twelve to fourteen hours. In the evening, the cheeses are unmoulded and left to drain again, brined, and dried in the drying room for one to two days. Finally, they go to the maturing room, where they are turned after five or six days, with care being taken at this stage not to disturb the growth of the rind by touching them (Kevin turns them like a cake, with a tray on top of them). They are wrapped a day or two later and can be eaten thereafter at any time over the next six weeks.

Nut Knowle Farm Cheeses

LYN AND JENNY JENNER, NUT KNOWLE FARM, WORLD'S END,
GUN HILL, HORAM, EAST SUSSEX TN21 0LA. TEL: 01825 872214

In an earlier existence, the Jenners lived in a large house in Woodmancote, near Brighton; they then spent twenty years at Nut Knowle Farm at the foot of the Sussex Downs. Now, because of the M23 and road improvements around Brighton, they have moved to World's End, near Horam, which – at least when I went there, on a dark, damp January day – seemed aptly named. From London, you approach via the A22, which could hardly be more of a contrast to the motorway; you turn off down a small side road and into a deeply rutted track leading past a farm on which there was no sign of people or animals and a pond so covered with weed that it was scarcely identifiable as such. You drive on, past another farm, and on, the track (labelled 'footpath') becoming ever more liquid with rich, sticky, almost black mud. Their house, which at that time they had only just finished renovating, similarly rose from what might have been primeval slime – the combined result, I gathered, of contractors' vehicles, cows, and an overflow from their pond.

In their Woodmancote days, Lyn was a successful dealer in antique silver, flying to sales all over the world and working with 'women who wore leather and men who wore mink'. Then one day they were held at gunpoint and robbed. Lyn is dismissive about this experience, saying only that it was 'unpleasant': one of their reactions, however, was to buy two German shepherd dogs. Although the dogs were in fact as gentle as possible, they frightened the milkman, who refused to deliver.

The Jenners therefore tried a carton of goats' milk, liked it, and after visiting various goatkeepers and viewing a number of goats with increasing excitement and enthusiasm, bought their first goat, a British Toggenburg called Treacle. As Treacle was lonely by herself, their next step was to find her a companion, Honey; Honey was followed by Sweetie, then Toffee, until the herd had increased to fourteen. They then accepted that their lives had changed, moved to Woodmancote, and began to make cheese, experimentally at first, but later with the same flair and professionalism as had distinguished them in the silver business.

They now have 250 Toggenburgs, British Alpines, and Saanens, with names beginning with the appropriate letter of the alphabet, like car registration numbers, according to year of birth. For the same reasons as others with large herds, they keep their goats indoors: Lyn remarked, rather despondingly, that if let out they will eat literally anything, making the production of a cheese with consistent flavour impossible. They live in open sheds carpeted with straw so sweet-smelling that it would be worthy of a scent and are fed on barley and hay grown on the farm plus a compound feed specially mixed to the Jenners' requirements.

Lyn is even more emphatic than Charles Westhead (page 172) about the importance of not disturbing the milk, which is pumped directly from the milking parlour to a tank above the cheesemaking room so that it need not be pumped again but runs into the vats by force of gravity. To offset the effects of differing weather conditions on the cheeses before they are matured, the dairy also includes a drying room, where the air is filtered by a sterilizing fan. Lyn and Jenny make ten different cheeses: one, however, is still at the experimental stage and three are aimed chiefly at the catering trade, including an ash-covered, pyramid-shaped cheese which is served on British Airways. Of the remaining six, three are made to their own recipes, one is French, one Swiss, and one, St George, made to a recipe which they bought when they first started cheesemaking. Another, Caprini, is marinated in rapeseed oil and comes in various flavours, including peppers with herbs, chillies, and spices; wild nettle and garlic; and lemon and black olives.

ST GEORGE

A Camembert-style goats' cheese; full-fat, unpasteurized milk except by request; vegetarian rennet. 150g/5¼oz or 280g/10oz rounds (boxed)

When ripe, St George is flowing and creamy, with a very crisp white mould rind. The taste is of herbs, earth, and mushrooms, quite strong and distinctive but with scarcely any hint of goat as such: the goat simply adds intensity to the other flavours. Altogether, interesting and delicious, but (like St Francis, page 38) hard to come by: if you find it, snap it up at once.

For all the cheeses listed, the milk is heated to 18°C/64°F before the starter is added. For St George, penicillin for the rind is also added, and the temperature is increased to 25°C/77°F before the addition of rennet. The curd is left to set for an hour, then cut very small, drained, and poured into moulds. The cheeses are salted and turned twice, once as they are moulded and again when the moulds have been piled; after unmoulding, they are diced and matured for two weeks. They can be kept (chilled) for up to a month.

SUSSEX YEOMAN

A hard, washed-rind goats' cheese; full-fat, unpasteurized milk except by request; vegetarian rennet. 2kg/4lb 6oz truckles

Sussex Yeoman has a pleasantly fudge-like texture and nutty taste overlaid by a gentle smoky tang just strong enough to hold its own against a medium Cheddar.

Rennet is added when the milk has been heated to 32°C/90°F. After an hour, the curd is cut very small and left for a further half-hour. It is then scalded over thirty minutes to 38°C/100°F, ladled into moulds, and turned within ten minutes; this is followed by pressing with a pound-for-pound weight overnight. Next day it is removed from the press and brined over the following night; finally, it is drained for a further twenty-four hours and the rind washed with water. During the two months the cheese is left to mature, it is turned once a week 'and loved'; the rind is scrubbed before each despatch. If stored at around 10°C/50°F, it will keep for some time.

WEALDEN

A semi-hard, black-rind goats' cheese; full-fat, unpasteurized milk except by request; vegetarian rennet. 200g/7oz or 450g/1lb truckles

Like St George, this is an unusual, quite strong cheese but with very little taste of goat: instead, it has a decided, cool herbal tang with earthy undertones. One example that I tried was slightly blued, which added an extra dimension to the taste.

For this cheese, the Jenners use a vat which can be tipped so that the whey drains from the top. Rennet is added when the milk is at 28°C/82°F and the curd left overnight. Next day the whey is tipped off and the curd transferred to moulds, which are turned after six to ten hours; the following day the cheeses are unmoulded and salted. They are then left for a period in the drying room before being matured for a month.

Mike Turner's Dairy

MIKE AND KAREN TURNER, THE OLD FACTORY BUILDING,
BATTENHURST ROAD, STONEGATE, EAST SUSSEX.
TEL: 01580 200355

The Old Factory Building, deep in the Sussex countryside, used to be the egg-sorting station for Stonegate Farm Eggs. When Mike took it over, it was simply a shell of four walls and a roof: in effect, therefore, he has been able to start from scratch in designing a purist but perfect hand-cheesemaker's dairy, forward-looking rather than merely up-to-date in terms of hygienic arrangements yet without a single labour-saving device. The cheesemaking room contains a large but not unmanageably large vat, plus a smaller, covered one for experimenting; on the wall hang a shining harp (a frame with vertical wires) for cutting the curd, a curd shovel for piling it, a stirring paddle, and rake. The only other items are a chemical air-sterilizer, which looks rather like an old-fashioned electric fire, and the sink, which is supplied with purified water so that when the floor is washed or the vat rinsed after disinfecting there is no risk of contamination by tap-water.

The Old Factory Building is his second attempt to create a dairy: when I went to see him, it had been in use for only a month, prior to which he had been out of production for nearly a year because an extremely rare but disastrous infection had forced him to abandon the first. This was in a former stables and at first had seemed ideal; however, for a reason which for some time no one could identify, all the cheeses blew, i.e. burst their rinds. The cause was finally established as hetero-fermentative *lactobacilli*, a bacteria allied to the sort used for starter, which had originally entered the building in the horses' feed. Since there was no way of eradicating it, he was obliged to close down, thus losing his investment in the premises and £50,000 in cheese. All he says now is: 'Well, yes – it was expensive, but it was all part of the learning process. None of us had ever come across it before.'

A dairy farmer's son, Mike started his career trying to sell his father's milk in bags, American-style, which at the time seemed a bright idea; as the bags leaked, the enterprise was doomed to failure, but he was constantly asked by would-be customers for cheese. This led first to wholesaling, which he still does, and then to the desire to make cheese as well. A cheesemaker called David Doble, who made a cheese called Castle Hill, lived in the same village: just as he and David had agreed to go into partnership, David's circumstances changed and he moved to Surrey (page 34). Mike therefore developed his own adaptation of the cheese, Myrtle Grove, which he says 'was never as good as it should have been ... because of the learning curve'.

A few years later he met James Aldridge (page 36), who was just beginning a period of intensive study and experiment. Between them, they turned Myrtle Grove into Olde Sussex, which has been a bestseller for nearly a decade; Mike then introduced a smoked version, Goodwood, and a variation flavoured with cider, garlic, and herbs.

He and James also began to develop a hard sheep's cheese, Lord of the Hundreds, made to a recipe of James's, which took them a long time to perfect but was finally launched four years ago. Mike, who makes it in larger quantities than James, won the Supreme Championship with it at the London International Cheese Fair in 1996, which particularly pleased him because, far from being specially made for the occasion (as cheeses often are), it was not even carefully chosen, but simply pulled from the racks at the last minute: thus, as he says, it genuinely represented the quality of the cheeses actually on sale. He now produces a smoked version called Danegate Gold, which is smoked twice, and has adapted the recipe to make an interesting, slightly peppery-tasting goats' cheese, Skeete.

OLDE SUSSEX

A hard cows' cheese; full-fat, unpasteurized milk; vegetarian rennet.
4kg/8lb 13oz wheels

Olde Sussex is surprisingly different from its sibling cheese, Olde Scotland (page 35): it has a similar, slightly crumbly texture but instead of a smoky tang, a deliciously light, refreshing, summery lemon-like taste, unusual and welcome in southern England.

LORD OF THE HUNDREDS

A hard, slightly grainy sheep's cheese; unpasteurized milk; vegetarian rennet.
3.6kg/8lb squares

The particular quality of the cheese is the salty/sweet balance of flavour: the taste is distinctly smoky but the smokiness does not overwhelm its rich, nutty undertones and the sweetness characteristic of sheep's milk. The maturing time is four to six months: at four months, the cheese is relatively soft-tasting, but at six has become strong enough for sprinkling on soups and pasta and flavouring other dishes in the same way as pecorino.

The Lord's Fish Soufflé

Cooking time: 50–60 minutes
For 2–3 as a main course or 4–5 as a first course

250g/9oz cod, washed, skinned, and boned
150ml/¼ pint or a little more dry white wine
salt and pepper
1 tbsp oil
2 cloves garlic, peeled and finely chopped
15g/½oz white flour
100ml/3½fl oz whipping cream
2 large free-range egg yolks, beaten
100g/3½oz Lord of the Hundreds, finely grated
1 tbsp basil, washed and finely shredded
4 large free-range egg whites

Place the fish on a piece of cooking foil large enough to wrap into a parcel, pour about half the wine over it, and season moderately with salt and pepper. Wrap and bake the fish in a pre-heated oven at 180°C/350°F/Gas 4 for 15–20 minutes or until it is opaque all the way through and can be flaked easily with a fork. Leave it in its liquor to cool.

Warm the oil over fairly low heat and fry the garlic until it begins to show signs of changing colour: it should not be allowed to brown. Remove the pan from the heat at once and stir in the flour. Drain the fish liquor into the pan, return it to low heat, and stir until the sauce starts to thicken. Pour in the rest of the wine and the cream. Season with 1 teaspoonful of salt and a moderate grinding of pepper, simmer gently for 3–4 minutes, and allow to cool. Stir in the egg yolks. Flake the fish finely, checking for bones, and add it to the pan; stir in the cheese and basil. The mixture should be of soft dropping consistency: if it seems stiff, add a little more wine.

Heat the oven to 200°C/400°F/Gas 6; butter an 18-cm/7-inch soufflé dish. Add a generous pinch of salt to the egg whites and whisk until they are opaque, close-textured, and stiff enough to hold their shape. Fold them into the fish mixture gently but swiftly: it is more important to mix them quickly, retaining as much air as possible, than to ensure that every lump of white is dissolved. Turn the mixture into the soufflé dish and bake in the middle of the oven, without opening the door while it is baking, for 35 minutes or until it has risen and turned golden: if a skewer inserted into the middle does not come out clean, bake it for a few minutes more. Serve immediately.

Ladywell Dairy Sheep Products

DUNCAN AND MONICA CRUNDWELL, LADYWELL DAIRY,
COBBLER'S YARD FARM, LEGG'S LANE, LANGTON GREEN,
KENT TN3 0RP. TEL: 01892 863448

Langton Green is only just outside Tunbridge Wells on a busy main road; Legg's Lane and the farm, however, are tucked well away in the fields behind and seem almost as remote as World's End (page 49). The first thing you notice in the tiny farmshop-cum-office is the display of rosettes, mostly red, won by the Crundwells' sheep, who are unique in being the only complete flock of British Milksheep used for dairy purposes (as opposed to breeding) in existence. When the Crundwells originally started at Cobbler's Yard, their decision to rear sheep was governed by their limited grazing area; they chose Milksheep, a cross between Poll Dorset Horn, Blue-faced Leicester, Lleyn, and Friesland, partly because Duncan likes them but also because they are dual-purpose and can be used for lamb as well as milk.

The flock now numbers 120 and in addition to selling milk and meat (by the carcass or half-carcass only), the Crundwells make ices, yoghurt, cheesecake based on yoghurt curd, and soft cheese. All their products are outstanding as examples of the particular qualities of sheep's milk, which because of its small fat globules is more digestible although higher in fat and more concentrated than cows'. Its richness means that ices can be made directly with the milk rather than cream; however, delicate and healthy as they are, even they do not compete with the lightness of the cheese.

LADYWELL SOFT CHEESE

A fresh sheep's cheese; unpasteurized milk; vegetarian rennet. 150g/5¼oz rounds

The cheese is unsurpassed for its airy, mousse-like texture; the taste is mild and fresh, with flowery overtones. It comes with various flavourings, including celery, chives and garlic, and pepper and garlic.

Ladywell is made by a simple, Coulommiers-type recipe: the milk (morning and evening) is heated to 85°C/185°F, starter is added, and the milk is left to ripen for thirty minutes before the addition of rennet. When the curd has set, it is ladled straight into moulds with salt and whichever flavourings are being used, and left to drain for four days. It is then ready to eat: chilled, it will keep for fourteen days, or if frozen for twenty days after defrosting.

Gedi Enterprises Ltd

GARY FREEMAN, PLUMRIDGE FARM, STAGG HILL, BARNET, HERTS
EN4 0PX. TEL: 0181 4490695

London is the last place where you would expect to find a cheese-farm
– and in fact Gedi is not quite in London: the turning to the farm is at the
edge of the Green Belt, a short distance from the last house in Hadley Wood.
If you continue along the road, you come to the M25. As it is relatively near
to where I live, I have visited it at intervals over several years. It used to be
run by Nahi Elkin, an Israeli with a pigtail, a long white beard falling in
ringlets, and a formidable sense of humour, though I have the feeling that I
missed his sharpest remarks because of his habit of lapsing into Hebrew
whenever he had something particularly significant to say. In those days, the
farm felt like a kibbutz; under Gary Freeman's management, this no longer
applies, but the Israeli expertise which Nahi brought with him remains.

The milk for the cheese is supplied by 400 goats, who include brown
Toggenburgs, white Saanens, and black and white British Alpines. As is the
practice at virtually all large goat farms, they are permanently kept in. For a
long time this worried me but I have now come to think that they do not
mind. They hate cold and rain, largely because their coats contain no
protective oil, and (like some dogs) are far more interested in socializing than
exercise. The overriding reason at Gedi for not letting them out is lack of
land, but there is also the fact that if they had the chance they would eat
everything they saw, and one of the reasons for the quality of the cheese is
that their diet is limited to the very best 'haute-cuisine' hay, which is more
digestible than a mixture of foods. In consequence, the milk has a relatively
high fat content, which promotes taste.

ROUBILIAC

Gold Medal, British Cheese Awards 1994; Bronze Medal, 1996
A soft goats' cheese; full-fat, pasteurized milk; vegetarian rennet. 150g/5^1/4oz log

When young, the taste of the cheese is mild, with a gentle flavour of mushrooms and slight hint of nuts, but if it is kept for a few weeks it will develop
a pronounced nutty taste. It comes plain or rolled in herbs or peppercorns.

The most interesting aspect of the Gedi cheeses is that the method of making them, devised by Nahi, goes against one of the cardinal principles of every other goat-cheesemaker: namely that to minimize the taste of goat the milk should be disturbed as little as possible. Here, it is agitated continuously for two hours after the starter is added and for another half-hour after renneting; the curd is also manipulated for a further half-hour during salting. Another generally upheld cheesemaking principle is that the milk should be used as soon as possible. Chiefly for commercial reasons, Gedi pasteurizes, which is carried out directly, but thereafter the milk is allowed to stand for eighteen hours; the type of pasteurization (i.e. the heat used, and in particular how quickly the milk is cooled afterwards) is carefully calculated to suit the different cheeses. The starter and rennet are not standard preparations but custom-made by a Swiss firm. When the curd has set, it is stuffed by hand into muslin bags rather like cushion covers, sealed, and drained by pressing first in a pressing tank, then manually; finally, it is chilled to make shaping easier, salted, and moulded by machine. All the cheeses are matured on the farm for three to seven days.

MOILLION

Gold Medal, British Cheese Awards 1994; Silver Medal, 1996
A soft goats' cheese log; full-fat, pasteurized milk; vegetarian rennet. 150g/5^1/$_4$oz log

Moillion is exceptionally smooth and fine-textured, with a full, rich nutty taste and a gentle, lemon-like tang. It is delicious grilled with a slight dusting of pepper or used as a stuffing for chicken breasts or tomatoes.

VELDE

Bronze Medal, British Cheese Awards 1996
A Camembert-style goats' cheese with an ash coating; full-fat, pasteurized milk;
vegetarian rennet. 120g/4^1/$_4$oz

The soft, flowing texture of the cheese contrasts with the crisp white penicillin rind; the taste is mild and sweet, with an undertone of mushrooms. Gedi recommend serving this cheese with grapes.

CHAVANNES

A Camembert-style goats' cheese; full-fat, pasteurized milk; vegetarian rennet.
125g/4½oz

Chavannes is stronger than Velde, with a taste of grass and mushrooms. It has quite a pronounced cheesy tang but almost no hint of goat.

CROTTIN

Bronze Medal, British Cheese Awards 1996
A fresh goats' cheese; full-fat, pasteurized milk; vegetarian rennet. 70g/2½oz rounds

I used to buy a matured Crottin regularly when it was almost the only relatively strong goats' cheese made in Britain. However, because strong goats' cheeses do not sell, it is now distributed fresh and competes as one of the lightest, most delicate, soufflé-like cheeses on the market. For a stronger version, keep it chilled and wrapped for four to six weeks. It is excellent for grilling.

GEDI SELECTION

A soft goats' cheese; full-fat, pasteurized milk; vegetarian rennet. 110g/3¾oz

The newest addition to the Gedi range is an attractively presented pack of six coated balls (green and red sweet pepper, crushed peppercorns, herbs, and plain). The cheese is exceptionally fine-textured and creamy, with a mild but distinctive lemon-like flavour: the goat taste is almost imperceptible.

CORINNA

A soft goats' cheese; full-fat, pasteurized milk; vegetarian rennet. 240g/8½oz

Corinna is sold as herb-flavoured balls (50g/1¾oz each) preserved in a jar of olive oil. It works because the cheese is sweet and the oil slightly sharp. The left-over oil can be used for salads or cooking. Store the cheese at room temperature rather than in the refrigerator.

CHAPTER 2

South-west England

SMART'S GLOUCESTER CHEESE

CHARLES MARTELL

CERNEY CHEESES

SLEIGHT FARM

PARK FARM CHEESES

R. A. DUCKETT

EXMOOR BLUE CHEESES

DORSET BLUE CHEESE COMPANY

J. A. & E. MONTGOMERY LTD

S. A. & G. H. KEEN

LUBBORN CHEESE LTD

PEVERSTONE CHEESE CO.

J. G. QUICKE AND PARTNERS

TICKLEMORE CHEESE

SHARPHAM CREAMERY

TALA

LYNHER DAIRIES

MENALLACK FARM

Smart's Gloucester Cheese

DIANA SMART, OLD LEY FARM, CHURCHAM, GLOUCESTERSHIRE GL2 8AR. TEL: 01452 750225

Diana Smart did not start making cheese until she was over sixty. For her, cheesemaking was the fulfilment of a wish which had grown over twenty years of living at Old Ley Farm; when she finally began, her aim was, as it still is, to make Gloucester cheese as authentically as possible.

In this, her first and remaining problem was the type of milk. The old Gloucester cattle, who are dark chestnut red with a white stripe down their backs and magnificent horns, are now very rare, and indeed might be extinct were it not for Charles Martell (page 63); she nevertheless acquired a couple of cows in the hope of gradually building up a herd. Unfortunately, the cows have not obliged, having produced only one female calf to date: all the rest have been male or the twins of males (which means that they are sterile), so that most of the milk for the cheese comes from four dozen Holsteins.

Like most cheesemakers, she uses commercial starter, saying that she does not dare to make her own, and the milk is piped from the milking parlour to the dairy; otherwise she makes few concessions to modern practices. Her recipes and some of her equipment, including a hand-operated Victorian mill, came from two old ladies, the Misses Smith, who used to make cheese between Cam and Berkeley in the Severn valley. She abandoned an acidometer when she found that the readings always coincided with her own judgement, and uses pieces of old sheet instead of cheesecloths (boiled and therefore perfectly sterile). She beamed with approval when I said that I had noted 'Moulds lined with old boiled sheets'.

She makes her three cheeses twice a week: Double Gloucester on Tuesdays and Single Gloucester or Harefield, her newest cheese, on Thursdays. Formerly, she was helped by her son Jamie, but he died suddenly and she now works with an assistant called Gary.

SMART'S DOUBLE GLOUCESTER

Silver Medal, British Cheese Awards 1994; Bronze Medal, 1997
A hard cows' cheese; full-fat, unpasteurized milk; vegetarian rennet.
1.4–1.6kg/3–3½lb and 3.2–3.6kg/7–8lb truckles

'Rich', 'mellow', 'powerful', 'earthy, almost smoky' are some of the adjectives used to describe Diana's cheese in my notes. The texture is slightly crumblier than Cheddar, becoming crumblier with maturity. In the early eighteenth century, Gloucester cheeses were celebrated, along with Cheddar, as the finest in England: if this is anything like the historical version, one can understand why.

The milk (morning and evening) is heated to 30°C/86°F; just before it reaches this temperature, Diana adds starter and annatto, the dye traditionally used to give the cheese its rosy colour. The rennet is added after about half an hour, when she judges that the acidity has risen sufficiently, and the milk is left to set for an hour and a quarter. Gary then cuts the curd, scalds it to 38°C/100°F over forty minutes, stirring continuously with a (new) hayrake, and continues to stir for a further twenty minutes. The curd is left to rest before the whey is drained off, to be fed in the old-fashioned manner to the pigs, including an enormous Tamworth sow and an old but splendid Gloucester Old Spot boar. While the whey drains, Gary and Diana have lunch; after lunch, they cut the curd into squares and pile and turn it a total of five times to drain it further. At this point, Diana tests it between her teeth to see if it 'squeaks', which denotes that it is ready for milling. To mill it, she divides it into three and peels it apart in layers, when it looks rather like mattress stuffing; afterwards, the milled curd resembles wood chippings. Salt is then carefully rubbed in by hand, which takes some time; finally, the cheeses are moulded and pressed for forty-eight hours, with turning after twenty-four. The maturing time is at least six months.

Trout and Double Gloucester Fish Cakes

It is better to bake than boil the potato because (as one would expect) baking gives a lighter, drier result, which is especially advantageous for fish cakes made with cheese. The cakes can be made the previous day.

Cooking time: 1 hour (potato only)
Makes 8 cakes

200g/7oz (1 small) baking potato, e.g. Cara, Marfona, Kerr's Pink, washed
240g/8$\frac{1}{2}$oz trout, filleted, skinned, and boned
salt and pepper
1 tsp green peppercorns, crushed
1 small onion (70g/2$\frac{1}{2}$oz), peeled and very finely chopped
115g/4oz mature Smart's or Appleby's Double Gloucester, finely grated
25g/1oz white flour

1 large free-range egg, beaten
55g/2oz fresh, finely grated breadcrumbs
oil for frying

Prick the potato and bake it at 200°C/400°F/Gas 6 for 1 hour, until it is soft all the way through. When it is cool enough to handle, scoop out the inside or peel it, removing the hardened flesh next to the skin.

Check the fish for bones, wash, and season it lightly with salt and pepper. Wrap it in a parcel of cooking foil and bake it at the same heat as the potato for 10–12 minutes or until the fish is pale and flakes easily with a fork. Thoroughly drain the parcel and mash the fish with the potato, green peppercorns, and $\frac{1}{2}$ teaspoonful of salt. Stir in the onion and cheese.

Spread the flour over a large plate, turn the egg into a small bowl, and spread the breadcrumbs over a second plate; season the flour and egg moderately with salt and pepper. Form the fish mixture into cakes, coat all over with the flour, egg, and breadcrumbs, and fry them briskly until golden.

SINGLE GLOUCESTER

Bronze Medal, British Cheese Awards 1997
A hard cow's cheese; low-fat, unpasteurized milk; vegetarian rennet.
675–900g/1½–2lb, 1.4–1.6kg/3–3½lb, and 3.2–3.6kg/7–8lb truckles

Single Gloucester cheeses were originally more economic than Double Gloucester because they matured quickly and were often made with a proportion of skimmed milk. Smart's Single Gloucester is of particular interest now as one of only three surviving examples of traditional handmade skim-milk cheeses of this type. The fact that, like Cerney Heart (page 69), it loses its flavour when hot perhaps explains why in the past cooked cheese dishes did not play a major part in the national diet. It has a deliciously light texture and beautifully balanced taste, with a cool, clean tang and grassy sub-flavours. It is not as strong as Harefield (opposite), but proves that low-fat cheeses can compete with whole-milk ones on perfectly equal terms.

The morning milk is separated and added to the previous evening's whole milk; it is then heated as for Double Gloucester. Relatively little starter is used; rennet is added half an hour after the starter and the milk left to set. After an hour and a half, the curd is cut, scalded to 34.5°C/94°F over thirty minutes, with continuous stirring, and allowed to settle before the whey is run off. The curd is then cut into sixteen squares, turned (but not piled), and left to rest for twenty minutes before being cut into sixty-four squares and turned again. Further cutting follows; finally, the curd is salted as for Double Gloucester, milled, pressed, and matured for three to four months.

HAREFIELD

Bronze Medal, British Cheese Awards 1995; Silver Medal, 1996 and 1997
A hard cows' cheese; low-fat, unpasteurized milk; vegetarian rennet.
2.7–3.2kg/6–7lb truckles

Harefield is made in a similar way to Single Gloucester but matured for at least a year. The long maturing gives it a hard, dry texture and a tang as salty/ sharp but grassier and without the smoky tones of Parmesan. Perhaps even more than Single Gloucester, it shows how excellent low-fat cheeses can be.

Charles Martell
CHARLES MARTELL, LAUREL FARM, DYMOCK, GLOUCESTERSHIRE GL18 2DP. TEL: 01531 890637

Laurel farmhouse is full of prints and pictures: in the time he never has, i.e. very occasionally, Charles paints, and in another life might have been an artist. He is a consummate cheesemaker: even cheese, however, is subservient to his passionate commitment to Gloucester cattle. When he moved to Laurel Farm in 1972, there were only sixty-eight Gloucesters in the world: he bought as many as he could find, revived the Gloucester Cattle Society, of which he is patron, and started making cheese as a way of publicizing his cause rather than for its own sake. The total number of female cattle has now risen to 450 and his own herd, which has been more co-operative than Diana Smart's two cows, has grown to twenty-five. Recently, he also took up the cause of Gloucester cheese: although, as Diana's case illustrates, it is at present impracticable to insist that it should be made of Gloucester milk, he has established that the name Single Gloucester can be applied only to cheeses made in Gloucestershire.

His great regret as a cheesemaker is that, with only twenty-five Gloucesters and 22ha/55 acres, he cannot produce enough milk for an economic quantity of cheese. He does not split his herd for winter milking: some of his cheeses are made from his own milk while it is available and the rest (Friesian) is bought from a neighbouring farm, which he feels obliged to pasteurize because it has travelled. However, like Paddy Berridge, Eugene Burns (pages 120 and 128), and a few others, his skill is such that without being told, I do not believe that anybody would know. This is not to say that if you tried them side by side, the difference between the pasteurized and unpasteurized versions of his cheeses would be unnoticeable, but in comparing them you would also have to allow for the difference in the type of milk.

SINGLE GLOUCESTER

Gold Medal, British Cheese Awards 1996; Silver Medal, 1997
A hard cows' cheese; full-fat, pasteurized and unpasteurized milk; vegetarian rennet.
3.6–4.5kg/8–10lb truckles

Charles's Single Gloucester is as traditional as Diana's but totally different because it is made with whole-milk and notable for its creamy texture and rich taste. The texture is miraculous: although technically hard, the cheese melts in the mouth like mousse or ice-cream. The taste is full of nuances, fresh but without a trace of sharpness, sweet and sunny without being flowery, and above all buttery.

Charles's three hard cheeses are all made by a similar method to Single Gloucester. The milk is heated or cooled, depending on whether it was pasteurized, to 32°C/90°F before the addition of starter; renneting follows after forty-five minutes. When the curd has set, after about another thirty minutes, it is cut and scalded for half an hour to a temperature which depends on the weather. It is then drained, milled and salted, and moulded; finally, the cheeses are pressed for two to three days and matured for up to two months.

HEREFORD HOP

A hard cows' cheese coated with toasted hops; full-fat, usually pasteurized milk;
vegetarian rennet. 3.6–4.5kg/8–10lb rounds

The cheese is smooth, moist, and creamy, with a soft but distinctive flowery rather than hop-like taste. It gains rather than loses flavour when heated and is delicious toasted.

Hereford Hop is pressed longer and heated to a higher temperature than Single Gloucester. It is matured in a crust of toasted hops: Charles says that he is not sure precisely how this affects the cheese, but, flavour aside, it presumably helps to keep it moist and contributes to its rich, creamy character.

Hereford Hop Chive and Bacon Creams

Cooking time: 12–14 minutes (excluding bacon)
For 5–6

5–6 rashers streaky unsmoked bacon (1 each), baked brown and crisp
1–1$^1/_2$ tbsp chives, washed, dried, and snipped finely
4 large free-range egg yolks
salt and pepper
270ml/$^1/_2$ pint less 2 tbsp milk
2 tbsp whipping or thin double cream
100g/3$^1/_2$oz Hereford Hop, cleared of any fragments of rind and finely grated

Pre-heat the oven to 190°C/375°F/Gas 5. Lightly butter five or six ramekin or similar baking dishes. Break the rashers of bacon into fragments and spread them over the bottoms. Sprinkle with the chives. Season the yolks lightly with salt and moderately with pepper, beat until smooth and homogeneous with a fork, and gradually stir in the milk and cream. Stir in the cheese. Ladle the mixture into the dishes, set the dishes in a bain-marie, and bake for 12–14 minutes or until firm and just showing signs of turning golden.

STINKING BISHOP

Gold Medal, British Cheese Awards 1994; Bronze Medal, 1996
A semi-soft cows' cheese; full-fat, usually pasteurized milk; vegetarian rennet.
1.5–1.8kg/3lb 5oz–4lb rounds

Like the French Epoisses, the cheese smells – slightly or strongly according to ripeness – of old socks. The smell is more potent than the taste, which is utterly different and totally delicious but impossible to describe except by saying that it is the essence of cheese. I am told that at the 1996 Besançon cheese fair, the French refused to believe that it was not made in France.

Instead of being drained, milled, and salted, the curds are washed in perry and ladled directly into moulds; to increase moisture content and encourage bacterial activity, salt is not added until the cheeses are turned out.

Stinking Bishop Fritters with Cider

Allow thirty minutes to an hour for the batter to stand. The cheese should be kept chilled until just before use so that it is firm when added to the batter. Serve with apple chutney or pear and apple cheese (page 24).

125g/4¹/₂oz white flour
salt and pepper
1 large free-range egg
125ml/4fl oz strong cider
1 large free-range egg white
about 50g/1³/₄oz Stinking Bishop per head, chilled, rind removed, and cut into 1.5-cm/¹/₂-inch squares
sunflower oil for frying

Sift the flour with the salt and pepper, make a well in the middle, and add the egg plus a little of the cider. Stir the flour into the liquids, working towards the outside: add more cider as needed until all the flour is taken up. Beat the mixture against the side of the bowl until no pockets of flour are left; then stir in the rest of the cider to make a thick paste. Leave the batter to rest for 30–60 minutes.

Set a plate lined with absorbent paper ready to draw excess oil from the fritters as they come out of the pan. Whisk the egg white until it is opaque and stiff enough to stand in peaks; fold it lightly into the batter. Gently stir in the pieces of cheese. Pour enough oil into a wok or frying pan to cover the bottom fairly generously; allow it to warm for a moment or two over medium heat, and fry the pieces of cheese to a deep gold on each side. Do not fry more at a time than will fit into the pan without touching. Drain the fritters on the paper and serve immediately.

DOUBLE BERKELEY

A hard cows' cheese marbled with annatto; full-fat, pasteurized and unpasteurized milk; vegetarian rennet. 3.6–4.5kg/8–10lb truckles

Like Single Gloucester, the texture is wonderfully light, delicate, and melting; the taste is mellow and very buttery but, again, surprisingly fresh. The overall effect is milder but richer than a matured Double Gloucester, as is consistent with history, since the Vale of Berkeley was considered a particularly rich grazing area. Double Berkeley is made in almost exactly the same way as Single Gloucester but annatto is added with the starter.

Cerney Cheeses

LADY ANGUS, CHEESEMAKER: MARION CONISBEE-SMITH,
CERNEY HOUSE, NORTH CERNEY, CIRENCESTER,
GLOUCESTERSHIRE GL7 7BX. TEL: 01285 831312

Originally, Cerney cheeses were made to a French recipe (as they still are) in the quintessentially English surroundings of a Cotswold country house. The house, redesigned by Decimus Burton in 1791, is situated deep in the hollow of a wold, surrounded on three sides by steeply wooded hillsides and a lawn which slopes upwards towards the main garden; in front, the former deer-park stretches down to the pond which in earlier times supplied the household with ice. The garden is best known for roses, but also remarkable for herbs, of which there are forty varieties, and a seriously gastronomic selection of fruit and vegetables.

Lady Angus was taught to make cheese by a farmer's wife at Valencay, near Tours; Marion Conisbee-Smith, who has managed the dairy for the past ten years, still uses the same basic recipe and goes to Valencay every year to buy the mixture of oak ash and salt with which the cheeses are coated. Even so, the English version differs from the French: for one thing, it tastes much less of goat. According to Marion, one reason for this is that, unlike the British, French goatkeepers do not segregate their male and female animals but keep them all together, which is said to give the milk a more distinctive taste. Lyn Jenner (page 49) explained why at the 1995 Goat Conference: 'If you put your male into the milking herd, this can cause tainted milk, because they spray everything in sight, including the goats' udders. Some won't agree with this, but it is certainly my experience.' (*Goat News*, Winter 1995)

The milk was produced on the premises in the early days but is now bought (frozen) from neighbouring farms, where the herds include Golden Guernseys and Anglo-Nubians: this gives it a relatively high fat content and partly accounts for the richness of the cheese. Similarly, Marion used to make all the cheese in the former butler's pantry in Cerney House; recently, how-ever, the ground floor of a nearby farmhouse was converted into a new, much larger, better equipped dairy. The pantry will not be abandoned, but will serve as an experimental area where, among other possibilities, she is plan-ning to develop a blue goats' cheese, of which to date only two (Brendon Blue and Harbourne Blue: pages 81 and 106) are made in this country.

At present, besides the original cheese, she makes a low-fat version called Cerney Heart, for which the milk is separated (although, because of the homogeneous nature of goats' milk, it is not fat-free). She was led to develop it more from a love of 'fiddling' than concern for health, but as the only reduced-fat goats' cheese on the market, it is a boon to anyone watching their diet. The cream is mixed with full-fat Cerney to make cream cheeses; she also makes a small, fresh cheese designed for grilling, Cerney Starter.

CERNEY

Bronze Award, British Cheese Awards 1994 and 1995; Silver Medal, 1996
A fresh goats' cheese coated with ash; full-fat, unpasteurized milk; vegetarian rennet.
250g/9oz truncated pyramid

The taste is full and rich, with flavours of cream, herbs, and nuts but only the mildest tinge of goat; the texture is similarly nutty, and much firmer and more concentrated than is usual for a fresh cheese.

The cheese is made over a period of five days. On the first morning, the milk is warmed to blood-heat and starter and rennet are added together; the starter, which is homemade, is part of the Valencay recipe. The following morning, the curd is ladled into cloths and left to drain for a further twenty-four hours; on the third morning, Marion transfers it to moulds, pressing it down fairly firmly, and sprinkles the top with the mixture of ash and salt. On the fourth day, the cheeses are unmoulded and the rest of the surface is salted; they are then left for a final day to dry. They can be eaten immediately or kept (chilled) for up to a month.

 ## Cerney Chicken in Pastry

Cooking time: 25 minutes
For 6

2 tbsp oil
3 cloves garlic, peeled and finely chopped
1 tbsp rosemary, washed and very finely snipped
6 small chicken breasts, skinned and boned *or* 6 small, thinly cut pork escalopes
salt and pepper
flour for dusting
1 quantity puff pastry (page 21)
150g/5$^{1}/_{4}$oz Cerney
1 small egg, beaten *or* milk for glazing

Warm the oil over medium heat and fry the garlic until it starts to change colour; add the rosemary, turn, and remove the pan from the heat.

Beat the meat with a pestle to tenderize and thin it, and season each breast or escalope moderately with salt and a little more generously with pepper. Dust the rolling-pin and board with flour, roll out the pastry very thinly, and cut it into squares about 5cm/2 inches larger than the width of the meat.

Set the oven to 200°C/400°F/Gas 6. Thoroughly mix the cheese with the rosemary, garlic, and oil; place a sixth of the mixture (about 1 tablespoonful) in a strip down the shorter side of each piece of meat, roll up the pieces (pork makes tidier rolls than chicken) and set each roll on one side of a square of pastry, leaving a margin of about 2.5cm/1 inch from each end. Moisten the edges, fold them over, and seal them securely. Trim or fold back the ends as for a parcel; brush with the beaten egg or milk and make two or three slashes across the top. Bake for 25 minutes or until the pastry is pale golden.

CERNEY HEART

Silver Medal, British Cheese Awards 1995
A fresh, ash-coated goats' cheese; skimmed, unpasteurized milk; vegetarian rennet. 200g/7oz

The cheeses are heart-shaped to indicate that they are good for the heart; except for being a little lighter and milder than full-fat Cerney, they are surprisingly like them in both texture and taste.

 ## Cerney Heart and Smoked Trout Pâté

Although it retains its texture, the Heart, like most other low-fat cheeses, loses much of its flavour when heated; however, it is excellent as a base for dips and pâtés. The following is healthy and almost instant.

For 4

25g/1oz shallot, finely chopped
135g/4³/₄oz smoked trout fillets
125g/4¹/₂oz (about ²/₃) Cerney Heart
juice of ¹/₂ small lemon
salt and pepper

Blend the shallot, trout, and cheese with 1 teaspoonful of the lemon juice, a moderate seasoning of salt, and a generous grinding of pepper. Add more lemon juice to taste (probably another teaspoonful). Serve with hot toast and/or crudités.

CERNEY PEPPER, ORANGE AND GINGER

Bronze Medal, British Cheese Awards 1997 (Cerney Pepper)
Flavoured fresh cream goats' cheeses; full-fat, unpasteurized milk; vegetarian rennet.
150g/5¼ oz cylinders

Cerney Pepper is coated with crushed black peppercorns; Orange is flavoured with orange essence, a little sugar, and Grand Marnier, and rolled in toasted almonds; Ginger is rolled in hazelnuts and made with puréed and stem ginger and Canton ginger liqueur. As with the original Cerney, the texture is firm and concentrated, but with a luxuriously smooth, satin-like feel. The peppercorn version is rich and intense, the orange subtle and barely sweet; the Grand Marnier gives the cheese a refreshing tang which offsets the richness of the cream. Personally, I much prefer it to the Ginger, but Marion says that people who like the one generally hate the other.

CERNEY STARTER

A fresh goats' cheese; full-fat, unpasteurized milk; vegetarian rennet. 50g/1¾oz buttons

Cerney Starter is primarily intended for grilling: each button is of a thickness and size to be cooked directly as an individual portion. As is needed for grilling, the texture is relatively dry; the flavour is fresher and more delicate than the other Cerney cheeses. The Starters are usually sold frozen: allow one and a half to two hours for defrosting.

Lady Angus suggests grilling the buttons with a little thick honey: set the cheese on croutons, add honey, pepper, and olive oil, place them under a hot grill to brown them lightly, and serve them with bitter leaves. Alternatively, grill them with fruit and apple or redcurrant jelly or sugar plus a tablespoonful of Jersey cream on top. Good combinations are Cerney Starter and grapes with pear and apple jelly or black cherries with demerara sugar.

Sleight Farm

MARY HOLBROOK, SLEIGHT FARM, TIMSBURY, BATH, AVON BA3
1HN. TEL: 01761 470620

Sleight Farm is on a hill with a view stretching over Bristol and the
Severn Bridge to South Wales on the one hand and Salisbury Plain on the
other: much of it was blotted out by rain when we arrived, and when we left
it was dark, but the vista of lights across Bristol was dramatic and gave an
exhilarating sense of space. The farm is one of the few that I visited outside
the organic movement which is still mixed, with a beef herd and pigs as
well as sheep and goats for cheese (Old Ley, where the Smarts keep pigs,
chickens, and sheep for lamb is another: page 60).

Mary used to be an archaeologist and then became a museum curator.
She originally started making cheese because she had two goats who gave
more milk than she could drink. She now has ninety, all bred on the farm,
plus 180 Friesland sheep, and is renowned throughout the cheese world for
her exquisite cheeses and profound knowledge of cheesemaking, gained from
a combination of personal experience and observation of practices in France
and other countries, notably Portugal. The quality of her cheeses is probably mainly due to individual judgement and skill, but other factors include a
traditional, near-organic approach to farming and her similarly traditional
cheesemaking methods. At the time of our visit, the exceptionally dry
summer had impelled the Holbrooks to use artificial fertilizer for the first
time in five year; normally, they do not need it, since they have rich clay soil
and abundant supplies of pig manure. There is no question of keeping the
goats permanently indoors, although Mary never lets them out until the dew
has dried as a precaution against worms; she has also given up producing
winter milk, which is less stressful for the animals and gives her a rest.

In the dairy, she uses very little starter and rennet, and no starter at all
for her latest cheese, Tilleys, which is also remarkable for being made with
an enzyme derived from cardoons instead of a conventional type of rennet,
according to an old Portuguese custom. The cardoons are infused in water
and the infusion added to the milk directly after milking, when the milk is at
a certain temperature: exactly the right temperature is vital if it is to work.
Like James Aldridge and a few others, she uses traditional, i.e. animal, rennet for the rest of her cheeses. The first was Sleight, a fresh goats' cheese: she
now makes two other goats' and four sheep's, all named after the fields on the
farm in which the animals graze.

SLEIGHT

A fresh goats' cheese; full-fat, unpasteurized milk; traditional rennet. 115g/4oz logs; seasonal: March–November

All Mary's cheeses have a warm, nutty, slightly mushroom-like taste: Sleight is distinctive but delicate, with a notably fine, creamy texture. It is sold plain or coated with pepper, rosemary, or garlic and herbs.

TYMSBORO'

Gold Medal, British Cheese Awards 1997
An unpressed goats' cheese coated with ash under a penicillin rind; full-fat, unpasteurized milk; traditional rennet. 225g/8oz truncated pyramids; seasonal: March–November

The rind may be tinged greenish-grey rather than white: the green is an invading strain of penicillin, as edible as the white and welcomed by Mary because it adds to the flavour. Directly underneath the rind, the cheese will have ripened to a cream; the middle is compact but quite wonderfully light and smooth. The taste is deep, rich, nutty, and sweet/sharp, with hints of earth, mushrooms, and herbs which vary with the season; without being strong, it has a pronounced tang, although of cheese rather than goat.

TILLEYS

A compact goats' cheese, hard or semi-hard according to maturity; full-fat, unpasteurized milk; extract of cardoon. About 1.2kg/2lb 11oz rounds; seasonal: March–November

The texture is fudgy when young but becomes harder as it ages, with a few small holes; the taste is salty/sweet with suggestions of nuts and earth and a definite tinge of artichoke. In particular, it is absolutely excellent toasted.

 Warm Salad of Tilleys with Hazelnuts

You can either grill the cheese on slices of baked bread or fry it in egg and breadcrumbs: the second looks more elegant but I recommend the first because the flavour of the cheese is more intense if it is left in one piece.

For 2

40g/1^1/$_2$oz whole (unskinned) hazelnuts

100g/3^1/$_2$oz Tilleys

2 half-slices of baked bread drizzled with oil and lightly seasoned with salt
and pepper for grilling (page 22) *or* 25g/1oz flour, 1 small free-range egg, and
25–40g/1–1^1/$_2$oz fresh breadcrumbs, plus oil for frying

2 tbsp virgin olive oil

^{1}/$_2$ tbsp red wine vinegar

salt and pepper

mixed sharp or bitter, or non-sweet salad leaves (batavia, spinach, oakleaf or
lambs' lettuce, land- or watercress, sorrel, rocket, mizuna), washed and dried

Crisp the nuts by toasting them in a moderate oven for 4–5 minutes or toss
them in hot oil (but do not use the oil in which you plan to fry the cheese).

If you are grilling the cheese, place it on the bread in thick slices, trim-
ming the bread if necessary so that none of it is exposed (if uncovered it will
burn). If you are frying the cheese, cut it into squares and coat them with
flour, egg, and breadcrumbs (page 23).

Beat together the oil, vinegar, and a slight seasoning of salt and pepper;
toss the salad leaves with the dressing and arrange them round the edge of
the serving plates. If you are grilling the cheese, place the bread slices under
a hot grill until they turn golden; for frying, line a dish with absorbent paper
to drain off surplus fat, fry the cheese squares until golden, and blot on the
paper. Place the cheese in the centre of the salad plates, sprinkle with
the nuts, and serve.

EMLETT

Gold Medal, British Cheese Awards 1997
An unpressed sheep's cheese; white or green and white penicillin mould rind;
unpasteurized milk; traditional rennet. 175g/6oz rounds; seasonal: March–November

Emlett is soft but compact rather than runny and, like Tymsboro', wonderfully smooth. The taste is gentle but positive, fresh and at the same time
nutty, with numerous variable undertones. Its many sub-flavours make it
exceptionally adaptable on the cheeseboard, where it will harmonize with a
wide range of cheeses; however, particularly good partners might be Montgomery's Cheddar and Harbourne Blue (both from south-west England).

LITTLE RYDING

An unpressed sheep's cheese; white or green and white mould rind; unpasteurized milk; traditional rennet. 200g/7oz rounds; seasonal: March–November

Little Ryding is larger and more powerful than Emlett, although, as with Tymsboro', one would not describe it as strong. It is superbly creamy and flows slightly; the taste is full, rich, deep, and telling, with quite a strong mushroom flavour. I have no favourite cheese; however, if I were forced to name one, this would be among the strongest contenders. With its depth and power, it would also be my choice if I were going to serve just one cheese.

TYNING

A hard, close-grained sheep's cheese; unpasteurized milk; traditional rennet. 2.3–3.2kg/5–7lb basket-shaped cheeses; made March–November but available all year

The flavours are predominantly of flowers and nuts, again varying with the season, with a slightly smoky overtone. At four to six months the cheese has a soft flavour; by the time it is a year old it has developed a tang which makes it excellent for sprinkling over pasta or soups.

FETA

A fresh sheep's cheese preserved in brine; unpasteurized milk; traditional rennet. 900g/2lb blocks; made March–November but available all year

If the cheese is too salty to eat directly after you have bought it, soak it in water for a couple of hours or to taste. The texture is firm and compact but deliciously soft; when excess salt is drawn out, the taste is surprisingly sweet and flowery, shot with a slight lemon-like tang. For cooking, you may prefer it slightly saltier than for straight eating: it is ideal for many dishes, including Greek spinach pie or moussaka.

Park Farm Cheeses

GRAHAM AND GABRIELLE PADMORE, CHEESEMAKER: PETER
HUMPHRIES, PARK FARM, KELSTON, BATH, AVON BA1 9AG.
TEL: 01225 424139

Although one tends to associate Camembert-style cheeses with France, the Padmore's first two cheeses, Bath Soft and York, are in fact revivals of traditional British recipes. Cheeses of this type used to be made in many parts of the country but did not become nationally known because of transport and storage problems (as still applies in the case of many fresh cheeses). I tried Bath Soft as soon as I saw it on sale, strikingly packaged in plain cream and black, and found that although it was perfectly ripe, with a soft, flowing texture, it had absolutely no taste at all. Another was the same: the entry in my tasting notebook ends plaintively: 'Why does anybody bother to make this cheese?' A year later, I tried it again – and was stunned: not only was it even softer and creamier but it was also brimming with sweet, summery, yet surprisingly intense flavours. After sampling several more equally triumphant examples, I could hardly wait to find out how they had brought about such a transformation. The answer is simple: experience.

Graham is a third-generation farmer, but no one in his family had ever made cheese before: he turned to it because of the milk quota, which prevented him from expanding quantitatively. Feeling that it was futile to compete in the Cheddar market, he looked through old books on cheesemaking and settled on Bath Soft as the obvious choice (Kelston is only 6km/4 miles from Bath). He and Gabrielle started by experimenting in the kitchen, like others new to cheesemaking, but with consistent lack of success: the cheeses remained obstinately hard and unripe. After some time, they gave up, but a few weeks later came across a couple which they had forgotten and which, to their astonishment, turned out to be delicious: they still had to find out why, but the knowledge that the recipe could be made to work was enough to encourage them to persist.

Graham equipped a dairy (which by now has cost £20,000), enlisted Peter's help, and began to make the cheese on a regular basis, although for the first year only once a fortnight. At this stage, they had by no means mastered it: as well as lack of taste, it went through a phase of being bitter. Graham, who is not given to complacency or sales' talk, said, 'Frankly, it was horrible – almost inedible. I can't think why anybody bought it.' Fortunately, however, they did, so that he and Peter have stepped up cheesemaking to three times a week and introduced two more cheeses, York and Kelston Park (Kelston Park is the adjacent stately home: hence the name Park Farm).

There are several points of interest about their cheesemaking process. One is that they use only evening milk, which is considerably richer than the morning's. Their method is basically the Coulommiers process: as is a common practice in France, they add the rennet in buckets rather than a vat, because the curd for soft cheeses should not be stirred but if left to set in a vat varies slightly according to whether it is at the edge or in the middle. Also, the cheese is salted by rubbing the dry salt over the surface after moulding, which delays the inhibiting effect of salt on bacterial activity and probably increases flavour.

BATH SOFT

A Camembert-type soft cows' cheese; full-fat, unpasteurized evening milk; vegetarian rennet. 10-cm/4-inch squares (about 280g/10oz)

Bath Soft is gloriously rich, flowing, and creamy, with a widely mixed bouquet of sweet, flowery flavours, sometimes cooler, sometimes warmer and more vibrant, depending on the season. Eating it is pure luxury. A 1906 recipe quoted on the label says that the cheese 'will demonstrate its ripeness by spreading on bread as butter does'; however, if you want anything with it at all, very thin, crisp wholemeal biscuits, such as Clarke's, seem to me to suit it better than bread.

The milk (Friesian) is left to stand overnight, warmed, and then starter and penicillin for the rind are added together. Before renneting, it is run into a total of twenty buckets, to each of which the rennet is added individually: when the curd is firm enough to 'break over the finger', usually in forty to forty-five minutes, it is cut once vertically with a knife, left to stand for twenty minutes, and poured into moulds, which, according to tradition, are square. The cheeses are then left in a warm place until the next morning, when they are turned out and set on racks in the maturing room. They are matured for three weeks, with wrapping after two to prevent the escape of moisture, and remain at a more or less perfect stage of ripeness for a further three to four weeks.

KELSTON PARK

Bronze Medal, British Cheese Awards 1997
A Camembert-type soft cows' cheese; full-fat, unpasteurized evening milk; vegetarian
rennet. 675g/1¹/₂ lb rounds

The new cheese is larger than Bath Soft, which gives it stronger, more intense flavours. It is made in much the same way, but is poured into round rather than square moulds.

YORK

A Camembert-type soft cows' cheese with sage; full-fat, unpasteurized evening milk;
vegetarian rennet. 10-cm/4-inch squares

York is similar to Bath Soft but made with just a hint of sage and a stripe of curd coloured with annatto in the middle (traditionally it was cream). The sage does not taste as such but causes the flavours to develop along a herbal rather than flowery path.

R. A. Duckett

CHRIS DUCKETT, WALNUT TREE FARM, WEDMORE, SOMERSET
BS28 4UJ. TEL: 01934 712218

Apart from the dairy, my chief memory of Chris Duckett's farm was of a family of llamas who, along with a small herd of chestnut alpaca goats, are Chris's especial pleasure and interest. The Ducketts have made cheese here for three generations: Chris's grandfather bought the farm, his father established the present firm, and he and his brother Philip now make the cheese; their mother still moulds butter with old-fashioned wooden pats in a little room at the end of the dairy. As the milk is not skimmed, the butter is made from the whey, which is rich in fat and gives a wonderfully sweet, distinctively flavoured result.

Until recently, the milk came from the Ducketts' own herd of 120 Friesians; now, however, it is delivered by Milk Marque from specific farms nearby. The cows graze on part of Tealham and Tadham Moor, which is peat and an area of special scientific interest because of its exceptionally wide variety of grasses and herbs; the land is untreated and effectually organic, which further contributes to the flavours in the cheese.

77

Nearly all the equipment in the Ducketts' dairy is inherited or old. The first items to catch the eye are a pair of magnificent double Victorian cheese-presses, dating from 1866, about 2½ metres/8 feet tall and decorated with mouldings of cows: together, they can take more than twenty cheeses at a time. The moulds are of the traditional shape, with clip-on lids which leave a mark on the side of the cheese; some have been handed down through the family, and the rest made to the same design by Chris. The only obviously modern item is the shining, stainless-steel vat, which is as large as a small swimming-bath.

Historically, Caerphilly was made and eaten locally, matured quickly, and, like Single Gloucester, often included a proportion of skimmed milk. The fact that the Ducketts make it in Somerset rather than Wales is typical of a pattern which emerged after the coming of steam-power and the easy transport of liquid milk. As elsewhere, the option of selling the milk direct discouraged the farmers in Wales from making cheese, and it was natural for the gap to be filled by those on the other side of the Bristol Channel, who had the advantage of richer grazing and were probably already making Cheddar.

DUCKETT'S CAERPHILLY

A semi-hard cows' cheese; full-fat, unpasteurized milk; vegetarian rennet. 900g/2lb, 1.8–2.3kg/4–5lb, and 3.6–4kg/8lb–8lb 13oz truckles

The Ducketts keep the cheeses for only a week, when they are firm and refreshing, with a slight youthful sharpness: further maturing is carried out by purchasers, who include James Aldridge and Neal's Yard Dairy. James uses them for Tornegus (page 37); Neal's Yard matures them for one to two months, until they have become almost semi-soft, with a deliciously smooth texture and mild, creamy, infinitely subtle taste which encompasses all the grasses and herbs of the moor. Like other Caerphillies, they melt beautifully: hence presumably the popularity of Welsh rarebit.

Cheesemaking takes about four hours, starting as soon as the milk is delivered in the morning. The milk is warmed to 20°C/68°F, starter added, and the milk heated to 26°C/79°F. It is then left to ripen for about two hours before being re-heated to 32°C/90°F for renneting. When the curd has set, which takes about forty-five minutes, it is cut and scalded a few degrees higher and stirred continuously for another forty-five minutes or until Chris can tell by the 'feel', which should be smooth and elastic, that the correct acidity has been reached and it is ready for draining. After draining, instead of being piled in blocks and milled, as for Cheddar, it is swept into heaps and cut first into 5-cm/2-inch, then 2.5-cm/1-inch squares. This is followed by a light salting, moulding in muslin cloths, and pressing for an initial half-hour before the surfaces are salted again; finally, the cheeses are pressed for sixteen hours and brined for twenty-four.

 ## Welsh Rarebit

For 2

15g/¹/₂oz butter
3 level tsp white flour
2 tbsp strong cider
salt and pepper
1 tsp Dijon mustard
1 tbsp double cream
200g/7oz Mature Duckett's Caerphilly, finely grated
2 whole or 4 half-slices baked bread (page 22), sprinkled with oil and pepper

Melt the butter in a small pan over low heat; stir in the flour off the heat. Add the cider, return to the heat, and stir continuously until thick. Season with a pinch of salt and a generous grinding of pepper, stir in the mustard, and simmer gently, stirring often, for 2–3 minutes to ensure that the flour is cooked: by this time, the mixture will be very stiff and gluey. Stir in the cream and remove from the heat. Thoroughly stir in the cheese. Put a thick layer of the mixture on each piece of bread, making sure that the bread is entirely covered (if exposed, it will burn). Grill until the cheese is well dotted with brown: it should spread just enough to trickle over the sides of the bread.

AVALON

A semi-hard cows' cheese flavoured with caraway seeds; full-fat, unpasteurized milk; vegetarian rennet. 1.8–2.5kg/4–5¹/₂lb truckles

Avalon is similar to the Duckett's Caerphilly but is matured for only seven to ten days. Not being particularly fond of caraway, I was surprised that I liked it: however, the seeds remove the sharpness characteristic of new Caerphilly and leave it with a pleasant, marshy, slightly salty rather than acid tang.

Avalon and Sultana Tea Bread

I suppose you might call this a version of Welsh *bara brith* ('speckled bread'). Lovers of caraway seeds may wish to add a few more; those who do not can use plain Caerphilly. Serve it at once, preferably while it is still warm.

Cooking time: 30–40 minutes, depending on the size of loaf
Makes 1 x 600g/1lb 5oz loaf or 2 smaller loaves

150g/5$\frac{1}{4}$oz plain, preferably organic white flour
100g/3$\frac{1}{2}$oz plain, preferably organic fine wholemeal flour
1 tsp salt
1$\frac{1}{2}$ tsp bicarbonate of soda
125g/4$\frac{1}{2}$oz caster sugar
25g/1oz butter, chopped small
150g/5$\frac{1}{4}$oz Avalon, finely grated
140g/5oz sultanas
about 225ml/8fl oz strong tea

Pre-heat the oven to 180°C/350°F/Gas 4. Sift together the first four ingredients and mix them with the sugar. Rub in the butter until it has disappeared; stir in the cheese and sultanas. Add most of the tea; pour in the rest gradually until the mixture is a light but fairly soft dough. Turn the dough into a loaf tin (or tins) lined with cooking foil: the tin should not be more than two-thirds full to allow for rising. Bake the bread for 35–40 minutes, until well browned, for a large loaf, or 30–35 minutes for smaller ones. Serve with cottage cheese, butter, or butter and marmalade.

DUCKETT'S SMOKED CAERPHILLY AND WEDMORE

A semi-hard cows' cheese (Wedmore: with chives); full-fat, unpasteurized milk; vegetarian rennet. 1.8–2.3kg/4–5lb truckles

The Smoked Caerphilly is moist, with a light texture and tiny holes. The smoking is carried out when the cheeses are only two to three days old, so that they are still slightly sharp; it seems to me a pity to smoke a cheese of such potential, but the taste of smoke, although pronounced, is not overwhelming and the result is surprisingly pleasing and delicate.

Wedmore is similar to Smoked Caerphilly but has a more pronounced smoky tang because of the added chives. If this sounds like overkill, it is not: although stronger than the other cheeses, the result is harmonious.

Exmoor Blue Cheeses

KAY AND ALAN DUFFIELD, WILLETT FARM, LYDEARD ST LAWRENCE, NEAR TAUNTON, SOMERSET TA4 3QB.
TEL: 01984 667460

Kay and Alan Duffield downshifted, not exactly from the city but Welwyn Garden City in Hertfordshire, where Alan used to work for ICI. He started out in the West Country farming sheep on the moors, but about ten years ago gave it up in order to take over the dairy at Willett Farm, in the valley between the Quantock and Brendon Hills. He and Kay now live in a listed early seventeenth-century house of traditional local design, with a roof sloping one way, like a lean-to, and a 'slee', a wide corridor which was once used as a dairy and for other outer-kitchen purposes, such as the laundry and salting pigs. On this side, which is north-facing, the roof reaches to within a metre/few feet of the ground; on the south side, where it is high, large windows give the rooms a cheerful, summery atmosphere even when, as on the day of my visit, the hills outside are covered with snow.

The farm is over 1.5km/about 1 mile from the house up a narrow lane with such high banks that you feel as if you are in a tunnel. When Alan first came to the dairy, only one cheese was made, a hard sheep's cheese called Coleford Blue; now, by using not only sheep's but goats', Jersey, and buffalo milk and adapting the recipe to soft as well as hard cheeses, he has extended the range to nine, which in addition to the ones given below include a hard, fairly powerful blue goats' cheese, Brendon Blue, a semi-soft sheep's cheese, Quantock Blue, which is relatively mild but will become stronger if it is kept (store at 4°C/39°F or in a cool, damp place), and small goats' cheeses marinated in oil, prepared by Kay.

The goats' milk comes from a farm on the other side of the Quantocks, near Bridgwater, and most of the sheep's from the Quantock Sheep Milking Centre at Nether Stowey, where the flock is based on British Milksheep; the Jersey milk is brought and quality-tested from three specific farms near Willett by Milk Marque. The buffalo milk is from a herd near Holsworthy, Devon, which also supplies the Minsons in Cornwall (page 114). Before he made the buffalo cheese, Alan, like Robin Congdon (page 104), suffered from conservatism over the type of milk: customers' preference for cows' milk was such that eighty per cent of his output was Jersey. However, the novelty of buffalo cheese may break the mould: so far, the Duffields' has been sold out continuously.

COLEFORD BLUE

A hard sheep's cheese; 33% fat, unpasteurized milk; vegetarian rennet.
2–2.5kg/4lb 8oz–5lb 8oz

The cheese is firm-textured and at two to three months' old rich and creamy-tasting, with only moderate blueing; lovers of strong cheese can keep it for up to two months more, when it will become progressively more powerful.

This is the original Willett Farm recipe. Initially, it is fairly simple, but the final stages stretch over a number of days. The milk is warmed slightly before starter is added, then heated to 31°C/88°F before the addition of rennet and *Penicillium roqueforti* for the blue. When the curd has set, which takes one and a quarter to one and a half hours according to the weather, it is cut coarsely in two directions with long flat knives. For the soft cheeses, it is moulded without draining; for the firm, it is heated a few degrees, drained, and turned until it is dry before the moulds are filled. After moulding, the cheeses are finished for the day except for turning in the evening.

The next morning, they are all turned again, and the soft cheeses are brined; on the third day, the soft cheeses are aerated by piercing. Thereafter, all the cheeses are taken to the maturing room where they are sprayed with white penicillin for the rinds: this shows less on the soft, more quickly matured cheeses, but gives a definite gloss to the firmer ones. The hard cheeses are left to drain for three days before brining, brined for two, and drained for another two before piercing; finally, they are drained for a further five days before being set to mature in rooms, which, to encourage mould, are kept at a humidity of around ninety-five per cent. Although they do not become exceptionally blue on the inside, the mould on the surface develops, not into a mere crust or moss but a veritable garden, with long, fine dark grey fronds reaching into the air. (The fronds brush off immediately: there is no trace of them once the cheeses are moved.) Maturing times are three to seven weeks for Baby Brendon and the soft cheeses and two to three for the hard.

EXMOOR JERSEY BLUE

A semi-soft blue Jersey cheese; 35% fat, unpasteurized milk; vegetarian rennet.
500g/1lb 2oz and 1.2kg/2lb 10oz truckles

Jersey Blue is Alan's most popular cheese: it is fairly firm-textured, with the sweet, buttery taste of the rich milk and gentle herbal undertones. The blue is just strong enough to be piquant without overwhelming the background flavours of the cheese.

 ## Butternut Squash and Tomato Soup with Jersey Blue

This is a thick, glowing orange soup with a mellow flavour which matches the character of the cheese. As only a little cheese is needed, it is an excellent way of using up a small piece. It can be prepared in advance.

Cooking time: 55–65 minutes
For 3–4

2 small or 1 large onion/s (about 200g/7oz), peeled and finely chopped
6 cloves garlic, peeled and chopped
700g/1lb 9oz ripe tomatoes, peeled, chopped, and the cores removed
salt and pepper
$^3/_4$–1 tsp caster sugar
$^1/_2$ butternut squash (about 350g/12oz when prepared), peeled, the seeds and pulp removed, and chopped into 1.5-cm/$^1/_2$-inch squares
4 tbsp double cream
70g/2$^1/_2$oz Exmoor Jersey Blue, coarsely grated or finely chopped

Pre-heat the oven to 190°C/375°F/Gas 5. Spread the onions and garlic over the bottom of a medium-sized baking dish; cover with the tomatoes. Season the tomatoes fairly generously with salt and pepper and sprinkle them with the sugar. Bake for 45–50 minutes, until they look slightly dry and shrivelled.

Transfer the contents of the baking dish to a saucepan, add 400ml/14fl oz water and the squash, and simmer for 10–15 minutes or until the squash is tender; liquidize until the soup is very smooth. If you are making it ahead of time, keep it chilled until needed.

When you are ready to serve, bring the soup to a simmer over low heat; simmer for 3–4 minutes, thinning with a little more water if necessary, and stir in the cream. Sprinkle the cheese into the bowls after serving.

PARTRIDGES

A semi-soft blue Jersey cheese; full-fat, unpasteurized milk; vegetarian rennet.
1kg/1lb 5oz drums

The blue is strong but the cheese itself deliciously rich and sweet, with a luscious, creamy texture. The name originates from the fact that it was originally made specially for Partridges of Sloane Street; now, however, it is widely sold.

SOMERSET BLUE

A firm Jersey cheese with a predominantly white mould rind; 40% fat, unpasteurized milk; vegetarian rennet. 2–2.5kg/4lb 6oz–5lb 8oz

Having been matured for longer, Somerset Blue is bluer and stronger than Exmoor Jersey; however, it has a similarly rich, buttery taste with a hint of herbs. It can be kept at 4°C/39°F for up to two months.

BABY BRENDON

A soft goats' cheese; full-fat, unpasteurized milk; vegetarian rennet.
About 400g/14oz rounds

Baby Brendon is unusual in that it is one of the very few goats' cheeses made in Britain which actually tastes of goat. However, it is also quite exceptionally sweet, with background flavours of herbs and a strong infusion of flowers. If kept, it becomes harder, with a slight grain, but retains its sweetness.

BUFFALO BLUE

A blue buffalo cheese; full-fat, unpasteurized milk; vegetarian rennet. 115g/4oz, 225g/8oz, 450g/1lb, and 900g/2lb rounds; 1.8kg/4lb rounds, Fortnum & Mason only

Buffalo milk is even richer than sheep's milk (eight per cent as opposed to six per cent fat). This is reflected in the rich, creamy texture of the cheese; like fresh sheep's cheeses, however, it is also wonderfully smooth and light. The taste, similarly, is sweet and creamy, with nuances of grass and flowers to which the blue adds just the right amount of zest to be interesting but not overwhelming. This is a delightful cheese: as well as on the cheeseboard, it is particularly good with plums and pears.

Dorset Blue Cheese Company

MICHAEL DAVIES, WOODBRIDGE FARM, STOCK GAYLARD,
STURMINSTER NEWTON, DORSET DT10 2BD.
TEL: 01963 23216; FAX: 01963 23063

Michael says that he had wanted to make cheese ever since taking a cheesemaking course as a student. For a long time he had been deterred by the fact that he lives in Cheddar country: cheese and Cheddar seemed synonymous and, like Graham Padmore (page 75), he did not feel that he could compete with the 'big boys' (although in Dorset, Woodbridge Farm is only about 16km/10 miles from the Keens). However, as a dairy farmer producing only liquid milk before the introduction of the quota, when the milk lake was deepening and the butter mountain soaring, he began to ask himself seriously whether there was any point in what he was doing. While he was in this state of uncertainty, his attention was drawn to a case involving the sale of second-grade Stiltons as Dorset Blue Vinneys.

Blue Vinney was a local hand-skimmed-milk cheese which had not been produced on a significant scale since the war, although Patrick Rance discovered several farms where it was still being made in very small quantities. The blue in the authentic cheese, so the story goes, was encouraged by maturing it with mouldy boots or old harnesses; the Stiltons were bought from Leicestershire and disguised by being left in a Dorset cellar to acquire a little genuine local mould. To Michael, the fact that there was clearly a demand for Blue Vinney was decisive. He found a number of recipes at the Ministry of Agriculture, Fisheries, and Food office in Dorchester and for the next two months experimented in his garage every Saturday, using cut-off pipes instead of moulds (as is practised regularly by at least two Irish cheesemakers) and maturing the cheeses in his larder, where, predictably, they turned even the cornflakes blue. Today, he employs two cheesemakers and produces 540kg/1,200lb of cheese a week.

Blue Vinny (he spells his version without the 'e') is interesting as an example of a traditional skim-milk cheese and one of the very few, possibly the only one, which was blue – the blue rectifying the hardness and lack of flavour for which many such cheeses were known; his recipe is a reminder that a crucial point about all of them was that the milk was skimmed by hand rather than machine. If you toast the cheese, you can see that it still contains an appreciable amount of fat: Michael reckons that it is about three per cent.

DORSET BLUE VINNY

A blue cows' cheese; hand-skimmed, unpasteurized milk; vegetarian rennet.
1.8–2.3kg/4–5lb cylinders and 6kg/13lb 3oz

The cheese has a nutty texture and because of its low fat content tends to crumble, particularly if, as some are, it is very blue. Even when very blue, however, it is not overwhelmingly strong, since the blue has a pleasingly soft taste which tingles rather than bites in the mouth. It keeps its flavour relatively well when heated; as the mould does not liquefy, it also retains little nutty clusters which are delicious on tomato soup or polenta. Apart from the blue, it melts smoothly, and is excellent toasted. It also freezes perfectly.

The cows (Friesian) are milked at 5 a.m. and the milk left for two and a half to three hours to allow the cream to rise before it is hand-skimmed. Unless the cheesemakers can find the time to turn it into clotted cream, the cream, sadly, is thrown away. The temperature and acidity of the milk are checked, starter and *Penicillium roqueforti* for the blue added, and the milk left for another hour before renneting. After a further one and a half hours, the curd is stirred and cut to the size of broad beans; it is then left to stand again, this time until the next morning, when it is drained and the whey fed either to the cows or the pigs. Michael and Mary Holbrook at Sleight Farm (page 71) are among the very few who still keep pigs to drink it, according to the custom when mixed farming was the norm.

The next stage is to texture the curd by cutting it into blocks and piling them at the end of the vat; this is followed by milling, salting, and moulding. Instead of being pressed, the cheeses are left at 15.5°C/60°F for four days, with turning every day: at this point, they look like pans of rather pale, dry scrambled egg. After four days, they are turned out and dressed with a flour paste mixed with a little more *roqueforti* so that the rinds also become blued. For the next five or six weeks, the cheeses are turned daily and some are pierced to introduce extra air: not all of them need it, but with some piercing may have to be repeated several times. Thereafter, they are matured for two and a half to five months, with turning every two or three days.

Polenta with Blue Vinny and Tomatoes

The porridge for the base can be made the day before.

Cooking times: 20 or 60 minutes (porridge), according to type; 5 minutes for grilling or 16–20 for baking before serving
For 6–10

125g/4$\frac{1}{2}$oz polenta meal
700ml/1$\frac{1}{4}$ pints milk, skimmed, semi-skimmed, or whole, *or* milk and water
1 tbsp cream (single or double)
salt
15g/$\frac{1}{2}$oz butter
about 300g/10$\frac{1}{2}$oz (4 fairly large) ripe tomatoes, skinned
pepper
150g/5$\frac{1}{4}$oz Blue Vinny, crumbled

Put the polenta meal into a cup or funnel so that it can be poured steadily. Bring the milk (or milk and water) and cream to the boil, add $\frac{1}{2}$ teaspoonful of salt and the butter, and pour in the meal gradually, stirring continuously. Reduce the heat to a simmer and continue stirring for 3–5 minutes, until the mixture thickens; simmer for an hour, stirring fairly frequently. Some brands of meal are quick-cooking and do not need simmering for as long, but in all cases I recommend at least 20 minutes. If the porridge sticks to the bottom of the pan, leave it while it cooks and soak the pan afterwards. Pour it into a lightly buttered 22-cm/8$\frac{1}{2}$-inch tart dish and leave it to cool.

Slice the tomatoes, discarding the stalk ends, and arrange them over the top of the polenta; season with pepper and cover with a thick layer of cheese. Bake at 220°C/425°F/Gas 7 for 16–20 minutes or grill until browned.

J. A. and E. Montgomery Ltd

JAMES MONTGOMERY, MANOR FARM, NORTH CADBURY, YEOVIL,
SOMERSET BA22 7DW. TEL: 01963 440243

Like the Ducketts and Keens (pages 77 and 90), the Montgomerys have
made cheese for three generations. Even more than most people who work
with it, James lives it and loves it; he is also exceptionally lucid about the
cheesemaking process and all that precedes it, i.e. the grazing, cows, and
quality of the milk. The business is a family concern shared by his mother
and brother; however, it includes two farms, and his brother Archie manages
the second, which is arable and not directly connected with the cheese.
James, at Manor Farm, produces milk for direct sale from a herd of Jerseys
and the cheese from 120 Friesians. Originally, his family made the cheese
from Ayrshire milk, which has a relatively high solids content: the Ayrshires
were switched to Friesians for the sake of the increased yield but the cows are
bred to give milk which as far as possible retains the Ayrshire characteristics,
in particular with regard to the protein ratio. He does not standardize it with
equalizing separators, as is the custom among larger cheese producers (page
92), but if necessary enriches it with skim-milk powder, although he dislikes
both the necessity and the result, since he says that if too much is used, the
cheese becomes 'chippy'. The farm is not organic, but the soil, which is silty
clay loam, is excellent and the grazing very rich.

MONTGOMERY'S CHEDDAR

*Gold Medal, also Best Cheddar Cheese and Best Traditional British Cheese, British
Cheese Awards 1996; Gold Medal, Extra Mature Traditional Cheddar, 1997*
A hard cows' cheese; full-fat, unpasteurized milk; traditional rennet.
26kg/57lb cylinders

At ten months old, Montgomery's Cheddar is relatively moist, with a slightly rough, granular texture; as it ages, it becomes drier and grainier. When
younger, the taste is deep but soft, more delicate and feminine than Keen's
or Quicke's (pages 91 and 102), with not quite such a strong tang; however,
at two years old, if you are lucky enough to find some, it is as powerful as
any cheese in the world. At this stage, it may have developed a few knots of
blue, probably near the rind, which is a recommendation rather than otherwise. I do not suggest it as a preference for cooking because the flavour loses
its subtlety. It is a cheese to savour as it stands.

The cheesemaking is carried out by a team of three, organized on a rota system to include weekends. It takes, or should take, four to four and a half hours, as measured from renneting to milling – which was the only absolute timing James would give because of the need for judgement at every stage. The evening's milk is chilled and added to the morning's while still warm from the cow; it is then heated to 35°C/95°F and Barber starter, which is incubated to a culture before use, is added: James prefers this to the usual kind straight from the packet because he finds that it makes the resulting cheese less acidic and gives a broader spectrum of flavour. When the acidity has reached the desired level, usually in about forty-five minutes, the milk is renneted. The curd, similarly, usually takes about forty-five minutes to set: cheesemaking does not proceed until it has 'a clean break'.

The next part of the process, which is carried out mechanically, is to scald it to 41°C/106°F, at the same time stirring and cutting it to the size of wheat grains. This is followed by draining, cutting a channel down the middle of it, and 'Cheddaring' (this is done by hand). The Montgomerys' method of draining is to run the curd into another vat; digging the channel and Cheddaring (i.e. cutting it into blocks and piling and re-piling) textures the curd and releases further moisture while the acidity begins to rise. When the acidity has reached the correct point, it is checked by salting, and the curd is milled with an old peg-mill which James favours because it gives an uneven result and makes for an interesting, slightly less than homogeneous texture to the cheese. A second salting follows, after which the cheeses are packed into moulds lined with linen, and pressed overnight.

The next day the cheeses are sealed by dipping in hot water, re-wrapped, and pressed for a second night. On the third day, they are rubbed with melted lard and wrapped in a final coat of muslin, which is firmly stuck to them by pressing briefly. The Montgomerys mature them for a year or longer on wood (rather than stainless steel), with turning as necessary to prevent them from sticking to the shelves.

S. A. and G. H. Keen

GEORGE KEEN, MOORHAYES FARM, VERRINGTON LANE,
WINCANTON, SOMERSET BA9 8IR. TEL: 01963 32286

When I visited the Keens, in April, Somerset looked as if it had just been created. The new season's grass was so short that the whole county might have been a lawn; the banks sparkled with freshly opened primroses and the hedgerows were clouded with white blackthorn blossom. Moorhayes Farm stood out against the newness like a symbol of continuity: the tall, gabled farmhouse is sixteenth century, and appears the more impressive as you approach because it is set back above the road on the hillside. Like the Montgomerys, the Keens are brothers whose family has made cheese on the same farm for three generations. Their grandfather came here in 1900, when everyone who farmed made cheese as a matter of course; the same dairy, traditionally placed next to the kitchen, was used until 1990. One of the old covered cheese vats now stands next to the Aga, serving a double purpose as a store-cupboard and table. A barn across the yard has been converted into a new, much larger dairy, enviably well equipped and carefully purpose-designed; nevertheless, when he moved into it, George was very worried about its effect on the cheese. One of his main concerns is that it should be 'genuinely traditional, just as it has always been. Otherwise, why do we bother to make it at all, when there are so many commercial Cheddars on the market?' He stressed that every circumstance influences it: not only the soil, grazing, cows, season, freshness of the milk, and method of making it, but also the position of the dairy, particularly the direction that it faces, which affects humidity, and the materials used for the cheesemaking equipment. In the event, he says that although the cheese has in fact changed, he thinks 'not for the worse'.

Rather like Archie Montgomery, George's brother Stephen raises cash crops; the livestock on the farm, however, now consists only of the dairy herd. George greatly regretted giving up the pigs but found that they did not pay. Despite this and his attention to every detail connected with the cheese, he regards himself as a farmer rather than cheesemaker, taking the old-fashioned view that making cheese is not a separate occupation but merely a branch of farming. 'I didn't choose to be a cheesemaker, I chose to be a farmer, and cheesemaking is part of that.' Consistent with this is his policy of never buying in milk to increase output, no matter how much demand for the cheese might rise; similarly, his commitment to his cattle, in their own right as well as in relation to the cheese, is paramount. With a few exceptions, his herd is closed, i.e. home-bred, and building it up has been his life's work; he knows all the cows personally, and his feeling for them obviously goes very deep. This was just at the time when hysteria over BSE was at its height: the aspect of it that most upset him was not the likelihood of a cull (which, as it happened, was announced that evening) but simply that he could not bear to see the cows ill. It seems that although they do not actually go mad, they become restless, neurotic, and unhappy; although he cannot be sure that they are in physical pain, he reckons that at least they must suffer from headaches.

KEEN'S CHEDDAR

Silver Medal, British Cheese Awards 1996; Gold Medal, Mature Traditional Cheddar, 1997
A hard cows' cheese; full-fat, unpasteurized milk; traditional rennet.
1.4kg/3lb and 29kg/64lb cylinders

The texture is moist, smooth, and surprisingly light; the taste, spicy and deep, striking the tongue at many levels, with a warm, powerful, distinctive tang. This is serious Cheddar, less sweet and summery than Montgomery's at the same age but an ideal partner to equally serious wines and, with Quicke's, probably the best Cheddar in the world for cooking.

The cheese is made by a method similar to but not quite the same as the Montgomerys': the most obvious differences are that the temperature used to warm the milk at the beginning is lower, the curd is scalded after rather than during cutting, and the cheese is pressed for an extra day. The milk arrives at the dairy at 8.30 a.m. and is warmed to 30°C/86°F. A cultured starter is added while it heats; it is renneted when it has reached the full temperature and left to set for about forty-five minutes. It is then cut to a size between a wheat-grain and a pea before being stirred and scalded to 40°C/104°F over about an hour, until the acidity has risen and the curd is 'firm and nutty: you can feel it knocking your fingers'. This means that it is ready for draining, which is carried out by running it into another vat, or 'cooler'; Cheddaring, milling, and salting follow. The cheeses are pressed for twenty-four hours, dipped in hot water (which helps the rind to form), and pressed for another twenty-four hours: they are then rubbed with lard and covered with two layers of muslin. Finally, they are pressed for a further twenty-four hours and matured for a year on wooden as opposed to stainless steel shelves, which George (like others) feels are detrimental to flavour.

Lubborn Cheese Ltd

PIERS FEILDEN, NORTH STREET, CREWKERNE, SOMERSET
TA18 7AS.

I had to ring Directory Enquiries for Piers's telephone number, which is not given on his labels, and was informed that they have no record of Lubborn Cheese. When I told him this, he laughed and said, 'Ah well, our policy of secrecy is clearly working', and added that I probably would not see the sign with their name when I arrived because it is small and very discreetly placed. However, he assured me that I could not miss them because they are in a large Victorian malt-house with milk storage tanks and a car-park in front. For once, the assurance was justified: the malt-house is tall, red brick, and distinctive, proudly utilitarian and beautiful because of it, and the milk tanks of a size consistent with processing up to 12,000 litres/2,640 gallons of milk three or four times a day. Inside, the white-painted spaces, too big to be called rooms, house huge pieces of shining stainless-steel equipment which dwarf the human occupants (of whom there are surprisingly few: Piers employs forty people, but only eleven are engaged in the actual cheese-making). Near the entrance are a machine for concentrating milk and a pasteurizer; towering twin cylinders in which the starter is prepared stand opposite. Further in there is a series of vats which look like the trucks of a goods train; beyond them, a curd pump separates the curds and whey. The moulds are filled on a long, slowly moving conveyor belt; later, the turned-out cheeses are similarly carried through a salting chamber where they are sprayed with a special French salt which has granules of exactly equal size. The only colour besides that of the steel and white is the blue of the women's overalls in the packing area, where thousands of cheeses are wrapped by hand every day and the scene is more in keeping with the date of the building.

Piers makes Bries, Camemberts, and Camembert-style goats' cheeses. The milk for the Bries and Camemberts comes from fifteen farms within 8km/5 miles of Crewkerne and the goats' milk from nine farms in the area. Unlike small producers, who accept that their milk may vary and modify their procedures accordingly, Piers ensures that his products are consistent by standardizing all the cows' milk before cheesemaking begins. This is done by removing and separating a proportion of the milk, perhaps a quarter of it, concentrating the skim, and returning an appropriate amount of the concentrate to the rest (in effect, the equivalent of James Montgomery's addition of skim-milk powder: page 88). The goats' milk, which tastes stronger the more it is disturbed, is not standardized; however, mainly in the interest of flavour, Piers insists that his suppliers' goats are kept in. I asked if he thought the goats minded: given his professionalism, I feared that he would consider it a sentimental point – but not at all. He replied that when he started it had often worried him but he has since satisfied his conscience about it, using the analogy of Londoners, who live in conditions which some would find intolerable yet feel that they live full and rewarding lives. Goats, he emphasized, are sociable animals, who will be happy so long they are with the herd.

SOMERSET BRIE

Silver Medal, British Cheese Awards 1996; Bronze Medal, 1997
A soft white mould rind cows' cheese; full-fat, pasteurized milk; vegetarian rennet.
1.1kg/2lb 7oz or 2.5kg/5lb 8oz wheels or pre-packed slices

The cheeses have an exceptionally crisp crust and rich, flowing texture, on which you can rely, since they are not distributed for sale until they are ripe. The flavour is fresh, sweet, and creamy, mild in the smaller size but fuller in the large. Especially in view of the very reasonable price, buying half or a whole large wheel is not as extravagant as it sounds, since it can be used for a salad dressing or stuffing, or fried in breadcrumbs (page 23).

One of the two cylinders for preparing the starter is used to mix, heat, and thus sterilize the solution in which it is cultured: the starter, which is laboratory-made, is added in the second. Under the direction of Piers's microbiologist, Matthew Organ, not only starter and penicillin for the rind but also yeasts are added to the cows' milk to aid the ripening process and promote the differences between the Bries and Camemberts; extra starter is also added to the milk for the Camemberts to produce a stronger flavour. Apart from this, all the cheeses are made in the same way.

After the starter and other preparations are added, the milk is left to stand for forty minutes before being pumped into one of the series of vats, where it is renneted and allowed to set: as cheesemaking is continuous throughout the day, each vat, or truck, contains milk at a different stage of setting. The cow curd is cut into 2-cm/$^3/_4$-inch squares and the goat curd into smaller pieces. Thick pipes at the bottom of the vats convey both curds and whey to the curd pump, and from there the curd is taken to the belt of moulds. At the end of the belt, the moulds, still raining whey from every hole, are piled in stacks of eight to drain; after being turned several times, they are transferred to an enormous tiled draining room.

In the morning, they are turned out and salted in the salting chamber, which looks like an enormous box. To encourage the growth of an extra crisp rind, the cheeses are sprayed with a further dose of penicillin by a 'fogging' machine. They are wrapped as soon as the rind has developed, partly, to use Piers's delightful phrase, 'to avoid earthy tastes from the air', partly to retain ammonia which is given off during ripening, and, most obviously, to keep them creamy and moist. As yet, only the Camemberts are machine-wrapped, but Piers is hoping to install a machine for the goat cheeses soon (which, he was careful to emphasize, would not mean redundancies but that staff are freed for further expansion: whether in terms of quantity or new cheeses, he did not say). After wrapping, the goat cheeses are sent out at once, the Camemberts after ten to sixteen days, and the Bries after sixteen days.

Somerset Brie and Garlic Mushrooms

Either the sauce or the complete dish can be prepared a day ahead.

Cooking times: 8 minutes for the sauce, 8–10 for the mushrooms
For 4

4 large mushrooms (400–450g/14oz–1lb combined weight), peeled and stalks removed
salt and pepper
6 cloves garlic, peeled, 2 roughly and 4 finely chopped
15g/$\frac{1}{2}$oz butter
1 tbsp oil
1 large shallot (about 55g/2oz), peeled and finely diced
100g/3$\frac{1}{2}$oz button mushrooms, washed and diced
125ml/4fl oz dry white wine
2 tsp dill, washed, dried, and finely chopped
150g/5$\frac{1}{4}$oz Somerset Brie (with rind), chopped
40g/1$\frac{1}{2}$oz Parmesan, Cwmtawe (page 145) or other pecorino, grated
4–5 tbsp fresh white breadcrumbs

Wash the large mushrooms and dry them with kitchen paper, squeezing out as much moisture as possible. Place gills upwards on a lightly oiled baking tray, or plate if you are preparing the dish in advance. Season moderately with salt and pepper.

Crush the roughly chopped cloves of garlic in a mortar; add and beat in the butter and set it aside. Warm the oil over fairly low heat and fry the shallot and the rest of the garlic for $1\frac{1}{2}$–2 minutes or until soft; add the button mushrooms, season with a little salt and rather more pepper, and fry, turning often, for 3–4 minutes or until they begin to colour. Pour in the wine, raise the heat, and cook away the liquid. Remove the pan from the heat and stir in the garlic butter and dill; add and stir in the cheeses, pressing the Brie gently against the bottom of the pan until it has melted sufficiently to mix with the other ingredients. Place a quarter of the mixture on top of each mushroom. If you are making the dish in advance, allow the mushrooms to cool, cover, and chill.

Pre-heat the oven to 200°C/400°F/Gas 6. Sprinkle the mushrooms with the breadcrumbs and bake them for 10–12 minutes, until the topping is brown and crisp. Serve at once, with bread or tagliatelle lightly dusted with Cwmtawe or other pecorino to mop up the juices.

SOMERSET CAMEMBERT

Silver Medal, British Cheese Awards 1996
A soft white mould rind cows' cheese; full-fat, pasteurized milk; vegetarian rennet.
220g/scant 8oz rounds

Like the Brie, the texture is deliciously rich and creamy and the rind thick and crisp; the taste is mild and fresh, with a tinge of grass and a hint of mushrooms which comes partly from the rind.

To make Somerset Camembert Fritters, follow the recipe on page 66. The flavour is improved slightly if you substitute red wine for cider; with red wine, serve redcurrant jelly or raspberry vinegar instead of apple chutney.

SOMERSET GOAT CHEESE OR CAPRICORN

A soft white mould rind goats' cheese; full-fat, pasteurized milk; vegetarian rennet.
100g/3$\frac{1}{2}$oz rounds

Both names apply to the same cheese, depending on where it is bought. The cheese has a crisp rind and creamy flowing interior. Unlike the cows' cheeses, it may not be ripe when purchased, in which case keep it chilled for a few days. To me, this is the Mars Bar of cheeses: small, cheap, easy to buy, and with just enough taste of goat to be interesting.

Peverstone Cheese Co.

JEREMY FRANKPITT, CHEESEMAKER: CATHERINE PYNE, PEVERSTONE, MUTTERTON, CULLOMPTON, DEVON EX15 1RW. TEL: 01884 35292

A feel-good factor prevails at Peverstone. The countryside is green and lush, with long hills and long views; the farm and eighteenth-century farmhouse are in impeccable condition, the dairy is new and spacious, and everyone I met was smiling, charming, and enthusiastic. Part of the reason for the atmosphere of well-being is perhaps that the farm is, in a literal sense, a family creation. The Frankpitts senior farmed in Western Australia before returning to England and buying Peverstone, which was in a very run-down, dilapidated condition: Jeremy and his two brothers restored it almost entirely themselves, only calling for occasional help from an odd-job man. One of the brothers, who now owns a second, small farm next door, is a design engineer, which was helpful; the other, Michael (the eldest), acts as financial director and runs Peverstone, supplying the milk for the cheese from a herd of 180 Friesian–Holsteins.

As his parents had not sold their original property, Jeremy farmed in Australia for a time, during which he bought his own farm, Tagon (hence the name of his newest cheese). Over this period, friends made him various attractive offers, including a career in merchant banking; however, the lure of cheese eventually brought him back to England, where he trained with a Cheddar-maker in Somerset. He then met Hilary Charnley, the maker of the herb-flavoured cheese Devon Garland, who was about to retire, and bought the Garland recipe from her. Now he makes six cheeses altogether, four based on the Devon Garland recipe, a Cheddar, and a new Swiss-style cheese rather like Gruyère.

KNIGHTSWOOD

Silver Medal, British Cheese Awards 1996
A semi-hard cows' cheese; full-fat, thermized milk; vegetarian rennet.
2kg/4lb 6oz and 3.6kg/8lb wheels

Just as the cheesemaker's touch affects the quality of a cheese, so it sometimes seems to me that cheeses reflect character: all the Peverstone cheeses except the one which Jeremy did not originate, Devon Garland, have a warm, accessible, sunny taste. Knightswood, called after a wood near the farm, is light and open-textured, with a creamy taste and flowery undertones: it is very much a cheese which you could eat every day. It is excellent with nuts, fruit, and plum and apple cheese (page 24), which brings out its sweet notes.

The Devon Garland recipe belongs to the Cheddar group but the curd is cut less finely than for Cheddar, the cheese is only lightly pressed, and the maturing time is relatively short. After starter and rennet have been added and the curd has set, it is cut into 1-cm/$^1/_2$-inch cubes rather than pea-sized particles; stirring and 'pitching' (leaving it to rest), draining, and piling in blocks follow. To ensure even distribution, Catherine salts the curd before, during, and after milling; for the three flavoured versions, herbs and other items are also added. Finally, the cheeses are moulded and pressed overnight. The flavoured versions are matured for six weeks; Knightswood is rubbed with lard after pressing, brine-washed a week later, and matured for three months.

DEVON GARLAND

A semi-hard cows' cheese; full-fat, thermized milk; vegetarian rennet.
2.3kg/5lb and 3.6kg/8lb wheels

This is the original cheese on which Knightswood is based; instead of being plain, it is flavoured with a band of herbs running through the centre. The herbs look decorative but in the samples I have tried tasted slightly bitter, in contradiction to the cheese itself.

TISKEY MEADOW AND HUNTING PINK

A semi-hard cows' cheese; full-fat, thermized milk; vegetarian rennet.
2kg/4lb 6oz and 3.6kg/8lb wheels

Tiskey Meadow (the name of a field on the farm) was Catherine's idea. Instead of a band of herbs, it is flavoured throughout with sun-dried tomatoes, oregano, garlic, and fresh basil. I admit that before tasting it, I was doubtful – but it works: the basil and garlic give the cheese a lift and the tomato adds a mellow quality which suits its character. The texture is moister and softer than Devon Garland, with the lightness of good flaky pastry.

Hunting Pink, which won a Silver Medal at the British Cheese Awards in 1996, is similar to Tiskey Meadow, but flavoured with pink peppercorns: the result is warm and spicy rather than hot. At present, it is exclusive to Fortnum & Mason.

Tiskey Meadow Courgettes

Chillies vary greatly in strength: try a tiny piece of the one you are planning to use, and if it is very mild, do not remove all the seeds. The courgettes can be prepared up to twenty-four hours in advance.

Initial cooking time: nearly 1 hour; final baking time: 10–12 minutes
For 4 as a vegetable

450g/1lb ripe tomatoes, peeled, chopped, and the hard cores removed
salt and pepper
white sugar
500g/1lb 2oz (4 medium) courgettes, washed and the ends trimmed
5 cloves garlic, peeled and finely chopped
100g/3^1/$_2$oz (2 large) shallots, peeled and finely chopped
1^1/$_2$ tbsp oil
40g/1^1/$_2$oz pine-nuts
1 green chilli, washed, dried, core and seeds (unless needed) removed, and finely diced
2 stems basil or enough for 2 tbsp when washed and shredded
100g/3^1/$_2$oz Tiskey Meadow, finely grated
extra virgin olive oil for drizzling

Pre-heat the oven to 190°C/375°F/Gas 5. Put the tomatoes into a small, shallow baking dish (do not spread out in a single layer or they will become too dry); season fairly generously with salt and pepper and sprinkle with a very little sugar. Bake for 40–45 minutes, until the tomatoes are dry but not charred.

Boil the courgettes in lightly salted water for 7–9 minutes, until they are tender when pierced with a blunt knife; drain, refresh in cold water, and leave for a few minutes to cool. Halve them lengthwise and score round the cut side about 5mm/^{1}/$_4$ inch from the edges to about the same depth, taking care not to penetrate the skin. Scoop out the flesh in the middle with a spoon; turn the shells upside-down to drain and tip the liquor into the baked tomatoes; chop the flesh into 1-cm/^{1}/$_2$-inch squares.

Fry the garlic and shallots in the oil over medium heat for 2 minutes or until soft, turning constantly; add the courgette flesh and fry for another 1–2 minutes or until the shallots start to be tinged with gold. Add the nuts and stir-fry for a few seconds; add the chilli and stir. Add the tomatoes and cook for 3–5 minutes or until liquified, pressing out lumps of tomato flesh against the bottom of the pan. Stir in the basil. Fill the courgette shells; store in the refrigerator until needed.

To bake, keep the oven at 200°C/400°F/Gas 6, set the courgettes closely together in a baking dish, and cover liberally with the grated cheese. Sprinkle with a few drops of ordinary oil and bake for 10–12 minutes or until the cheese begins to brown. Drizzle with a little virgin olive oil before serving.

PEVERSTONE 'TASTY' CHEDDAR

A hard cows' cheese; full-fat, thermized milk; vegetarian rennet. 2kg/4lb 6oz and 3.6kg/8lb wheels; also blocks

The cheese has a fairly moist, clean texture and a clean, light rather than deep taste; it is pleasant on the cheeseboard and strong enough to give a pronounced flavour when used for cooking.

Cheddar and Sweetcorn Pancakes

The Cheddar gives the pancakes a wonderful crispness. With the proportions I have given, the taste of the cheese is fairly positive: if you prefer the sweetness of the corn to predominate, use less cheese – which, however, will mean sacrificing some of the crispness.

The pancakes can be thick or thin: for thinner, more delicate ones, add a little extra milk before frying.

The batter should be made at least half an hour in advance. A non-stick frying pan is essential.

Makes 12–14 small pancakes

salt
125g/4$^{1}/_{2}$oz maize meal
1 large free-range egg
150ml/$^{1}/_{4}$ pint milk, plus 3–4 tbsp for thin pancakes
125g/4$^{1}/_{2}$oz fresh sweetcorn kernels, stripped from the head and rinsed
100g/3$^{1}/_{2}$oz 'Tasty' Cheddar or Old Plaw Hatch (page 40), finely grated
oil for frying

Sift a small pinch of salt into the meal, make a well in the middle, and add the egg. Stir the egg into the meal, working outwards; add milk as needed to prevent the mixture from becoming dry. Stir in the rest of the milk and leave the batter to sit for at least 30 minutes. Simmer the corn kernels for 7–10 minutes or until tender; drain and leave them to dry.

Stir first the corn kernels, then the cheese into the batter. After the cheese has been added, it will become very stiff; add extra milk if you wish. The pancakes should be fried over moderate heat in enough oil to cover the bottom of a wok or frying pan fairly generously. Use about 1 tablespoonful of the mixture per pancake: make sure that they have room to spread a little in the pan without touching. Fry the pancakes until they are deep brown on both sides; turn them carefully, as they tend to be fragile. Place them on absorbent paper after you remove them from the pan. Serve immediately.

TAGON

Gold Medal, British Cheese Awards 1996
A hard cow's cheese; full-fat, thermized milk; vegetarian rennet. 2kg/4lb 6oz and 3.6kg/8lb wheels; also blocks

Tagon has a smooth, slightly elastic texture with medium-sized holes and a taste rather like Gruyère but lighter and fresher. At present, it is the only cheese of its kind made in Britain: Jeremy reckons that there is almost no possibility of competing successfully with Cheddar, but says cheerfully that a Gruyère-type cheese should at least hold its own in the sandwich market. It should be added that it is also excellent on the cheeseboard and for cooking: like its Swiss counterpart, it melts in strings and is suitable for fondue.

The procedure for making Tagon is quite different from the Devon Garland recipe. Several starters are used because the curds are heated to a high temperature and bacteria are needed which can survive the heat; also, one of the starters is propionic, i.e. it contains gas-producing organisms which give the cheese its characteristic round holes. The curd is cut to the size of peas, stirred for forty-five minutes, and partly drained; it is then stirred for another five to ten minutes before being heated to 52°C/126°F. This is followed by further stirring for about an hour, after which the curd is pressed for around twenty minutes with perforated sheets, which reduces it to a solid mass. After the rest of the whey has been run off, it is cut into blocks, moulded, and, like the Garland cheeses, lightly pressed overnight. Next morning, it is brined; thereafter, it is kept in a relatively warm atmosphere for two to three weeks while the bubbles of gas which make the holes are formed. Finally, it is matured at 7°C/45°F for six to seven months.

J. G. Quicke and Partners

Tom Langdon Davies, Woodley Farm, Newton St Cyres, Exeter EX5 5BT. Tel: 01392 851222

The Quickes have made cheese on the same farm, not just for three generations, like the Keens and Montgomerys, but for over 450 years. During and after the Second World War there was a long lapse, which initially was due to the ban on farmhouse cheesemaking and afterwards because, when the ban was lifted, Mary's father agreed to sell the milk to another cheesemaker who continued in business for nearly twenty years. The present dairy was set up by Mary's mother, Prue, in 1973, when the cheesemaker finally emigrated to Australia. At that time, cheesemaking was still regarded as part of the normal business of a mixed farm, as it had always been; the success of the dairy enabled the Quickes to continue mixed farming for a few more years, but eventually, like almost everyone outside the organic sector, they felt obliged to specialize. However, they do not concentrate solely on the cheese; instead of giving up their pigs, they have turned them into a second profitable enterprise (their pork is sold via Peninsula Pigs to Marks & Spencer).

The dairy herd consists of 550 pedigree Friesian–Holsteins, which is large but still not large enough: restrained from enlarging it still further by the milk quota, they buy in an extra supply of quality-tested Friesian–Holstein milk from Milk Marque. Their own cows are genetically based on Ayrshires so that, like the Montgomerys', the milk has Ayrshire characteristics, including a high solids content. Their method of making Cheddar is also similar to the Montgomerys': they differ, however, in pasteurizing most of the milk, in using vegetarian rennet for some of their cheeses, and making a range of products, including smoked and flavoured Cheddars, Double Gloucester, Red Leicester, a soft lactic cheese, and whey-butter and ice-cream as well as plain Cheddar (the butter-maker is Val Rowe).

Unpasteurized cheeses are made only on particular days, when there is no mud and the milk is especially suitable; Mary, who is in charge of the cheesemaking, prefers to use traditional rennet for long-matured cheeses because she finds that the vegetarian version gives a metallic taste to those matured for more than six months. The Gloucester and Red Leicester are made in almost the same way as the Cheddar but at different acidities. The soft cheese is rich and creamy, and is ideal for cooking or making dips and pâtés; at present, because of its short shelf-life (seven to ten days), the Quickes sell it only from their farmshop.

QUICKE'S TRADITIONAL CHEDDAR

Bronze Medal for Mild Traditional Cheddar, British Cheese Awards 1996;
Silver Medal for Extra Mature Traditional Cheddar, 1997
A hard cows' cheese; full-fat, pasteurized and unpasteurized milk; vegetarian
and traditional rennet. 25.2kg/55¹/₂ lb truckles

The texture is smooth, moist, and more compact than either Montgomery's or Keen's; the taste is deep, clean, and true. The strength of the cheese depends on its age, which varies from six months for the Mild to eighteen months for the Extra Mature, which is very powerful. After trying one sample (from Neal's Yard Dairy) I noted: '*Really* strong ... leaves the mouth tingling'; another time, however, when both were labelled Extra Mature, Keen's was the stronger. Like Keen's, the cheese is superb on the table, and the two can be used interchangeably for cooking.

Mary Quicke's Celeriac Chowder

Mary gave me only the rough outline of this recipe, so it may not be precisely as she intended: it is nevertheless extremely good. If you can buy organic celeriac, use it, not only because it will probably be fresher than when conventionally grown but may also be sold complete with leaves, which add flavour (those left over are delicious in salads).

A vital point about celeriac is to peel it carefully, removing inlets of skin and tough flesh under the surface, which otherwise will remain as abrasive edges in the soup, rather like bits of core in apple pies.

Cooking time: 40–45 minutes
For 4

1 medium onion (about 150g/5¹/₄ oz), peeled and finely chopped
15g/¹/₂ oz butter
¹/₂ tbsp oil or a little more
1 small leek (85–100g/3–3¹/₂ oz), finely sliced, washed, and left to dry
1 medium (250g/9oz) floury potato, e.g. Estime, Cara, or Kerr's Pink, peeled and diced into 8-mm/¹/₃-inch squares
1 smallish root celeriac (500g/1lb 2oz), prepared in the same way as the potato

salt and pepper

1 litre/1³/₄ pints vegetable (page 22) or chicken (page 21) stock, skimmed of fat

2 fronds celeriac leaves if available, washed

2 tbsp double cream

125–140g/4¹/₂–5oz Quicke's, Keen's, or Peverstone Cheddar, finely grated

Sweat the onion in the butter and oil over low heat for 10 minutes or until soft but not brown. Add the leek and stir-fry for 1–2 minutes: moisten with extra oil if necessary. Add the potato and celeriac, season with 1 teaspoonful salt and a fairly generous grinding of pepper, and pour in the stock. Throw in one stem of celeriac leaves, bring just to the boil, cover, and simmer for 25–30 minutes or until the potato and celeriac (root) are tender.

While the soup simmers, pull 6–8 celeriac leaves from the second stem and shred them finely. Add the cream to the soup; remove the pan from the heat and take out the cooked stem of celeriac. Stir in about two-thirds of the cheese and sprinkle the soup with the shredded leaves. Serve the rest of the cheese separately.

QUICKE'S TRADITIONAL OAK-SMOKED CHEDDAR

Bronze Medal, British Cheese Awards 1996
A hard cows' cheese; full-fat, pasteurized milk; vegetarian and traditional rennet.
6.8kg/15lb truckles

As smoked cheeses go, this is one of the best: the taste of smoke, though strong, does not overwhelm that of the relatively mild, young cheese. When used for cooking, for which it is excellent, both flavours intensify.

QUICKE'S TRADITIONAL RED LEICESTER

Gold Medal, British Cheese Awards 1996; Bronze Medal, 1997
A hard cows' cheese; full-fat, pasteurized milk; vegetarian rennet. 16kg/35lb truckles

Quicke's is one of the best Red Leicesters currently made, with a light, open texture and rich, buttery, but very mild flavour. (The deep orange colour is produced by annatto.) All the Red Leicester produced at the moment is pasteurized; however, at the time of writing Richard Calver of Milton-Westcombe Farms Ltd, Evercreech, Shepton Mallet, Somerset BA4 6NR is planning to make an unpasteurized Cheddar, which should be on sale by now, and is considering following it with an unpasteurized Red Leicester.

Ticklemore Cheese

ROBIN CONGDON, SHARPHAM BARTON, SHARPHAM ESTATE,
ASHPRINGTON, NEAR TOTNES, DEVON. TEL: 01803 732737

Our visit to Robin Congdon was especially memorable not only for the location of his dairy but also because of his all-expressive way of talking about cheese, which conjures up the densely populated world of micro-organisms in the minimum of words. To reach his house, which is house and dairy combined, you go up a hill via the usual narrow, twisting West Country lane enclosed by walls or high banks. The hill is steep but not remarkable and in no way prepares you for the view of the Dart valley which suddenly spreads out before you at the top. The river winds northwards between convex slopes patchworked with woods which at that time of year were bare and dark, interspersed with fields dusted with snow: in the summer I am sure that it is very pretty, perhaps too pretty, but on a winter afternoon, with an evening mist gathering, it had the drama of a slightly blurred black and white photograph. Robin's house is almost on the summit, overlooking the river: he certainly does not make cheese for the sake of living here, but he chose the site and put up the house himself rather than moving into an existing building in a less inspirational spot.

Before becoming a cheesemaker, he had farmed on the estate (which includes four farms) and during that time started milking sheep, not with any particular aim but simply because in the 1970s nobody else had thought of it except Olivia Mills. This led to making yoghurt for Harrods, which he delivered himself: cheese was the obvious next step. Like Alan Duffield (page 81), he eventually gave up farming to concentrate on cheese and now makes blue cows', sheep's, and goats' cheeses plus a non-blue hard and a fresh goats' cheese – and, again like Alan, bemoans the fact that the cows' cheeses are much the most popular. With his partner, Sarie Cooper, he also runs a cheese-shop in Totnes at the bottom of the hill.

As he showed me round the dairy and explained his cheesemaking processes, his descriptions were so rich in aphorisms that I can only remember a few. The most memorable was: 'Cheesemaking is almost farming bacteria', but 'There are so many generations of life in a cheese' was a close runner-up. He also stressed that cheesemaking is very much what you feel with your hands, and that it calls for judgement at all times because there are so many variables: the weather, the field in which the animals are grazing, the animals' state of mind, and luck – and, he added, a cheese needs love as well.

DEVON BLUE

Silver Medal, British Cheese Awards 1997
A blue cows' cheese; full-fat, unpasteurized milk; vegetarian rennet.
3kg/6lb 10oz cylinders

Devon Blue has a moist, slightly crumbly texture and a soft, many-tiered taste which includes flavours of grass, flowers, cream, and butter, with earthy hints. The blue is just strong enough to be lively without overwhelming the other flavours.

To make the blue cheeses, the milk is warmed, starter added, and the milk heated to 34°C/93°F before the addition of rennet and *Penicillium roqueforti* for the mould. He and Debbie Mumford at the Sharpham Creamery down the hill (page 108) are among the very few who have as yet adopted the genetically engineered vegetarian rennet Chymosin, with which Robin is very pleased. The curd is left to set for thirty to sixty minutes, cut twice, once coarsely and once finely, with a harp (a set of vertical wires instead of a blade) and stirred at intervals for twenty to eighty minutes according to the kind of cheese. It is then left to rest and, like Alan Duffield's soft cheeses (page 82), moulded without draining; instead, the cheeses are turned several times on the first day and once on the second. For two days, they are kept very warm (20–22°C/68–72°F), after which they are rubbed with salt and spiked to allow extra air to enter. When enough blue has developed, in three or four weeks, Robin wraps them in foil or plastic, according to the French rather than the Stilton method (instead of wrapping, Stilton is not pierced until it is five to six weeks old). The goats' cheese, Harbourne Blue, is matured for four months, and the cows' and sheep's cheeses, Devon and Beenleigh Blue, for six to eight.

BEENLEIGH BLUE

Gold Medal, British Cheese Awards 1996
A blue sheep's cheese; unpasteurized milk; vegetarian rennet. 2.7kg/6lb cylinders;
scarce in winter

The cheese is slightly crumbly, with tiny, bubbly holes. Cheese addicts are divided between those who prefer Beenleigh and those who prefer Harbourne: Beenleigh, being sheep, is richer and sweeter, with hints of grass and flowers and a distinct tang of the sea. As with Devon Blue, the blue, although strong, complements rather than overwhelms the other flavours.

Beenleigh Blue Pâté with Sage

For 4–6

1 fair-sized clove garlic, peeled and chopped
225g/8oz goats' curds or Perroche (page 174)
115g/4oz Beenleigh Blue, chopped
8–10 sage leaves, washed and finely chopped

Crush the garlic to a paste in a mortar. Add and mash the two cheeses; stir in the sage. Serve with pears or fresh figs.

HARBOURNE BLUE

Silver Medal, British Cheese Awards 1996 and 1997
A blue goats' cheese; full-fat, unpasteurized milk; vegetarian rennet.
2.7kg/6lb cylinders; scarce in winter

The texture is creamy and melting; the taste includes suggestions of the sea and moors. It is a wonderful cheese, but with the background of goat the blue can be very powerful. As Robin acknowledges, its strength varies considerably: more than most blues, it is better eaten last rather than first on the cheeseboard.

TICKLEMORE

A hard goats' cheese; full-fat, unpasteurized milk; vegetarian rennet.
1.8kg/4lb basket-shaped cheeses; scarce in winter

Ticklemore is very light and delicate, with small holes; the taste is mild, fresh, and sweet, with a mixture of moorland flavours and only the faintest trace of goat.

Ticklemore is made by heating the milk to 30°C/86°F, adding starter, followed by rennet, and leaving the milk to set for half an hour. The curd is then cut into large chunks and left to stand for twenty minutes before being cut again, stirred, and heated by 2°C/36°F. After being left to rest for another twenty minutes and cut again, it is moulded, not in conventional basket moulds but Woolworth's colanders. Finally, it is left in a warm place for two days, salted, and left at cool room temperature (14°C/57°F) for another two days before being matured for two to three months.

TICKLEMORE SOFT GOAT

A fresh goats' cheese; full-fat, unpasteurized milk; vegetarian rennet.
50g/1³/₄ oz buttons; scarce in winter

This is an exceptionally smooth, delicate goats' cheese, with a mild, sweet, but fresh flowery flavour. Unluckily for those who do not live in the area, it is sold only at Ticklemore Cheese, Ticklemore Street, Totnes.

Ticklemore and Apple Mousse

Cooking time: 8–10 minutes, plus 4–5 to crisp the nuts just before serving
Allow at least 3 hours for chilling
For 4

400g/14oz Bramley apples (2 medium), peeled and chopped fairly small
125g/4¹/₂ oz Muscovado sugar
1 Ticklemore soft goats' cheese (50g/1³/₄ oz)
150ml/¹/₄ pint whipping cream
25g/1oz pecans

Set the apples over very low heat with the sugar and allow them to cook until the sugar has started to melt; stir gently and continue to cook for 7–8 minutes more or until the fruit is soft and submerged in liquid. Blend or sieve it, pressing as much of the pulp through the mesh as possible. Sieve or blend in the cheese. Whip the cream until it stands in peaks; fold it in gently and chill for at least 3 hours.

Shortly before serving, pre-heat the oven to 200°C/400°F/Gas 6, and toast the nuts for 4–5 minutes. Coarsely crush or very finely chop them and sprinkle on top of the mousse.

Sharpham Creamery

DEBBIE MUMFORD, SHARPHAM CREAMERY, SHARPHAM HOUSE, ASHPRINGTON, TOTNES, DEVON TQ9 7UT. TEL: 01803 732600

Sharpham House is dramatically situated on the side of a hill above the Dart, which here, only about 8km/5 miles from Dartmouth, is meandering and tidal. The house was designed by Sir Robert Taylor in 1770; in front, on the edge of a steep slope down to the river, framed by trees and perfectly placed to give scale and focus to the view, is quite a large statue by Henry Moore, who was a friend of Maurice Ash, the former owner. Inside, Oriental rugs on the landings are a reminder that for a time the house was occupied by a Buddhist community and is still used as a Buddhist educational centre, with a printing press, library, and programme of lectures and meditation retreats. Behind the house are gardens, possibly laid out by Capability Brown, and 200ha/500 acres of farmland, most of which is on a peninsula made by a bend in the river. The privacy given by the hill at the back and the river on the other three sides, the timelessness of the Moore, and perhaps the atmosphere lent by Buddhism, produces an almost tangible sense of calm.

The estate is now owned by the Sharpham Trust and, besides the house, consists of four farms, one organic and one biodynamic, the Sharpham vineyard, and the creamery, which is in the stableyard next to the house. The milk comes from a herd of fifty-five Jerseys kept on permanent pastures which Debbie and her partner, Mark Sharman, are in the process of converting to organic; conversion will be completed next year. When I visited her, she only made Sharpham, although she had already developed her second cheese, Elmhirst; since then, she has also taken over Devon (now Sharpham) Rustic, a rich, moist, semi-soft cheese which used to be made by Robin Congdon (page 104), with whom she trained for two and a half years before moving down the hill to Sharpham.

SHARPHAM

Bronze Medal, British Cheese Awards 1996
A soft, white mould rind Jersey cheese; full-fat, thermized milk; vegetarian rennet.
250g/9oz squares or 1kg/2lb 4oz rounds; 500g/1lb 2oz rounds occasionally or to order

When ripe, the cheese is gloriously rich and creamy; the taste is grassy and herbal rather than sweet, very individual and stronger than one might expect, particularly slices from the large size (small cheeses tend to be milder).

Every morning, Debbie collects the milk in a Land Rover fitted with a cooled milk tank. Her first step is to thermize it by heating it to 68°C/154°F: she says that she has tested the treated against the raw milk and the only difference thermizing makes to the cheese is to slow down its development slightly. Sharpham is made by a fairly classic version of the Coulommiers method. After starter is added, the milk is left to ripen for one to one and a half hours, or longer in winter, before the addition of rennet and penicillin for the rind. The curd sets in about an hour; Debbie then cuts it twice, with half an hour between each cutting, and ladles it into the moulds to free-drain. The cheeses are turned four or five hours later and the next morning are taken to a draining room kept at 14°C/57°F; the following day they are brined and for the next three days they are turned daily. They are then moved to a room kept at 10°C/50°F, where they stay for a further twelve days while the rind develops. Thereafter, they are kept chilled until they are ready for eating at seven to ten weeks. If bought unripe, the cheese should be kept in its wrapping, wrapped again loosely in plastic to prevent loss of moisture, and stored at 4°C/39°F, i.e. in the refrigerator, until soft and flowing.

ELMHIRST

A soft Jersey cheese; full-fat, thermized milk and added cream; vegetarian rennet. 250g/9oz squares and 1kg/2lb 4oz rounds

Elmhirst has a very smooth, silky texture and is soft as opposed to runny, with a taste of butter and cream mingled with grass, wild flowers, and sunshine. It is unusual in that, so far as I know, only four other handmade cream cheeses are produced in Britain.

SHARPHAM RUSTIC

Silver Medal, British Cheese Awards 1997 (Chives and Garlic)
A hard Jersey cheese, plain or flavoured with herbs; full-fat, thermized milk; vegetarian rennet. About 2kg/4lb 6oz flattened spheres

I have tried both Robin Congdon and Debbie's versions of this cheese and, despite a possible difference in touch and texture, found both equally exceptional. Like Elmhirst, it tastes of butter, cream, grass, and wild flowers, but, because it is matured and drier, it is sweeter and the flavours more concentrated. To my palate, few more delightful cheeses of the milder, less challenging type are to be found anywhere.

Tala

HANS AND HEATHER WHITE, NORTH BEER FARM, BOYTON,
LAUNCESTON, CORNWALL PL15 8NR. TEL: 01566 785607

On the way to North Beer Farm, in July, I counted over a dozen different types of wild flower on the hedgebanks: pink campion, red clover, yellow toadflax, foxgloves, sheep's-bit scabious, speedwell, mallow. This is not irrelevant to the cause of cheese, since it shows that here at least the herbage is still mixed despite the use of agrichemicals.

Hans and Heather White embarked on professional cheesemaking only five years ago and their problems have included most of the difficulties that a cheesemaker is likely to face (short of a court case such as Humphrey Errington's: page 234). Hans was in the Navy and retired at fifty with a pension which needed supplementing: having decided to dairy-farm but disliking goats' milk and feeling unable to cope with cattle, they settled on sheep. They began with twenty British Friesland ewes, a ram, and a cheesemaker in Devon who agreed to take their milk. Before long, the cheesemaker went 'rather seriously' bankrupt, leaving them with an unpaid account and no alternative outlets.

They had both taken cheesemaking courses before starting out, but, as Heather remarked, only a certain amount can be taught in a classroom situation. Having tried freezing and storing the milk, which proved uneconomic, they 'fiddled' with cheesemaking until they produced a cheese which sold. Before long, success prompted them to buy in extra milk: it also soon became obvious that they did not have enough time both to milk their own sheep and fulfil their orders. They therefore gave up the sheep and relied entirely on bought-in milk, which Hans said made him uneasy from the start. His fears were justified: 'We had a lot of trouble, going back over three years, with thousands of pounds of cheese going off (i.e. "blowing") because of dirty milk.' However, Hans's next-door neighbour, Terry Perkins, is a farmer who at that time was raising sheep for lamb: moaning over the fence to him about his troubles, Hans eventually persuaded him to branch out into milking, with the result that he now has milk as fresh as his own and Terry supplies the Minsons and Robin Congdon as well (pages 115 and 104).

The dirty-milk period, however, has left its mark on Hans, who has kept an entire storeroom of failed cheeses to study: gazing at row after row of them, all coated with black mould, some with staring white patches cut out of them, was a strange experience. Also, when the cheeses first started 'blowing' he thought that it might be because he hedged, ditched, and did other farm work as well as making cheese, thus contaminating the milk with undesirable yeasts and moulds. He therefore withdrew from the actual cheesemaking, leaving it to Heather, and restricted himself to packing and marketing. Although he now knows that the milk itself was the problem, this arrangement continues, with Heather making the cheese twice a week (she also teaches deaf children); in addition, she occasionally makes small fresh cheeses which are not sold as such because of distribution difficulties, but which Hans preserves in olive oil and is planning to launch under the name Davatty.

TALA

A hard sheep's cheese; thermized milk; vegetarian rennet. 450g/1lb and 2.3kg/5lb truckles

The texture is fine, compact, and velvety; the taste is surprisingly strong and completely unique. As always, it is impossible to give a true idea of flavour in words, but it is grassy and perhaps the earthiest cheese that I have yet come across. The unusual taste means that you may need to give it a little time: if you are not quite sure about it at first, try it again. It is particularly delicious toasted, when it browns and melts to a toffee-like consistency, with a flavour which if anything is even more intense than when it is uncooked; for best results, drizzle it with a little fruity olive oil.

The particular flavour of Tala is partly due to the fact that it is a washed-curd cheese, like Waterloo and cheeses of the Gouda type. Understandably, in view of their earlier difficulties, Heather takes the precaution of first therm-izing the milk, which is heated to 65°C/149°F; rennet is added about an hour after the starter and the curd is left to set for about another hour. It is then cut very small, heated by about 10°C/50°F to give it a firm coating, and washed by gradually replacing the whey with boiled water, which reduces the acidity in taste of the final cheese. Draining and moulding follow, after which the cheeses are pressed and turned several times, with increasing pressure after each turn. The next day they are moved to a drying room, brined the day after, and finally dried for another twenty-four hours, by which time a firm crust has formed. The maturing time is three to four and a half months, or six weeks for the small size; some are also smoked.

Lynher Dairies

MIKE HORRELL, NETHERTON FARM, UPTON CROSS, LISKEARD, CORNWALL PL14 5BD. TEL: 01579 362244; FAX: 01579 362666

Netherton is the largest of a cluster of farms most of which are rented by Mike from the Duchy of Cornwall – who are a helpful landlord except that he feels that they would be happier if he farmed organically (which he does not). The farm is open to the public, with a barn which has been converted into a coffee-shop, a farm trail, ornamental poultry, wild boar, and a few pigs. Very properly, the first to greet visitors when they arrive are the pigs, who (deliberately) are kept in the field opposite the car-park.

Serious farming, however, is concentrated on the dairy. Mike, who has been at Netherton since the 1960s, switched from mixed farming about twenty years ago and now has a herd of 500 pedigree Friesian–Holsteins. Cheese was brought to him by the Duchy: aware of the need for a value-added product, he had already been thinking about it when they telephoned to ask if he would take in a couple of cheesemakers who were in need of a home. He said, 'Yes. When?' and they replied, 'Now. Today.' Alan and Jennie Gray from Wales thus arrived with a very old recipe, possibly dating from the thirteenth century, and made the cheese, Yarg (Gray spelt backwards) three days a week for nearly two years. At this point, since the cheese had become popular, Mike asked them to step up production to five days a week: they departed soon afterwards but left the recipe.

Although virtually all the milk comes from his own herd, he pasteurizes, partly to ensure that the cheese has a consistent flavour. Like some others, it nevertheless retains its individuality to a surprising degree: when I asked him why, he answered, 'I don't know', adding that he did not feed the cows for any special effect (at the time of my visit, one of the most eye-catching features of the farmyard was a stack of silage as high as a house).

The dairy, where half a dozen people or more are now employed, makes not only Cornish Yarg but also flavoured soft fresh cheeses, Cornish Pepper and Cornish Herb and Garlic, for which the curd is simply drained in cloths. In the past distribution was limited, but Mike is now planning to market them more widely and, because of the lack of plain, fresh cheeses for cooking, add an unflavoured version to the range.

CORNISH YARG

A hard cows' cheese coated with nettle leaves; full-fat, pasteurized milk; vegetarian rennet. 1kg/2lb 4oz and 3kg/6lb 10oz rounds

Cornish Yarg is a moist cheese which tastes fresh and creamy, with a gentle tang and surprisingly wide range of strong yet subtle herbal, grassy, and flowery undertones. The nettle coating, which is dark, greenish grey, is truly artistic, especially when seen on a whole cheese: whether it adds to the flavour is open to question. Mike thinks not; his wife is convinced that it does. I would be inclined to agree with her because of the importance to flavour of the other sorts of rind; however, as the Lynher Dairies soft cheeses show, much of the taste is certainly due to the milk.

The cheese is made by a method half-way between Caerphilly and Cheddar, although it differs from both in that it is not scalded, which means that it sets less firmly; also it is covered with its distinctive coating of nettle leaves rather than a rind. After pasteurization, the milk is cooled to blood-heat, starter is added, and the milk is left to ripen for about an hour before renneting. When the curd has set, it is cut very finely with a curd knife (which has vertical blades) and drained. The next stage is cutting it into blocks and piling; this is followed by milling, moulding and pressing overnight. Finally, the cheeses are brined for twenty-four hours, the nettle coating dipped in a sterilizing solution, and applied to the cheese with paintbrushes. The nettles are picked by children and others and frozen, not merely for convenience and to deaden the sting, but because when defrosted they are limp, which makes sticking them neatly over the cheeses much easier.

CORNISH PEPPER AND CORNISH HERB AND GARLIC

Gold Medal, British Cheese Awards 1996 (Cornish Pepper)
A fresh cows' cheese; full-fat, pasteurized milk; vegetarian rennet. 500g/1lb 2oz or smaller and 1kg/2lb 4oz rounds

Both cheeses are rich, creamy, and close-textured; the herbs and garlic in the one are quite strong but, despite pasteurization, you can still taste the natural grassy and flowery flavours of the milk.

Menallack Farm

CARYL AND JOHN MINSON, MENALLACK FARM, TREVERVA, PENRYN, CORNWALL TR10 9BP. TEL: 01326 340333

Besides making cheese, Caryl Minson acts as a wholesaler for cheeses all over Cornwall and part of Devon, which sometimes involves driving 480km/300 miles a day; she also keeps a farmshop selling chutneys and cheeses, bread, pottery, and anything else 'genuine', makes bread for her own and another local shop, and offers bed and breakfast plus good home cooking with no corners cut (I know because we stayed there). She is helped in all this by John, who, after a job which took them all over the world, retreated to Cornwall with the aim of living a life of leisure and sailing.

They bought the farm because their son wanted to keep cows: Caryl accordingly experimented with cheese and came up with Menallack, which is based on a recipe for Cheshire from Val Cheke and A. Sheppard's *Butter and Cheesemaking*. This proved so popular that she decided to employ a cheese-maker, which gave her the time to develop her other activities. Meanwhile, the son fell in love with the cheesemaker and carried her off to Kent, leaving Caryl and John with the cows as well as everything else. The cows, except for one or two who were kept for pleasure, were sold: Milk Marque agreed to supply quality-tested milk from a particular farm, and John turned out to be an excellent cheesemaker. Soon after, a couple who made a cheese called Nanterrow, which Caryl sold in her shop, announced that they were giving up; not wishing to lose the cheese, she took it over. By now, she has evolved three more cheeses, St Laudus, a cream cheese called Mrs Finn's Farmhouse Cheese, and a cheese made from buffalo milk. She has also taken on another cheesemaker, Wendy, and a part-time assistant called Kate, who is a sculpture student – which struck me as completely appropriate, since cheese-making and sculpture are both tactile. However, with orders for five cheeses flowing in, John's skill in the dairy is needed as much as ever.

MENALLACK

A hard cows' cheese; full-fat, unpasteurized milk; vegetarian rennet. 10-cm/4-inch, 15-cm/6-inch, and 17.5-cm/7-inch truckles

Menallack has a dryish texture and mild flavour, with a gentle, grassy tang and herbal undertones. It is a good all-purpose cheese suitable for lunches and snacks as well as the cheeseboard; it is excellent toasted.

After slightly warming the milk and adding starter and rennet, Caryl cuts the curd into 1-cm/^{1}/$_2$-inch cubes, stirs it for twenty minutes, and scalds (heats) it to 35°C/95°F over another twenty minutes, stirring continuously; she then holds it at 35°C/95°F, still stirring, for a further twenty minutes or until 'the cubes feel like tender, cooked peas ... they should be sufficiently scalded to take on the imprint of your fingers.' Having reached the right point, the curd is left to rest for an hour before being cut into blocks and worked for one and a half to two hours. Draining, milling, and salting follow; finally, the cheeses are packed into moulds, pressed, and matured for a minimum of two months.

NANTERROW

Silver Medal, British Cheese Awards 1996
A fresh sheep's cheese; unpasteurized milk; vegetarian rennet. Made in 1.4kg/3lb
disks; sold in 450g/1lb slices

Nanterrow has the delicate, insubstantial, almost trembling texture characteristic of fresh sheep's cheeses; the taste is equally delicate, with the sweetness of the milk balanced by hints of herbs and grass and a very slight tinge of lemon. It comes plain or flavoured with herbs: the herb-flavoured version, which focuses the natural flavours of the cheese without altering its character, is particularly successful.

The milk comes (frozen) from Terry Perkins, near Launceston (page 110). Nanterrow is made by a version of the Coulommiers method: watching John, I was reminded of Charles Westhead at Neal's Yard Creamery (page 172), since both are equally insistent on the need to disturb the curd as little as possible. When set, the curd is very gently lifted into the moulds, not with a ladle but with a plate: John then covers the mould with gauze and deftly turns it upside-down to drain, like turning a cake to cool on a rack. The herbs for the flavoured cheeses are sprinkled over the curd in layers; the cheeses are then left to drain for twenty-four hours, during which they are turned three times. Finally, they are lightly salted, cut into three, and vacuum-packed.

ST LAUDUS

A semi-hard cows' cheese; full-fat, unpasteurized milk; vegetarian rennet.
17.5-cm/7-inch truckles

St Laudus is notable for its light, crumbly, almost frothy texture; the taste is mild and fresh, with a suggestion of lemon.

The Minsons' third cheese (named after an early Cornish saint) is given its character by leaving the curd in the whey as it drains for the first two hours and thereafter pressing it only by means of a tight cloth. The curd when set is gathered into muslin and left to drain in a container; the whey is emptied after an hour and the process repeated. After the second hour, the muslin is tightly tied and the curd left until it is solid enough to hold its shape; it is then cut and left to rest and drain further until the correct acidity is reached. Milling and salting in the usual manner follow; when moulded, however, the curd is laid lightly in the moulds, rather than firmly packed, and covered with a damp cloth. It is turned daily for the next three or four days and matured for two months.

MRS FINN'S FARMHOUSE CHEESE

A fresh combined cows' and sheep's cheese; full-fat, unpasteurized milk with added cream; vegetarian rennet. 175g/6oz rounds, boxed

Elizabeth Finn founded the Distressed Gentlefolks Aid Association Home-life, a charity which provides care for the old: the cheese was devised by Caryl and John to celebrate its centenary. They have come up with a winner: Mrs Finn's combines the lightness and delicacy of Nanterrow with a slightly stronger, yet overwhelmingly creamy taste in which the sweetness of the milk and cream are offset by a gentle lemon tang. The result is refreshing rather than rich, and I think delicious. I tried it with a washed-rind cheese, Gubbeen (page 140): the two cheeses set each other off perfectly. All profits will go to DGAA Homelife; available by mail order from the farm.

SOFT CHEESE WITH GARLIC AND HERBS

A fresh buffalo cheese; full-fat, pasteurized milk; vegetarian rennet. 115g/4oz, 225g/8oz, 450g/1lb, and 900g/2lb rounds

The buffalo milk, which is even richer than sheep's, gives a nutty, concentrated, but deliciously light, soufflé-like texture; the taste of the cheese is creamy and very garlicky.

CHAPTER 3

Ireland

CROGHAN GOAT FARM

CARRIGBYRNE FARMHOUSE CHEESE CO.

COOLEENEY FARMHOUSE CHEESE

CASHEL BLUE FARMHOUSE CHEESE

INAGH FARMHOUSE CHEESES

ARDRAHAN CHEESE

MILLEENS

DURRUS

WEST CORK NATURAL CHEESE

GUBBEEN

ORLA

CARRAIG

COOLEA CHEESE

Croghan Goat Farm

LUC AND ANN VAN KAMPEN, CROGHAN FARM,
BALLYNADRISHOGUE, BLACKWATER, COUNTY WEXFORD.
TEL: 00353 53 29331

The first thing to strike us about Ireland was its greenness. We arrived at the end of May, when Britain is green too, but because of the extent and continuity of the grass if not because of the actual colour, the Irish green is much more noticeable and insistent. In the flat basin around Wexford, the land seemed entirely given over to grazing, the grass being interrupted only by equally green trees and the white, blue, and yellow splashes of wild flowers. Cattle were everywhere – but few people and hardly any traffic.

In terms of cheese, one of the major differences between Ireland and Britain was clearly illustrated by our first two visits. Here, the Cheddar and Cheshire tradition does not hold and inspiration tends to come from France, Holland, or Switzerland. Like several other leading cheesemakers, Luc van Kampen is from Holland: one of his cheeses is of the Gouda type, the other French. To reach him, we drove along a narrow but straight and empty road and turned down a track which reminded me of World's End (page 49). The dairy is small and we would probably have missed it without the tell-tale milk churns outside: if it were bigger, Luc said, they would make more cheese, but at present they are limited by storage space (however, when I spoke to him some months later, he had already begun to extend the storeroom).

He has been interested in cheese for as long as he can remember, having been brought up in a cheesemaking area, Albusset-Waard; after meeting Ann in Dublin and deciding to stay, he started making it himself because at that time (1975) there was very little good cheese of any kind in Ireland. Counting 'everybody', i.e. kids, he and Ann have fifty goats, who supply about half their milk: the rest is bought from two specific farms, one of which is organic, bringing the total on a busy day to about 135 litres/30 gallons. Although their land is organic, the goats, strictly speaking, are not, since the van Kampens cannot afford organic feed; however, they are organic in spirit and do not stagger kidding for winter milk, which means that they make no cheese from November to May. Luc spends the winter equipping the dairy, where he has made his own press and all the wooden shelves, and very occasionally, when he has time, paints. From a large picture hanging in their bathroom, it is clear that he has unusual ability: he has designed their cheese labels and says that one day he would like to take a course in graphic design.

CROGHAN

Gold Medal, Best Semi-Soft Cheese, British Cheese Awards 1996
A semi-soft goats' cheese; full-fat, unpasteurized milk; vegetarian rennet.
400–450g/14oz–1lb cakes or 1–1.4kg/2lb 4oz–3lb basket-shaped rounds

Croghan has an exceptionally fine, velvety texture with a few small holes; the flavour is mild, creamy, and herbal, with a slight tang, not of goat (which is barely detectable) but of herbage and sea breezes (the farm is only 5–6km/3–4 miles inland).

The previous evening's milk is cooled and mixed with the morning's straight after milking; commercial starter is added and the milk is renneted at a temperature of 30°C/86°F, where it is held until the curd has set. It is then cut with a double-pronged curd knife into 1-cm/$^1/_2$-inch squares, partly drained, and scalded (heated) to 36°C/97°F for about half an hour, by which time it looks like very small white polystyrene balls. These are moulded and pressed for four hours, after which the cheeses are turned out and brined; the maturing time is one month.

MINE-GABHAR

Gold Medal, Best Irish Cheese, Best Soft White-rind Cheese, British Cheese
Awards 1996; Bronze Medal, 1997
A soft white mould rind goats' cheese; full-fat, unpasteurized milk; vegetarian rennet.
225g/8oz

Mine-Gabhar (pronounced Gower) is notably smooth and velvety but firm-textured; it has quite a strong, very distinctive taste, again not of goat but of blossom and sweet new leaves, with nutty and earthy undertones. The overall impression is rich and luxurious but at the same time sunny and fresh. To suggest using it for cooking seems like libel, but it is wonderful grilled, when the flavour becomes even sweeter and more distinctive: if I had to nominate a Best Cheese for Grilling, this would be my choice.

For this cheese, very little starter and rennet are used and the curd is allowed to set very slowly, which maximizes the natural flavours; in this instance, the starter is homemade. The curd is left for twenty-four hours, drained in a cloth, and moulded for a further twenty-four hours; finally, the cheeses are sprayed with penicillin for the rind and matured for four weeks.

Carrigbyrne Farmhouse Cheese Co.

PADDY AND JULIE BERRIDGE, CARRIGBYRNE FARMHOUSE,
ADAMSTOWN, COUNTY WEXFORD. TEL: 00353 544 0560

Carrigbyrne is gracious and manorial, with a large, gabled, partly Victorian house and farmyard almost as big but much more orderly than a town square, with a tree in the middle. Round two sides are stables with wooden doors, all painted bright blue; the woodwork on the house is also bright blue. Perhaps because of the blue, and possibly also because of the size and formality of the yard, my instant reaction, before I had seen or spoken to anybody, was that it was French: I felt as if, instead of crossing St George's Channel to Ireland, we were in Brittany. The French impression is not entirely subjective or chance: although Paddy was brought up on the farm, his mother is Belgian, he speaks French like a native, and has a French cheesemaker, Alan Girot.

Before he went into business, two attempts to make Camembert in Ireland, in 1963 and 1972, had already failed; however, a cheesemaker who was involved in the second came to fish in the Berridges' river and taught Paddy, then aged seventeen, to make the cheese in the kitchen. He started out professionally ten years later (on 16 March 1982): everything went 'swimmingly' until the cows came in for the winter. Then, because of the change in the milk, disaster struck: 'The cheese just melted through the racks.' Having by then established that there was a good market for Camembert, he promptly advertised for a cheesemaker: Alan replied and has been with him ever since. After sixteen years, he says that the main lesson he has learnt remains the often-repeated maxim that there are no rules in cheesemaking: judgement has to be exercised afresh every day.

Alongside his commitment to cheese, Paddy loves machines. In the dairy is a French stainless-steel washing-up machine, at least 3.6 metres/12 feet long, which washes up and sterilizes all the cheesemaking equipment. When I asked what happened to the whey, he replied, like everyone else, that he used to keep pigs but that they were uneconomic, and without saying more led the way to a barn at the corner of the yard. Inside, an enormous and astonishingly elegant sixty-five-year-old engine with a huge, red-painted fly-wheel generates enough electricity from the whey to service the house and farm and have some left over to sell to the national grid. He later admitted that this probably was not economic either, but I was suitably impressed, feeling, like him, that the machine was sufficient justification in itself.

Not surprisingly, the cheesemaking process is mechanized: only the wrapping is carried out by hand. The cows are a closed, i.e. entirely home-raised, herd of 160 Friesians: the fact that none are bought in obviously reduces the risk of infection from outside, although, as Paddy acknowledges, should disease strike they will be the more vulnerable. Besides the Camembert-sized St Killian, a larger version called St Brendan Brie is also made.

ST KILLIAN

Gold Medal, British Cheese Awards 1996
A Camembert-type soft cows' cheese; 45% fat, pasteurized milk; vegetarian rennet.
Boxed: 250g/9oz hexagonal rounds; St Brendan Brie, 375g/13oz rounds

The original quality of the milk combined with Paddy and Alan's expertise have produced a first-class result: the cheese has a spectrum of flavours ranging from herbs and grass to mushrooms (mould) and earth. In my tasting notebook, several samples from different shops are marked 'A1 delicious' or 'Wonderful'. Like Somerset Camembert (page 93), yeasts ensure slow ripening, which means that the cheese will almost certainly be at the correct stage when sold.

To encourage the development of yeasts and moulds, the milk is left unchilled for twenty-four hours before use; it is then warmed slightly, a special starter devised by Alan is added, and it is left to ripen for another hour before being 'flash' pasteurized at 72°C/162°F for sixteen seconds. The rennet and penicillin for the rind are added at the same time: until recently, Paddy and Alan used the traditional calves' rennet, but they are among the few so far to have switched to the genetically engineered vegetarian equivalent, Chymosin. When the curd has set, it is cut into cubes and left to drain, with turning at intervals, at 25°C/77°F, depending on the time of year, until it has contracted to about half its original volume. Finally, it is moulded, turned out and brined in salt which does not contain iodine (iodine inhibits mould), and ripened for about ten days at 10–12°C/50–54°F before packing.

St Killian is excellent in a pie (page 228), fried in egg and breadcrumbs (page 23) and served with redcurrant jelly, or simply baked in the oven and served as a hot dip with biscuits or crudités.

Cooleeney Farmhouse Cheese

BREDA, JIM, AND PAT MAHER, COOLEENEY, MOYNE, THURLES, COUNTY TIPPERARY. TEL: 00353 504 45112

Cooleeney farmhouse is approached via a handsome gateway crowned with urns and a long drive curving through parkland. Breda Maher, who is in charge of the cheese, is secretary of the Irish Cheesemakers Association and had been called away when we arrived, but I was shown round by her son Pat, who, having watched her efforts in the early years, when she had to 'push, push, push' to establish the cheese, has recently taken over as marketing manager. He told me that she had originally trained in hotel management with the idea of starting a restaurant; however, having married a farmer, she found herself with cows to manage rather than a kitchen. This made me wonder whether, as I do, she looks on cheesemaking as a parallel to cooking: when I spoke to her later, she said very positively, 'Cheese and cooking go hand in hand. They are both part of the same creative process.'

Her immediate incentive to make cheese was supplied by the milk quota, which interfered with the Mahers' plans for expansion. Almost directly after it was announced, she took a cheesemaking course in Cork, and went into production two years later. She now employs four full-time cheesemakers, who process nearly 2,000 litres/440 gallons of milk a day; all of it comes from a herd of 110 Friesians, the only livestock kept on the farm.

COOLEENEY

Gold Medal, British Cheese Awards 1996; Bronze Medal, 1997
A soft, Camembert-type cows' cheese; full-fat, unpasteurized milk; vegetarian rennet.
200g/7oz rounds (boxed) or about 1.6kg/3lb 8oz wheels

A wonderfully soft, creamy interior contrasts with the crisp, thick rind; the flavour is full and rich, striking the palate at different places and encompassing all the elements of the Irish pastures: sun, rain, wind, grasses and herbs, and flowers – a tribute, if you like, to unpasteurized milk. It loses some of its complexity when heated but is nevertheless delicious fried in breadcrumbs (page 23) or in a pie. For Cooleeney Pie, follow the recipe on page 228 but, to balance the rich flavour, sprinkle a teaspoonful of finely chopped sage over the cheese before wrapping it in pastry.

As the Mahers do not pasteurize, the cheesemaking process is more straight-forward than at Carrigbyrne. The morning and evening milk is warmed, starter and penicillin for the rind are added, and the milk is left to ripen for two hours before renneting. At the time of my visit, calves' rennet was still being used, but because of BSE this has now been replaced by vegetarian rennet (not Chymosin, but the usual version based on fungus). The curd is cut into 2.5-cm/1-inch squares, moulded, and left to drain for twenty-four hours, with turning after fifteen minutes and an hour. The cheeses are then brined and matured for two weeks, until the rind has developed, before they are wrapped; thereafter they are kept at 4°C/39°F, either on the farm or by the distributors, for four to six weeks in the case of the smaller size or eight to ten for the larger, until fully matured and ready to eat.

 ## Cooleeney and Fish Salad

Cooking time: 12–20 minutes (for the fish)
For 2 as a main course or 4–6 as a first course

175g/6oz turbot, halibut, or salmon, skinned and boned
salt and pepper
100g/3$\frac{1}{2}$oz Cooleeney straight out of the refrigerator
100ml/3$\frac{1}{2}$fl oz double cream
1 tsp dill (fresh) or 1$\frac{1}{2}$ of sorrel, washed and finely chopped or shredded
$\frac{1}{2}$ or 1 lettuce, according to the number of servings, washed and left to dry
cucumber and other salad ingredients to taste, washed and dried

Pre-heat the oven to 180°C/350°F/Gas 4. Wash the fish in cold water, check for bones, and season it lightly with salt and pepper. Enclose it in a parcel of cooking foil and bake for 12–20 minutes, or until it flakes easily with a fork (salmon cooks slightly more quickly than turbot or halibut). Drain the fish and leave it to cool.

Scrape the rind from the cheese and chop it into small pieces. Either beat the cream into it by hand, pressing out lumps on the side of the bowl, or process it, but do not over-whip the cream. Stir in the dill or sorrel.

Arrange the lettuce on the serving plates. Flake the fish into bite-sized pieces and place it on top of the lettuce; cover with the cheese dressing. Finely slice the cucumber and arrange it with the other salad ingredients round the edge.

Cashel Blue Farmhouse Cheese

JANE AND LOUIS GRUBB, BEECHMOUNT, FETHARD, COUNTY
TIPPERARY. TEL: 00353 5231151

No one could fail to be impressed by the extreme cleanliness of the dairies everywhere, both in Ireland and Britain: the Grubbs' was so spotless that I swear you would have noticed a single grain of salt on the floor. Louis observed that the hygiene regulations are adhered to here particularly strictly because agricultural products are Ireland's chief export. All his equipment except his cheese mould and a hand-beaten copper vat is stainless steel (which, being non-corrosive, resists moulds as well as rust); some of it is new, including a remarkably elegant spiking machine for pricking the cheeses and the racks in his storeroom, which are fitted with rollers to turn the cheeses automatically. Both were custom-made by a local craftsman, the racks to his own design. However, he takes equal pleasure in other pieces which, far from being new, he picked up in scrapyards and has lovingly restored to pristine condition such as the copper vat, which is at least 100 years old and, although replaced for everyday purposes, is still used from time to time. Similarly, his cheese moulds are waterpipes pierced by local schoolchildren.

When we came to the subject of flavour and pasteurization, he said that as far as he was concerned, the crucial factors were the original quality of the milk and maturity. At that time, he left ten per cent of his cheeses unpasteurized but pasteurized the rest: he was thus able to offer a comparative tasting which, although not decisive because the cheeses were of different ages, illustrated very clearly how the flavour develops. The immature cheeses were hard and sharp whether pasteurized or not, and although the oldest unpasteurized example was soft and subtle, it was not so deep-tasting and interesting as a pasteurized one three weeks older; not surprisingly, he now pasteurizes them all. He emphasized that if the cheeses had been made in the winter, even maturity could not compensate for the inferiority of milk.

CASHEL BLUE

Bronze Medal, British Cheese Awards 1996
A blue cows' cheese; full-fat, pasteurized milk; vegetarian and traditional rennet.
175g/6oz, 350g/12oz, and 1.5kg/3lb 5oz rounds

The cheese becomes increasingly soft and creamy as it matures; the taste is about as strong as Colston Basset Stilton (page 188) but softer and sweeter, with overtones of sun, rain, and flowers similar to the flavours in Cooleeney (page 122). As well as being outstanding for the table, it is one of the very best blue cheeses made anywhere for cooking, since it melts smoothly and easily and retains its depth of flavour.

The cheese is made three or four times a week by a staff of six; the milk comes from a pedigree herd of 110 Friesians. It is pasteurized, cooled, and starter and *Penicillium roqueforti* for the blue added and cultured at 30–32°C/86–90°F; renneting follows, after which it is left to set for an hour. The curd is then cut and left for another hour before being removed from the vat in scrim (raw Irish linen) cloths, drained, and tipped straight into the moulds. For the next two to three days, it is left to drain, with turning at intervals, until it is sufficiently dry for salting and piercing: the pierced cheeses, before the mould has grown, look like enormous, very thick Bath Oliver biscuits. To develop the blue, they are kept at 10°C/50°F for two weeks, after which the external mould is washed off and the cheeses dried and wrapped to inhibit the growth of further mould. Maturing is carried out at 4°C/39°F: some are sold young, but to reach their full potential, the cheeses need to be kept for four or five months.

 ## Cashel Blue and Fish Salad

This is the same as Cooleeney and Fish Salad but as the cheese is stronger, you need less; also, it suits cod better than salmon. Follow the recipe on page 123, cooking the cod as for salmon and using 40g/1½ oz Cashel Blue and 3 tablespoonsful of cream: since these quantities are too small to process, beat the cheese into the cream by hand.

The cream, cheese, and dill mixture is also excellent spread over turbot steaks: bake them at 180°C/350°F/Gas 4 for 5–25 minutes according to thickness, until the cheese mixture is brown and the fish is opaque all the way through.

Inagh Farmhouse Cheeses

MEG AND DERRICK GORDON, INAGH, COUNTY CLARE.
TEL: 00353 653 6633

It may have been at this point that straight roads gave way to bends: at any rate, we seriously underestimated the time it would take to reach Inagh and were dramatically late. We started to apologize but Meg cut us short. 'You haven't been in Ireland long, have you? It isn't like England. With us, it is bad manners *not* to be late. Relax!'

Here, only about 16km/10 miles from the west coast, the soil is peat or sandy and the Irish green interrupted by dark shrubs and pine trees; the other trees are tall but bent inland by the Atlantic wind. The farm, however, is protected by a slight hill; at the moment it is only organic but Meg and Derrick are aiming to become biodynamic (as yet, they do not grow all their own feed). Their animals consist of two Connemara ponies, sixty-eight white Saanen goats plus two Toggenburgs, three dogs, seven cats, and an unknown number of hens. The hens include chocolate-coloured speckled Marans, whose eggs are deep brown, and white Arkenet with large black spots, like Dalmatians, one of whom lays turquoise eggs. All the goats have names and, despite not knowing how many hens there are, Meg's feeling for them extends to giving them rum punch to drink when they are dying (of old age: none of them are killed for eating) so that after a happy life, they have a happy ending. The ponies are a reminder of the past: Derrick's grandfather bred racehorses, and after a spell of growing tea in India, Derrick returned to keep up the family tradition. When racing became big business, however, he had to give up because he could no longer afford the inflated stud fees. Livestock farming was the obvious alternative: they chose goats because Meg was already familiar with them and Derrick did not want to handle cows.

Her dairy is tiny, considerably smaller than the kitchen, and she works alone, chiefly because of hygiene. She has once or twice employed assistants, but said: 'I know exactly what I'm doing. People helping don't tuck their hair into their caps properly or realize how really *very* often they ought to wash their hands.' Before coming to Ireland, I had tried only one of her cheeses, a log called St Tola, but she also makes a hard cheese, Lough Caum, and little fresh buttons rolled in flavourings. We tasted them with coffee and soda-bread, watched by the goats, who were consuming twigs, dock leaves, and nettles in a field outside the window. Meg said that they eat everything except grass; she never mentioned consistency of flavour.

LOUGH CAUM

A hard goats' cheese; full-fat, unpasteurized milk; vegetarian rennet.
1.8kg/4lb rounds

Lough Caum has an exceptionally fine, smooth texture; the taste is sweet and nutty, with a gentle tang suggestive of the sea and undertones of peat. It is delicious toasted: serve it with peppery or bitter leaves.

CROTTIN

Fresh goats' cheeses, plain or flavoured; full-fat, unpasteurized milk; vegetarian
rennet. 85–100g/3–3^1/$_2$oz buttons; seasonal: April–December

The texture is silken smooth and surprisingly compact, much more like matured cheeses than fresh; the taste is of the varied flavours of rich, sweet, organic milk, with the same suggestions of peat and the sea as Lough Caum.

ST TOLA

A soft goats' log; full-fat, unpasteurized milk; vegetarian rennet. 1kg/2lb 4oz;
seasonal: April–December

St Tola is remarkable for its light, smooth, fine-grained texture: you would hardly recognize it as goat. The taste is creamy and sweet but with any number of sub-flavours, including peat and the sea. It becomes even sweeter when grilled: Meg and Derrick serve it with redcurrant jelly, honey, or pesto.

St Tola and Avocado Salad

For 2

2 tbsp oil
^{1}/$_2$ tbsp red wine vinegar
salt and pepper
1 ripe avocado
1 rosy grapefruit, skin and all pith removed
about 85g/3oz St Tola

Beat the oil and vinegar with a little salt and a moderate grinding of pepper. Halve and slice the fruit: arrange it along each side of the serving plates and pour the dressing over the avocado. Place the cheese in the middle.

Ardrahan Cheese

EUGENE AND MARY BURNS, ARDRAHAN HOUSE, KANTURK, COUNTY CORK. TEL: 00353 29 78099

I was particularly curious about Ardrahan because, even allowing for the fact that the rind is washed, it is one of the two or three most unusual and distinctive-tasting cheeses produced in Britain or Ireland. Although we had never met them, Eugene and Mary invited us (complete with dog) to stay the night. Our visit, delightful and memorable as it was, bore out the theory that cheeses imbibe something of the character of their makers; however, it revealed very little about how Ardrahan acquires its flavour, which one can only conclude is a product of the place, perhaps communicated via the water: a possible clue lies in the name 'Ardrahan', which means 'height of the ferns'. The country around is lush, with large trees and rich grazing; the house is Georgian, looking over a wide valley, and the farmyard large and immaculate, decorated with pots of red geraniums.

The dairy has a glass screen so that visitors can watch the cheese being made without entering; also, like Louis Grubb (page 124), Eugene has racks which turn the cheeses automatically and uses lengths of pierced piping as moulds, although only for the smaller cheeses. All the milk comes from his own herd, which was lovingly built up by his father from choice imported UK stock and is the oldest registered pedigree herd of Friesians in Ireland.

ARDRAHAN

Bronze Medal, British Cheese Awards 1997
A semi-soft washed-rind cows' cheese; full-fat, pasteurized milk; vegetarian rennet.
300g/10¹/₂oz and 1.5kg/3lb 5oz rounds

The cheese when ripe is creamy all the way through, with a few small holes; it should be soft enough to spread slightly over the knife when cut. The taste, as best I can describe it, is a heady mixture of sea, rain, mushrooms, flowers, oranges, and red wine: the overall effect is powerful but warm and persuasive rather than challenging. Although not an obvious candidate for cooking, it is in fact excellent, retaining its strength and individuality almost unchanged.

The cheesemaking involves both washing the curd, as for Gouda and the soft cheeses made further south, and brine-washing the rind, which has something to do with the flavour but does not in itself account for it. Rennet

(Above) Anglo-Nubian kids. Anglo-Nubians, from Africa, produce the richest goats' milk.

(Right) A Toggenburg goat. Toggenburgs originally came from the Alps.

Friesians grazing in parkland on Manor Farm, where Montgomery's Cheddar (page 88) is made.

Leon Downey adding rennet to the milk for Llangloffan (page 152). It will take about thirty minutes for the curd to set.

Testing the curd for Llangloffan to see if it breaks cleanly, which means that it is ready to cut. The next stage is stirring and heating.

Stirring the curd in the oblong vat at Keen's (page 91); while being stirred, it is heated to 40°C/104°F.

Andy Wigmore testing the curd for Waterloo (page 29). The cheese was originally made with milk from the Duke of Wellington's estate.

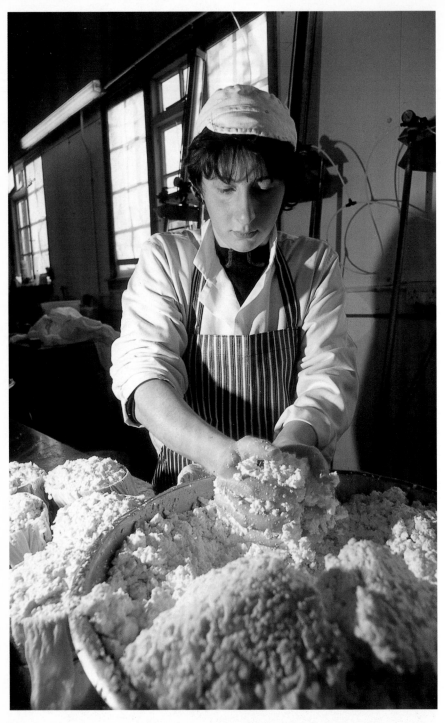

The curd for Cornish Yarg (page 113) being transferred to moulds after milling. Once moulded, the cheeses will be pressed and then brined.

Anne and Andy Wigmore's Spenwood in the cheese press.

Cornish Yarg remains in a brine-bath for twenty-four hours before being coated with nettle leaves.

Frozen nettle leaves for coating Cornish Yarg. The effect when finished is very artistic; whether it affects taste is more questionable.

Coolea (page 143), Tyning (page 74), and Spenwood (page 30). Coolea is a Gouda-style cheese; Tyning and Spenwood are hard sheep's cheeses.

*Blue Vinny (page 86), one of the very few traditional
low-fat cheeses to have survived.*

*Ardrahan (page 128), a washed-rind cheese made by
Eugene and Mary Burns in County Cork.*

Robin Congdon with his signature cheese, Ticklemore (page 106). As well as this hard goats' cheese, he makes a soft goats' cheese and three blue cheeses.

is added about fifty minutes after the starter and the milk left for another forty-five to fifty minutes to set; the curd is then cut by hand into 2.5-cm/ 1-inch squares, washed, i.e. some of the whey skimmed off and replaced with water, and scalded to blood-heat (37°C/98.6°F). This is followed by moulding and turning at half-hourly intervals for several hours; after unmoulding, the smaller cheeses, which emerge from the lengths of piping in continuous logs, are cut into rounds (the larger ones are made in ordinary moulds). The last stage is brining in sea-salt and washing twice over the next three days. When first made, the new cheeses look like white iced birthday cakes: as they grow older, the rind becomes crinkled and takes on an orange tinge, caused by *B. linens* mould, which proliferates in south-western Ireland. Other cheesemakers encourage it by spraying: Eugene sprayed his cheeses once, but having introduced it into his storeroom has never needed to add it again.

Ardrahan Potato Casserole

This is Mary's own favourite recipe for Ardrahan. It is extremely simple: she describes it as 'just an everyday, family sort of dish' – which it can hardly be for anyone else, since the rest of us do not have her access to the cheese; however, I promise that the result is fully worthy even of the quite large amount of cheese is needed. The quantity is flexible: you can use less if you wish.

Cooking time: 1 hour
For 4

300g/10^1/$_2$oz Ardrahan
625g/1lb 6oz waxy potatoes, peeled or scrubbed
a little butter for greasing the dish
pepper

Wipe but do not remove the cheese rind and slice the cheese and potatoes. Butter a soufflé or similar ovenware dish and arrange the cheese and potatoes in it in alternate layers, starting with potato and finishing with a thick layer of cheese; season each layer of potatoes very lightly with pepper. Bake at 110°C/225°F/Gas ^{1}/$_2$ for about an hour.

Milleens

NORMAN AND VERONICA STEELE, EYERIES, BEARA, COUNTY
CORK. TEL: 00353 27 74079

Although we had been told that the country is 'very pretty', I was
utterly unprepared for the drive over the West Cork mountains and up the
Beara peninsula to Eyeries. The mountains do not have the grandeur of
the Highlands nor the forbidding quality of the moors and crags of North
Wales, but are bright with grass, gorse, and rocks so pale that they catch the
sun: little rocky outcrops and boulders scattered all over the slopes shine like
white marbles. The first sign of water is the lake at Muckross: once you have
ascended the hills beyond, it is never absent from view. The coastline round
Beara is so jagged and intricate that land and sea seem inseparably entwined:
inlets too land-locked to be penetrated by the tide look like ponds or lakes,
with trees, bushes, and flowers growing right down to the water's edge. Here
and there, white-washed farmhouses gleam among the boulders on the
slopes; in the villages, the houses are painted pastel blue, turquoise, green,
yellow, and pink. The area is completely unspoilt: we passed not a single teashop, take-away, hotel, or caravan site on the entire route. Despite Veronica's
protest at the arrival of supermarkets, little can have changed since Norman
first brought her here nearly thirty years ago.

The story of the transformation of the local shop and the origin of
Milleens, to which in effect it gave rise, is told by Veronica herself:

> There was nothing to eat ... I mean nothing interesting. The old
> shop in Castletownbere with its saucepans and shovels and
> Goulding's Manures clock wagging away the time, and smoked
> hams hanging from hooks in the ceiling, and great truckles of
> Cheddar on the wooden counter with their mouldy bandages and
> crumbs of cheese strewn around, scrumptious, tempting, melt-in-
> the-mouth crumbs which you could nibble as you queued to be
> served, with your message list. And then she would cut a fine big
> chunk, golden or white, and what I miss most is the way it crumbled.
>
> So they closed it, gutted it, extended it, and re-opened it. Enter
> the trolley. Spotless. Sterile. Pre-packed portions perspiring in plas-
> tic. Tidy piles. Electronic scales. Keep moving. Don't block the
> aisles. No idle chatter. Big Brother is watching you. Don't ask for
> credit. Oh boy.

And then one day we bought a farm and a cow. Her name was Brisket and she had only one horn. She lost the other one gadding down a hill, tail-waving, full of the joys of spring. Her brakes must have failed. We had to put Stockholm tar on the hole right through the hot summer. And all the milk she had. At least three gallons a day. Wonder of wonders and what to do with it all. For two years I made Cheddars. They were never as good as the ones in Castletownbere had been but they were better than the sweaty vac-packed bits. Very little control at first but each failed batch spurred me on ... I was hooked.

One day Norman said, 'Why don't you try making a soft cheese for a change?' So I did.

Now while all this was going on we had a mighty vegetable garden full of fresh spinach and courgettes and French beans and little peas and all sorts of things you couldn't buy in a shop for love or money. And we would sell the superfluity to a friend who was a chef in a restaurant and took great pains with her ingredients. Annie would badger fishermen for the pick of their catch and come here on a Monday morning to root through our treasurehouse of a garden for the freshest and best. Now I was no mean cook myself and would have ready each Monday for her batches of yoghurt, quiches, game pies (made with hare and cream – beautiful), pork pies, skate pies, all adorned with pastry leaves and rosettes and as light and delicious as you can imagine, and my speciality, gâteau St Honoré – profiteroles oozing with cream and chocolate and freshly roasted almonds.

So there was the soft cheese beginning to run. We wrapped up the last of it and away it went with the vegetables and the pies and all the other good things to Sneem and the Blue Bull restaurant where it made its debut. As luck would have it Declan Ryan of the Arbutus Lodge Hotel in Cork was having dinner there that very night. Attracted no doubt by Annie's growing reputation, Declan had ventured forth to sample the delights of Sneem, and the greatest delight of them all was our humble cheese. The first, the one and only, Irish Farmhouse Cheese. At last, the real thing after so long.

Since then, vast quantities of learning have been ingested and applied, from the many journals of dairy science through *Scientific American* and even pamphlets from New Zealand on bacteriophage.

All grist to the mill. The making of Milleens is not a slap-happy matter but a carefully controlled scientific process. Thermometers have replaced elbows. Note is taken of pH and acidity. Milk quality is carefully monitored. Starters are recognized as a most important influence on flavour and quality and are as well looked after as the crown jewels, and to better effect.

Having established Milleens, Veronica became aware not only of the commercial potential of cheese in Ireland but also the advantage of conditions in Cork, where the growth of moulds is fostered by humidity of 100 per cent; she remarked that moulds rather than bacteria were the determinant factor for cheeses made in this part of the world. Partly by dint of a personality which Giana Ferguson (page 139) describes as 'visionary', she encouraged others to make cheese, notably Giana and Jeffa Gill (page 134), and consolidated their position by founding the Irish Cheesemakers' Association. The Steeles themselves have progressed from their first one-horned cow to a herd of twenty-four which includes 'mad, bad' black Kerry cattle, whose milk, according to Veronica, has fat globules almost as small as goats': with two assistants and additional milk from neighbouring farms, she now makes 72kg/158lb of cheese a day. Norman, who used to be a lecturer in philosophy, has given up his job to manage the farm; they no longer keep pigs, to their great regret, but still have hens and a large flock of ducks.

MILLEENS

Gold Medal and Supreme Champion, British Cheese Awards 1997
A semi-soft washed-rind cows' cheese; full-fat, unpasteurized milk; vegetarian rennet.
225g/8oz and 1.4kg/3lb rounds

The texture is rich and creamy, not as runny as Camembert but soft enough to flow over the knife when cut. It tastes of mushrooms, sun, the flowers which grow here in astonishing profusion, and the freshness of the sea: in themselves, the flavours are mild, but the combination is surprisingly powerful. Veronica's word to describe it is 'bold'; mine, as noted in my tasting book, is 'sexy'. The rind is a deep marigold yellow, caused by the growth of *B. linens* mould.

Veronica Steele's Puff-Balls

Entirely by chance, I met Veronica's daughter Jenny soon after returning to London: she says that of all the dishes her mother cooked when she was a child, this is the one she remembers most vividly. In fact, it is simply tiny choux buns fried very crisp and stuffed with Milleens while still hot. It is essential to eat them as soon as they are ready, before the cheese has had time to liquefy. They literally melt in the mouth. The dough, which should be chilled before frying, can be made the previous day.

Makes 24–30

85g/3oz butter, chopped small
salt
125g/4$^1\!/_2$oz plain white flour
3 large free-range eggs, broken and beaten in separate cups
about 225ml/8fl oz sunflower oil for deep-frying
a deep-fat thermometer *or* a few squares of bread to test the oil
about 100g/3$^1\!/_2$oz Milleens straight out of the refrigerator, cut into
1.25-cm/$^1\!/_2$-inch squares just before use

Put the butter, 225ml/8fl oz water and a moderate pinch of salt into a small saucepan. Set it over low heat until the butter has melted; then raise the heat and bring it to a brisk boil. Remove the pan from the heat, tip in all the flour at once, and beat until the mixture is smooth and comes away from the sides of the pan. Return the pan to very low heat and continue beating for 1–2 minutes, until the dough is stiff and cohesive and no tiny pockets of unmixed flour remain. Leave it to cool for a moment or two. Add the first egg and beat until it is completely amalgamated; the mixture will again become stiff. Repeat with the second and third eggs; after the third, the dough will be as soft as paste. Chill until needed.

Line a plate with absorbent paper to drain surplus fat from the puff-balls after they have been fried. Heat the oil to 175°C/350°F or until squares of bread brown in 40 seconds. Adjust the heat to maintain the temperature and slide heaped teaspoonsful of the dough into the oil: take care to avoid splashing and do not add more at a time than will fit into the pan without touching. Fry to a deep golden brown (if fried only to pale brown, the centres of the balls will be spongy instead of hollow). Roll the puff-balls on the absorbent paper, make a slit in the side of each and stuff with the cheese. Serve directly, while you fry the next batch.

Durrus

JEFFA GILL, COOMKEEN, DURRUS, COUNTY CORK.
TEL: 00353 27 61100

On the way to Durrus from Goleen, the roadside verges were covered with violets, lady's-smock, stitchwort, clover, dandelions, buttercups, large, yellow-centred daisies, and wild garlic; on marshy land were yellow flags, on patches of moorland, gorse. Jeffa's farm is in the armpit of the Sheep's Head and Mizen peninsulas, up a long moorland track which makes it seem very remote; the house when you arrive, however, is immaculate and welcoming – though we were not welcomed by Jeffa's Connemara pony, who had given birth that morning and was guarding her foal against all comers.

When Jeffa bought the farm, twenty-four years ago, she hoped to run it organically and sell a mixed range of produce, but was forced to revise her ideas by lack of demand: inspired by Veronica Steele (page 132), she experimented with cheese, starting, like almost everyone else, in the kitchen. With the support of local shops and restaurants, the business gained momentum slowly but steadily. Unable to manage both cows and the cheese, she sold the cows and now buys milk from a nearby farm: although not organic, the wide variety of flora means it is probably the equivalent in terms of taste.

DURRUS

> *Bronze Medal, British Cheese Awards 1995 and 1997*
> *A semi-soft cows' cheese; low-fat, unpasteurized milk (morning only); vegetarian rennet. 375g/13oz or 1.5kg/3lb 5oz rounds*

The cheese varies considerably according to age and season. At a few weeks old, it bends slightly over the knife when cut; at three months, it flows slightly. The taste is mellow and fruity, with a distinct hint of russet apples in the autumn; when young, the cheese is mild, but the more mature version can be quite strong.

Like Bill Hogan's (opposite), Jeffa's method is based on Swiss principles: like him, she uses a copper rather than stainless-steel vat and a 'harp' with vertical blades to cut the curd. As with Ardrahan (page 128), the curd is washed; when made, the cheeses are sprayed with a preparation which encourages *B. linens* mould. The maturing time on the farm for three to five weeks but they remain in good condition for up to five months.

West Cork Natural Cheese

BILL HOGAN AND SEAN FERRY, ARDMANAGH, SCHULL, COUNTY
CORK. TEL: 00353 28 28593

In his own way, Bill is as visionary a personality as Veronica Steele (page 132); he is also a practised and adroit interviewee and I swiftly abandoned any thought of asking why he became a cheesemaker, although he gave full details of how. He was trained in Costa Rica by the late Josef Dubach, a well-known Swiss cheesemaker who, under the auspices of the Swiss Development Corporation, made it his mission to teach sound, hygienic principles of cheesemaking in developing countries where it could substantially raise standards of living (as the production of Gruyère, Emmental, and other cheeses had in the Swiss valleys). Subsequently, Bill translated Dubach's book, *Traditional Cheesemaking*, and instead of payment spent a summer at Dubach's farm in Switzerland. He set up his dairy in West Cork partly because, with its cheeses, fish, and several good restaurants, it is the accepted gourmet centre of Ireland, but also because of its varied herbage and exceptional grazing. There was never any question of producing his own milk since, according to Dubach, the milk for first-class cheese should be taken only in high summer, when the grass is at its best and the stage of lactation most favourable. Thus Bill makes all his cheese in four months of the year, which means that in order to be economic he needs creamery-sized quantities over this period. He buys from seven farms in the area: as with Durrus, the milk is not organic but the quality of the grazing means that it tastes as if it were.

His house and dairy are just across the bay from Schull: at the time we went, the house was being converted and little more than a shell, as was his dairy for making butter, but the cheese dairy and maturing room were unaffected and more than enough to absorb on one visit. Before looking over them, however, we went for a walk round his reed bed, or, in less polite language, organic cesspool. It was laid out more than three years ago and treats both the household waste and the whey. It is striking not only for its magnificent bulrushes but also the slightly unnerving size and succulence of all the other plants growing around: were it not for this, it would look like an ordinary, if somewhat overgrown ornamental pond.

We then went into the cheese dairy, or rather, as I wrote in my notes by mistake, studio, which is really what it is. In the centre is a huge, round, gleaming copper vat – copper because, according to Bill, the very slight reaction of the copper with the acid of the curd gives the cheese a deeper, livelier taste than stainless steel, which he says has a deadening effect. At the far end is an elegant Victorian boiler, dating from about 1880, which he uses for scalding the curd (all his cheeses are hard and scalded to a high temperature). As the entire cheesemaking process except separating some of the milk is carried out by hand, a Swiss harp for cutting the curd and a forty-year-old Swiss separator are the only other items in the room. Both are worthy of being there solely for their aesthetic value, but they are not its most remarkable feature, since, unlike any other dairy I have seen, it is painted from floor to ceiling in bright turquoise. This is not (or not only) for decorative reasons but because the colour repels flies.

The maturing room is in a large, outwardly shabby barn with one small window half blacked out by gauze. Inside, having shut the door immediately lest a baby, new season's fly might slip past us, we could see nothing: the smell of cheese and the almost disinfectant fragrance of wood were sufficiently powerful to convince me for ever after that wood must surely contribute to taste, but still not enough to prepare us for the display of cheeses revealed when Bill switched on a single, dim light. From end to end of the barn, great, dark sculptural wheels of cheese, some as large as 31kg/68lb, and one or two (Mizen) of 45kg/100lb or more, were laid out at an angle on tilted wooden racks. Instead of labels, each was embossed with its name on top in black. As they are all matured from one summer to the next, the whole of the last season's production was on view – worth perhaps £35,000. Any cheese bought will therefore be almost a year old; some are matured for two.

GABRIEL

Bronze Medal, British Cheese Awards 1996
A hard cows' cheese; 85% fat, unpasteurized milk; traditional rennet (at time of writing). 6.8kg/15lb and 27kg/60lb wheels

In texture, this is hard and grainy, rather like Parmesan; the taste is deep and powerful, with the tang of the sea at one level, earthy undertones at another, and a warm peppery, almost spirituous aftertaste. Like other cheeses of this class it melts in strings; because of its dryness, it is better not heated alone, but is marvellous for fondue or sauces made with wine.

Bill cultures his own starters, skims fifteen per cent of the milk, and uses relatively little rennet to produce a soft curd from which a large proportion of the moisture can be expelled (for soft cheeses, a firm curd is needed). Also to expel moisture, the curd is cut progressively smaller the harder the cheese: for Gabriel, it is cut to the size of rice grains, i.e. slightly smaller than for Cheddar, and for Mizen, the hardest (which he only makes occasionally), 'as fine as dust'. The curd is then stirred for a considerable time and scalded, respectively, to 46°C/115°F, 53°C/127°F, and 57°C/135°F. By the time the cheeses are matured, their yield per gallon of milk is less than nine per cent and weight for weight they contain three times as much protein as steak.

DESMOND

A hard cows' cheese; 85% fat, unpasteurized milk; traditional rennet (at time of writing). 6.8kg/15lb and 27kg/60lb wheels

This is the least hard of Bill's three cheeses: though dry and grained, the texture is slightly fudgy. All three taste of the elements, i.e. sun, rain, earth, and the sea, as much as herbage. Although like the classic definition of a good soup, the flavours are mingled and balanced, Desmond is more on the side of grass and herbs than the others. When heated, the taste intensifies: it is delicious toasted, excellent for fondue, and also very good for sprinkling, although it is not as salty as pecorino and Parmesan.

At a tasting in London, Bill (who was once a chef) made a fondue which was universally acclaimed: this is the recipe as he later sent it to me.

 A Theory of Cheese Fondue

A true cheese fondue must be made with thermophilic cheese. Gruyère, Emmental, Appenzell, Gabriel and Desmond are all suitable. A fondue may be cooked with a single kind or any combination of these, depending on the flavour and effect that is desired. The word fondue simply means sauce.

Many white wines blend perfectly with thermophilic cheeses. I suggest light, crisp wines like Swiss Fendant or Alsatian and Luxembourgeoise Riesling or Pinot Blanc, the latter two embellishing the taste with special tone and glow. Personally, I avoid sharp or steely wines because they can overpower the dish.

Formula

Cut at least 2kg/4lb 6oz of thermophilic cheese into half thumb-sized chunks, removing the hard outer rind. Heat a cup and a half of white wine [350ml/12fl oz] nearly to the boil, preferably in a ceramic pot which may be pre-scented and rubbed with a dot of garlic. Add half the cheese and stir slowly at first with a flat wooden spoon.

Keep the heat fairly high for eight to ten minutes, until the cheese suddenly begins to melt. As the cheese dissolves, stir very briskly and lower the heat. Later, more wine may be added if the fondue becomes too thick. Or more cheese added if it gets too thin. The flame should be adjusted accordingly. A second batch may be prepared forthwith, if the pot is not scorched.

A small quantity of soft cheese may be added near the finish to achieve an extra layer of aroma. I often create a party fondue using Milleens, Gubbeen and Durrus as special taste ticklers. Try adding a few cubes of your favourite soft cheese. At this point a few drops of Kirsch or other spirit may be thrown in the pot, just as the fondue is being served...

The Meal

Traditionally fondue is eaten with small lumps of bread skewered on long forks or sticks. Each guest or family member gets an individual fork which is tipped with bread then dipped into the pot, twirled to gather the sauce, then eaten as quickly as possible to avoid drips.

Cheese fondue is perhaps the only European dish still eaten out of a communal pot. For this reason and the wonderful wine fumes which rise from it, fondue parties can be amiable and intimate occasions.

Instead of bread, I sometimes serve fondue over lightly sautéed or steamed vegetables like leeks, cauliflower, or tomatoes. An exciting modern choice is to offer raw or lightly cooked asparagus and broccoli spears for dipping in the hot fondue. Usually, I accompany a cheese fondue with a tart green salad and give simple ice-cream or sorbet with fruit for dessert.

To drink with the meal, I enjoy Pinot Gris for perfect resolution and clarity. But this is a matter of mood and fancy. Experiment yourself with fine white wines and thermophilic cheeses. Devise your own stratagems...

Gubbeen

Tom and Giana Ferguson, Gubbeen House, Schull, County
Cork. Tel: 00353 28 28231

Gubbeen House is on a blunt peninsula just to the west of Schull, surrounded by trees so that one's chief impression is of luxuriant foliage rather
than proximity to the sea. The Fergusons have farmed here for five generations but Giana, who is partly Hungarian, was brought up on a Spanish
mountain-top where her father, a writer and believer in what she terms
'Kitchen-culture', encouraged the family to gather in the kitchen every
evening to drink wine, watch their gypsy cook preparing their meal, eat, and
talk. Since they kept goats, the cook would make curd cheese; Giana was also
able to watch cheese being made at her uncle's house in the south of France,
near Nice. After she married Tom and had constant access to milk, making
cheese thus seemed obvious and natural; she did not start seriously, however, until Veronica Steele (page 132) had convinced her of its possibilities
and she had taken a course in hygiene and microbiology at University
College, Cork. Now, having made cheese for eighteen years, she says that she
finds it 'obsessional' but as creatively satisfying and personal as writing or
painting. However, she considers eighteen years not nearly long enough: a
lifetime, she declares, might be too short to come to know and develop
a cheese to its full potential. It took her five or six years simply to become
used to the characteristics and seasonal variations of her milk – and she now
wishes that she did not feel obliged to make cheese during the winter, when
the cows live on silage and the milk is correspondingly inferior. She also
sometimes regrets the need for consistent quality because of the barriers to
excellence that it imposes: as an example, she cited the fact that she uses a
commercial starter because a home-cultured one is less reliable, although in
certain conditions it gives much better results.

The milk for Gubbeen is from a mixed herd of Jersey, Friesian,
Simmenthal, and the local (but now very rare) black Kerry cattle. The two
most distinctive points about the cheesemaking are that the whey is diluted
to slow down bacterial activity (as opposed to washing the curd, which
implies draining off some of the whey) and that particular trouble is taken
over maturing or 'curing' the cheeses. It goes without saying that humidity
and temperature are carefully controlled, but the cheeses are also turned and
washed frequently to discourage the growth of all but *B. linens* mould, which
is promoted by daily applications of 'goo'. This system is time-consuming

and labour-intensive: partly because of it, Giana employs a staff of ten, which, given her output, nevertheless seems generous. When I commented on it, she smiled happily and said, in the melodious voice which is the first thing you notice about her, 'Well, yes, we *do* over-employ, but then, you see, the people round here need the work.'

GUBBEEN

Silver Medal, British Cheese Awards 1995 and 1997
A semi-soft washed-rind cows' cheese; full-fat, unpasteurized milk; vegetarian rennet.
1.4kg/3lb discs

The texture is slightly firmer and more elastic than that of the other semi-soft Cork cheeses, with small holes; the rind is temptingly crisp and crinkled, greyish but overlaid with a pink blush. In taste, the cheese is probably an accurate reflection of the West Cork flora, with flowery tones overlaid by grass and savoury herbs. Bill Hogan (page 135) once described Durrus as tasting like 'violins' – in which case Gubbeen resembles violas. A smoked version is also produced.

Orla

Iris Diebrok and Oliver Jungwirth, Manch Estate, Ballineen, County Cork. Tel: 00353 23 47507

Orla is a relative newcomer and one of only three sheep's cheeses currently made in Ireland. Oliver visited the farm on a 'placement' while he was studying agriculture in Germany and was told by the owners of the Manch Estate that he could rent it when he had finished his course so long as he farmed organically. He returned in 1991 and was joined by Iris and a cheesemaker, Janet, soon afterwards. They decided to raise sheep because they could neither afford nor had sufficient accommodation for cattle and at that time hoped to combine cheese with produce, which effectually eliminated goats, since they could be expected to eat anything that grew. Armed with Olivia Mills's book (page 32), they bought eleven Poll Dorset–Friesland crosses and a Friesland ram, from whom they have built up a herd of eighty-four. Even without goats, the produce has not fulfilled their original expectations, partly because the sheep and cheese have taken up most of their time, but also because the farm is low-lying and frost is possible for nine months of the year: Oliver therefore now grows only leeks, potatoes, and cabbages. As well as the sheep, they keep a few pigs to drink the whey and hens in the summer only (in winter, they need all their shelf-space for the cheese, and so sell the hens and buy more in the spring).

For their first couple of years, they could not make cheese because they had too few sheep, but in 1993 they started experimenting and the next year developed three prototypes: a fresh cheese, a Camembert-style cheese with a *B. linens* rind, and the future Orla. They dismissed the idea of the fresh cheese because of the problem of marketing and the Camembert-type because it was very strong and they felt would not appeal to the Irish public. However, they test-marketed Orla at agricultural shows and went into production the following year, by which time Janet had left because of health problems and Iris had taken over the cheesemaking. They anticipated that initially sales would be only local, but they won a gold medal at the first Cheese Awards, which led to the cheese being stocked at Neal's Yard Dairy and Barstow and Barr in London, and Iain Meliss in Edinburgh and Glasgow. Production last year was 1,515kg/1½ tons; this year it will be 2,020kg/2 tons and thereafter will increase with the rate of the milk supply.

ORLA

Gold Medal, British Cheese Awards 1995; Silver Medal, 1996; Bronze Medal, 1997
Washed-rind sheep's cheese; unpasteurized, organic milk; vegetarian rennet.
1.5–2kg/3lb 5oz–4lb 6oz rounds

When young, the cheese is mild and relatively soft, but the flavours become more intense and the cheese harder with age. It is sold at two to twelve months: a mature cheese has a slightly gritty texture and complex taste of earth, peat, and the sea, with a strong, spicy, slightly hot, almost fruity tang. At this age, it is quite powerful enough to use as a substitute for Parmesan, although the flavours are by no means the same.

Carraig

LIEKE AND AART VERSLOOT, BALLINGEARY, COUNTY CORK.
TEL: 00353 26 47126

The farm is up a narrow track off the road from Bantry to Macroom in the Shehy Mountains. After driving along the track round a frighteningly tight hairpin bend, you bear left up a hill until you come to a gate, with goats on the other side. Some of them look not exactly thin but unusually bony, with slightly bedraggled coats, as though they led a hard life: however, when I talked to Lieke, I found that the reason for their appearance was simply age. The Versloots' feeling for them overrides commercial considerations and instead of culling them when they are too old to milk, they keep them until they die naturally. In fact, they probably lead an ideal life, since the farm is in a sheltered situation and the hillsides are wooded, with a wide variety of tasty shoots and twigs.

CARRAIG

A Gouda-style goats' cheese; full fat, unpasteurized milk; traditional rennet (imported from Holland). 400g/14oz, 800g–1kg/1lb 12oz–2lb 4oz rounds

Carraig has a velvet-smooth texture with small holes; at six to eight weeks it is moist and elastic but becomes harder as it ages. The taste is a blend of sweet, flowery flavours, including gorse, with hints of herbs and nuts; the cheese has a gentle tang when young which becomes stronger with maturity. Virtually the only indication of goat is that the flavours are fuller and more intense than the usual Gouda-style cows' equivalent. To my mind, it is one of the most interesting hard goats' cheeses made. Unfortunately, it is only sold locally, notably in Bantry market on Fridays, but mail orders are welcomed (Lieke will send it anywhere: it has even been to Japan).

Lieke makes the cheese alone and entirely by hand to a recipe which she says is much the same as the Willems' (opposite) but adapted to goats' milk. As the goats' curd is more delicate than cows', she does not heat it to such a high temperature nor stir it for so long. After moulding and pressing, the cheeses are brined and matured for a minimum of six weeks, with daily turning for the first two or three; Lieke also brushes and washes them at intervals to prevent mould from developing on the surface. Although she herself prefers the cheese at six to eight weeks, it can be kept for up to a year.

Coolea Cheese

HELEN AND DICK WILLEMS, COOLEA, MACROOM, COUNTY
CORK. TEL: 00353 26 45204

From Schull to Coolea, in the hills west of Macroom, is a slow journey: there was hardly any traffic, but I shall never again comment on the straight roads of Ireland. Of all the farms that I have visited, including the Versloots' just across the hills, the Willems' seems the most isolated, although in fact it is only about 5km/3 miles from the main road to Killarney. It is in a spectacular situation facing a wide valley, with a skyline of hills. The Willems come from Linburg, in Holland, where Helen ran a pub and discotheque until she came to feel the need for silence and space. Her intention in coming to Ireland was to paint: for fifteen years, her time and attention were monopolized by the cheese, but her son Dick, after training in Belgium, has now effectually taken it over, leaving her with the leisure to pursue her ambition.

COOLEA

> *Gold Medal and Best Modern British Cheese, British Cheese Awards 1997*
> *A Gouda-type cows' cheese; full-fat, unpasteurized milk; traditional rennet.*
> *1kg/2lb 4oz, 2kg/4lb 6oz, 4kg/8lb 13oz, and 10kg/22lb rounds*

Louis Grubb of Cashel Blue (page 124) remarked that the reason for the popularity of Gouda-type cheeses in Ireland is that they are sweet and fairly mild, so that one can eat them continuously without getting tired of them: this certainly applies to six-month-old Coolea, which tastes subtly but positively of grass and flowers. When matured for longer, the flavour becomes deeper and richer, with a strong note of peat which gives it a sweet/salt tang that can compete with a blue or mature Cheddar on the cheeseboard.

The milk comes from a herd of twenty-three MRI cows. Starter is added half an hour before the rennet, which is calf, imported from Holland. When the curd has set, it is cut to the size of peas and washed twice to remove some of the lactose, which speeds up acidity and makes for a sweeter-tasting cheese; it is then scalded twice over about two hours, with continuous stirring (by machine). This is followed by moulding, pressing for six hours, and brining for up to four days. To keep the surface free of mould and promote ripening from the outside inwards, the cheeses are sprayed with a coating which dries into a hard skin. The maturing time is a minimum of six months, but for the large cheeses can be up to two years.

CHAPTER 4

Wales

Cwmtawe Cheese

GIOVANNI IRRANCA, CWM CYRNACH UCHAF FARM, GRAIG Y PAL, GLAIS, SWANSEA SA7 9PH. TEL: 01792 844637/01639 842703

The farm is hidden high up in the foothills of the Brecon Beacons above Glais, just north of Swansea. I had some trouble finding it: I went first by mistake to the Irrancas' house, which is distinctly Italianate, with a colonnaded terrace for sitting outside – realistically roofed over (that day, it was raining with that peculiarly wet, fine, misty rain which I always associate with Wales). A kindly van driver led the way to the turning for the farm at hair-raising speed: the next stage was an equally hair-raising ascent up a narrow valley on a small, unfenced road which winds its way along the edge of an almost vertical drop into the river which is presumably at the bottom. The hillsides are thickly wooded with twisted, wind-blown oaks which at that time of year (April) looked skeletal and sinister; the ground is a continuous carpet of bilberry plants. The final stretch, near the top, is a mud-and-stone track which caused me to grit my teeth and try not to think about tyres, suspension, or sticking in the mire.

Giovanni did not start making cheese until he retired, eight years ago; before that, he ran a delicatessen and Italian restaurant. As the position of the farm might suggest, he raises sheep only; altogether, he has 600, but 450 of them are for lamb and live out, protected by fleeces which before shearing almost sweep the ground. For the cheese, he keeps 150 Frieslands, who have spacious sheds into which they can retreat at will and, except when the grass is richest, in May, June, and July, are fed concentrates in the form of barley and soya meal. The grazing is effectually organic, since Giovanni uses nothing on the land except lime to counteract acidity; the concentrates, however, are not (he observed that it would be extremely difficult to find organic barley). He does not stagger lambing and so makes no cheese in the winter; when the milk yield is at its peak, i.e. from May to July, he usually makes it every day, and in early spring and autumn every other day.

CWMTAWE

*A pecorino-style sheep's cheese; full-fat, unpasteurized milk; vegetarian rennet.
1kg/2lb 4oz and 2kg/4lb 6oz rounds*

The texture of the eight-month-old cheese is still fairly moist, with small holes; the taste has a smoky, moorland tang but is also surprisingly delicate and sweet. It is not as salty as a piece of pecorino Romano, with which I compared it, but is still strong enough for grating when a very powerful flavour is not needed. A large piece wrapped in cheese-paper and kept for a further eight weeks in a cold room became sufficiently strong and dry to be used for sprinkling.

Both Giovanni's cheeses, Cwmtawe, which is hard, and its accompanying ricotta (produced from the whey) are made to exactly the same recipe as was once used by his grandfather in Sardinia. After starter and rennet have been added, the curd is drained and the whey set aside for the ricotta; the curd is then cut and instead of being milled, is spun by two blades, one sharp and one blunt. This is followed by moulding, pressing lightly for twenty-four hours, and brining (in sea-salt). The whey, meanwhile, is heated in a kind of bain-marie to 75°C/167°F (above pasteurization point), until the solids rise to the surface. They are then scooped out, left to drain naturally for twenty-four hours, and packed into tubs; the ricotta should be used within a week. The Cwmtawes are matured for between eight months and three years, which Giovanni says is the proper age if they are to be used for sprinkling. He also remarked, not very usefully for those of us who live outside the area, that the cheese is excellent for ravioli and other pasta fillings when aged two or three days (as is the ricotta, which is also only available locally). As maturing proceeds, the Cwmtawes become covered with a dark mould, sometimes with a bright orange one underneath; these are scraped off and the cheeses washed before sale.

 ## Sage and Mushroom Risotto with Cwmtawe

If the chicken stock is homemade, reserve the chicken fat and use it for the risotto instead of oil. The more mature the cheese, the less you will need.

Cooking time: 55 minutes
For 3–4 as a main course or 4–6 as a first course

15g/¹/₂oz dried porcini, soaked for 20–25 minutes in hot (not boiling) water
about 850ml/1¹/₂ pints fresh vegetable (page 22) or chicken (page 21) stock
2 tbsp chicken fat or oil

4 cloves garlic, peeled and finely chopped
250g/9oz button mushrooms, stalks trimmed, caps washed, diced, and sliced
salt and pepper
4–6 sage leaves, washed and chopped
150ml/$^1/_4$ pint dry white wine
300g/10$^1/_2$oz arborio rice
about 25g/1oz butter
55–100g/2–3$^1/_2$oz Cwmtawe, preferably 10 months old or more, finely grated

Drain and roughly dice the porcini, keeping the liquor; add the liquor to the stock and set the stock to heat slowly: it should be simmering very gently by the time the rice is added to the mushrooms. Adjust the heat so that it continues to simmer very gently while the rice cooks.

Warm the fat or oil over moderate heat in a large wok or frying pan and fry the garlic until it starts to change colour; add the button mushrooms and porcini, season with 1 teaspoonful of salt and a generous grinding of pepper and continue to fry, turning frequently, until they have exuded and reabsorbed their juice. Add the sage and turn; pour in the wine and allow it to cook away. Add the rice and turn for 1–2 minutes, until every grain is coated with oil. Pour in about a third of the simmering stock, stir, and reduce the heat to low so that the rice is just simmering. Allow it to cook until the stock has been absorbed; then add about another 100ml/3$^1/_2$fl oz, stir, and repeat until the rice is just tender but still firm and nutty in the middle. Add another couple of tablespoonsful of stock and the butter, and remove from the heat. Gently stir in about half the cheese; serve the rest separately.

RICOTTA

A soft, sheep's whey cheese; pasteurized milk; vegetarian rennet. 500g/1lb 2oz and 1kg/2lb 4oz tubs

The cheese has the texture of thick cream and a fresh, sweet, and, despite heating to above pasteurization point, surprisingly lively taste, particularly if used while it is still very fresh. It is excellent not only for pasta and similar fillings but also for tarts, cheesecakes, and other sweet dishes. At present, Giovanni sells it only to restaurants and friends in the area, but he is prepared to distribute it more widely on request.

Orange and Ricotta Tart

When the orange segments are boiled for only one minute, they are tender-ized by the syrup but remain plump and juicy. It is desirable that the oranges should be organic because the peel is used for setting the glaze; however, to ensure that it sets firmly, I also advise using pectin sugar.

Cooking time: 35–40 minutes
For 8–10

short pastry made with 115g/4oz white and 55g/2oz wholemeal flour (page 20)
2 large or 3 small oranges, preferably organic
200g/7oz pectin sugar
250g/9oz Cwmtawe or other ricotta (e.g. Sussex High Weald: page 43)
100g/3$\frac{1}{2}$oz caster sugar
1 tbsp Grand Marnier
1 tbsp freshly squeezed lemon juice
1 tbsp double cream if the ricotta is stiff

Set the oven to 200°C/400°F/Gas 6. Line a 22-cm/8$\frac{1}{2}$-inch tart dish with the pastry and bake blind until well browned (page 20). Turn down the oven temperature to 150°C/300°F/Gas 2.

Wash or scrub and peel the oranges; roughly chop the peel and put it into a medium to small (but not very small) saucepan. Divide the fruit into segments, removing the pips and all traces of pith, and add the pith, pips, segments, pectin sugar, and 100ml/3$\frac{1}{2}$fl oz water to the pan. Set the pan over low heat until the sugar has melted and the water is clear; then bring it to a fast boil, boil for exactly 1 minute, and remove the pan from the heat.

Beat together the cheese, caster sugar, Grand Marnier, and lemon juice, and cream if needed; spread the mixture over the pastry base, and bake it for 10 minutes. Allow it to cool.

Lift the orange segments from the syrup with a perforated spoon, hold them over the pan until they have drained thoroughly, and arrange them over the cheese. Bring the syrup, with the peel and pips, to the boil and allow it to boil for 4–5 minutes, until the quantity is reduced to about 5 tablespoons-ful. Pour the syrup over the tart, through a coarse sieve to catch the pips and peel; take care to cover all the segments. Serve cold.

Penbryn

Ty Hen Farm, Penbryn, Sarnau, Dyfed SA44 6RD.
Tel: 01239 810347

Ty Hen is just behind Penbryn beach, a National Trust property and presumably for this reason totally unspoilt: a small road twists down one of the narrow wooded valleys which are typical of this part of Wales to a car-park and beach where there are no beach huts, no motor boats, and, even on a fine Saturday in August, very few people. The farm, perched on the hill above, is in rolling country similar to that around Glynhynod (page 154): one is also reminded of Glynhynod by the fact that Andrea is Dutch and makes Gouda-type cheese. Neither she nor her partner, Paul Knifton, come from cheesemaking backgrounds: Paul used to be an antiques dealer in London and Andrea was a nurse to psychiatric patients. However, she began to feel the need to exercise the body as well as the mind, and as she loves cheese took a cheesemaking course which led her to work for a time with psychiatric patients on a Steiner farm. Here, she was converted to Steiner philosophy and biodynamism: 'You give more and get more out of the land'. However, for the moment she and Paul are content to be merely organic. They keep twenty-five Friesians for the cheese, six pigs, and just five hens to supply eggs for their own use; in addition, sheep from a neighbouring farm crop the grass and contribute manure. The cheese is made four times a week in the summer and three times in winter, usually by Andrea but once a week by Paul, who has also equipped the dairy remarkably economically and efficiently with a pair of bulk milk-tanks costing about £100 each instead of a brine-bath and jacketed vat (which would cost about £3,000).

PENBRYN

A Gouda-type organic cows' cheese; full-fat, unpasteurized milk; vegetarian rennet. 1kg/2lb 4oz and 2.7kg/6lb rounds

At two months, it tastes very distinctly of butter, grass, a wide variety of herbs, and the sea; by eight or ten, it has developed a powerful, characteristic tang and, like Teifi, leaves a strong peppery, almost spicy aftertaste. It is excellent toasted and for cooking (one of Andrea's favourite ways of eating it is in a toasted sandwich buttered on the outside).

The recipe for the cheese is a modified rather than strictly traditional form of the Gouda method. A home-cultured starter is added at the same time as the rennet; when the curd has set, it is cut for ten minutes, left to rest for ten minutes, and washed and scalded once, to 37°C/98°F. This is followed by draining, moulding, and pressing for an hour, after which the edges of the cheeses are trimmed (although rounded when finished, they are pressed in truckle moulds). They are turned and pressed for a further two and a half hours, trimmed again, and brined; the maturing time is two to ten months.

Llanboidy Cheesemakers

SUE JONES, CILOWEN UCHAF, LOGIN, WHITLAND, DYFED SA34 0TJ. TEL: 01994 448303

Rather as Charles Martell has devoted his life to Gloucester cattle (page 63), Sue is the saviour of Red Polls, a cross between the rare-breed Norfolks and Suffolks and, like other older breeds and MRIs, dual purpose. She started out as a teacher rather than farmer but kept goats and made goats' cheese in her spare time; then one day her husband, a TV journalist, gave her four Red Polls as a result of working on a feature. This unusual present led to their moving to Cilowen, where they kept a few other cows besides the Red Polls and sold beef and the milk direct. A few years later they divorced, and she agreed to stay at the farm so that she could keep the cows. It was a brave decision, since it left her to run the farm without help between, as she put it, a bank manager and two children. Having already made cheese, she was aware of its worth as a value-added product but also of the fact that she could not both make it and manage the cows single-handedly: she therefore called on her sister, at that time a 'scientific cook', who duly became her cheesemaker – and is still with her. She now has thirty-three Red Polls in milk, plus four Friesians; a man is employed for the milking and a cheesemaker alternates with her sister. As well as sitting on several National Farmers' Union committees, she is President-elect of the Red Poll Association.

LLANBOIDY

Silver Medal, British Cheese Awards 1997
A hard cows' cheese; full-fat, unpasteurized milk; vegetarian rennet. 4.5kg/10lb wheels

Perhaps partly because of the homogeneous nature of the milk, the texture is exceptionally smooth, almost silky, in contrast to the more robust flavour.

The taste varies according to maturity and season but is herbal and buttery with an almost spicy tang which appears to be characteristic of the area, since it is similar to that of nearby Teifi and Penbryn. When young, the cheese is mild, but as it matures the tang becomes increasingly powerful.

The Red Poll milk is higher in protein and has smaller fat globules than Friesian, rather like Ayrshire, and is thus especially suitable for cheese. After starter and rennet have been added, the milk is top-stirred; when the curd has set, it is cut and blocked and piled, as for Cheddar. Draining, milling, and salting follow; it is then packed into muslin-lined moulds and pressed for thirty-six hours. The maturing time is from two to ten months.

 # *Llangloffan Farmhouse Cheese*

LEON DOWNEY, LLANGLOFFAN FARMHOUSE, CASTLE MORRIS, HAVERFORDWEST, PEMBROKESHIRE. TEL: 01348 891241

Leon Downey ties with Lyn Jenner (page 49) as the cheesemaker with the most unlikely background; also, in line with the TV chefs, he has turned cheese into theatre and his farm into the perfect set – though, as the results of the British Cheese Awards show, without sacrificing quality in the slightest degree: indeed, it would seem that the opposite is true. The farm, which is about 3km/2 miles from the sea, is spruce and welcoming but in no way prettified: the various alterations he has made, which include converting some of the buildings into a shop, teashop, and house for his daughter and son-in-law, who helps him with the cheese, are scarcely noticeable from the outside. The dairy is in a former barn and quite the most attractive I have seen, with a warm-coloured stone floor, smooth for easy cleaning rather than flagged, and the original rafters, which to conform to hygiene standards have to be scrubbed regularly – but Leon does not mind: given the importance of the look of the dairy both to himself and to his demonstrations, the extra work is well worthwhile.

Before he made cheese, he spent fifteen years as the co-principal viola player with the Hallé Orchestra, where he performed with Barbirolli and Menuhin: he left because he was afraid of becoming stale, perhaps even ending up hating music. He chose to make cheese instead, he says, because it is just as creative and 'a natural progression' for a musician. However, cheesemaking *per se* lacks the performance element of music: he has remedied this by inviting the public to watch him – and people come, sometimes 150–200 in a morning. One may wonder how he can make first-class cheese and entertain at the same time, but he can. I stayed at a hotel further up the coast where a girl on a walking holiday had sprained her ankle: unable to walk, she went to Llangoffan instead and came back declaring that she had never seen anything so interesting and wanted to train as a cheesemaker herself.

Until recently, all the cheese was made from his own herd, which, because he has only 7ha/18 acres, is kept to fourteen: five Jerseys and nine Brown Swiss, whose milk is similar to Ayrshire; now, however, he buys a further supply from a Friesian herd nearby. Like Giovanni Irranca's (page 145), Leon's land is organic, fertilized in this instance by the cow-dung and seaweed; however, he too feeds the cows inorganic barley, and the milk he buys in is not strictly organic.

LLANGLOFFAN

Gold Medal and Dougal Campbell Memorial Trophy for the Best Welsh Cheese,
British Cheese Awards 1996
A hard cows' cheese; full-fat, unpasteurized milk; vegetarian rennet. 1.4kg/3lb,
4.5kg/10lb, and 13.5kg/30lb

The texture is light and slightly crumbly; the taste is fresh, buttery, and mild or deep according to age, with a mixture of grassy and herbal flavours. Of all cheeses, it is one of the most adaptable, with enough character to serve alongside potent partners on the cheeseboard but not too strong to be eaten every day. It is also surprisingly effective as a flavouring in cooking, when it adds vivacity and interest without the obvious tang of Cheddar. Some of the cheeses are flavoured with garlic and chives.

The starter is home-cultured and the milk left to ripen for an hour and a half before the addition of rennet; when the curd has set, after about another half-hour, it is cut with multiple-bladed curd knives. For the next hour it is stirred and scalded (heated) slightly according to acidity; it is then drained and milled. The salt, plus chives and garlic for the flavoured versions, is added during milling. Finally, it is packed into cloth-lined moulds and pressed again until the following day. At the time of my visit, the maturing time on the farm was ten weeks, although stockists such as Neal's Yard Dairy may mature the cheeses on for another one and a half to three and a half months; Leon said that he is aiming to mature them himself for up to nine.

Llangloffan and Spinach Pies

Total cooking time: just over 20 minutes; baking time: 13–15 minutes
Makes 12–14

200g/7oz spinach, picked over and washed
salt
$^1/_2$ tbsp oil
15g/$^1/_2$oz butter
3 cloves garlic, peeled and finely chopped
$^1/_2$ mild green chilli, washed, core and seeds removed, and finely diced
1 large free-range egg, beaten
4 tbsp single cream
1 tsp Dijon mustard
2 tbsp dry white wine
pepper
150g/5$^1/_4$oz Llangloffan, finely grated
1$^1/_2$ quantities short pastry (page 20)

Pack the spinach into a saucepan with $^1/_2$ teaspoonful of salt (but no water). Cover and set over medium heat for 4 minutes; stir and cook (still covered) for another 1–2 minutes, until the spinach is submerged in juices and tender. Drain in a sieve, pressing out as much liquor as possible with the back of a spoon, and chop.

Warm the oil and butter over medium heat and fry the garlic until it begins to show signs of changing colour (it should not be allowed to colour further because it will continue to cook in the hot oil). Add the chilli, turn it briskly, and remove the pan from the heat. Stir in the spinach.

Beat together the egg, cream, mustard, wine, a pinch of salt, and a fairly generous grinding of pepper. Stir in the cheese and spinach. Roll out the pastry thinly and line a patty tin or tins; fill just to the top of the cases with the spinach mixture. Do not add more because it will overflow during cooking. Set the oven to 200°C/400°F/Gas 6. Cut out tops for the cases, moisten the edges on the undersides to ensure that they stick, and cover the pies, pinching or stamping the edges firmly together. Make air-holes in the middle and bake for 13–15 minutes, until the pies are well browned. Serve them hot.

LLANGLOFFAN COLOURED CHESHIRE

Gold Medal and Dougal Campbell Memorial Trophy, British Cheese Awards 1997
A semi-hard cows' cheese; full-fat, unpasteurized milk; vegetarian rennet. 4.5kg/10lb
or 13.5kg/30lb

This cheese was originally made as a joke. Leon had never made Cheshire before, but his grandmother had, and he decided to try, partly to show that Cheshire cheese can be made outside Cheshire. He then entered it for the British Cheese Awards, where (as at all similar events) the cheeses are judged blind, so that no one knew who had made it until afterwards. It won not for its Cheshire-like qualities but simply because it was so delicious. The texture is quite wonderfully light, flaky, and melting, while the taste hits the palate at so many levels that you could call it mild and powerful simultaneously. The overall impression is rich and piquant, but the piquancy is not the salty/sweet tang of Appleby's (page 179) but a slightly peppery, mellow tang with (as one might expect) affinities to Llangloffan.

Teifi

JOHN AND PATRICE SAVAGE-ONSTWEDDER, GLYNHYNOD FARM,
FFOSTRASOL, LLANDYSUL, DYFED SA44 5JY. TEL: 01239 851528

Even though they are now as hooked as everyone else, John and Patrice set out to make cheese simply in order to live where they do. This area is not mountainous, but broken by sudden, convex, irresistibly pretty river valleys densely wooded with oak trees. Their farm is high up on the side of a wide valley (Glynhynod means 'remarkable valley') with a view across rolling, fertile country sloping down to the sea, only 10–11km/6–7 miles to the west.

John met Patrice in Holland, where he taught at the Small Earth, a leading organic farming and alternative living centre. As a result of translating a book into Dutch, *The Complete Book of Self-Sufficiency*, he and Patrice were invited to stay with the author in Pembrokeshire. This prompted their decision to move to Wales: before moving, however, Patrice spent a year in Brabant as an apprentice to a Dutch cheesemaker, Mrs Vermeer, who made the first post-war organic farmhouse Gouda in Holland.

As the farm is very small, they only keep six organically reared Jerseys, whose milk is used for butter and buttermilk; the milk for the cheese comes from a herd of about forty-five Friesians on the other side of the valley.

Patrice makes the Teifi to an allegedly 500-year-old recipe, using the traditional wooden vat; as from about two years ago, she now also makes Caerphilly. This was originally made for them by a cheesemaker called Cyril Woolley, who celebrated his fiftieth anniversary of cheesemaking while he was working with them; he has since retired but taught Patrice his method (and, as his experience was only with British territorial cheeses, she taught him in return to make Gouda).

TEIFI

Silver Medal, British Cheese Awards 1997; Bronze Medal, 1997 (Herbs); Bronze Medal, 1997 (Garlic)
A Gouda-style cows' cheese; full-fat, unpasteurized milk; vegetarian rennet. 450g/1lb, 900g/2lb, and 3.5kg/7lb 11oz truckles or 7.2–11.3kg/16–25lb wheels

Teifi has a very wide range of flavours which includes grass, flowers, earth, and a selection of herbs. When it first hits the tongue, it seems sweet and mild, but the flavours develop as you eat it and it ends by being surprisingly strong, with an almost spicy tang which, like that of Llanboidy (page 150), resembles cheese made nowhere else. Patrice may have begun to make cheese for practical reasons but she is a natural: both her cheeses are delicious. Sometimes she flavours them, e.g. with garlic, herbs, garlic and herbs, cumin, or peppercorns with sweet red pepper: I have not tried all the flavours, but rather to my surprise found that I liked the peppercorns with red pepper as much as the original, since the sweet pepper brings out the spiciness of the cheese and the peppercorns its herbal tones. John also matures some of the smaller sizes into Celtic Promises (page 38). The cheese loses none of its power when heated and is excellent toasted or as a flavouring; as it melts in strings, it is also suitable for pizza.

For both Teifi and Caerphilly, Patrice uses a homemade starter, added when the milk (morning and evening) is at 20°C/68°F. For Teifi, she adds rennet when it has been left to ripen for twenty minutes and warmed to 29°C/84°F. When the curd has set, she cuts it to the size of peas and washes and scalds it twice, to 32°C/90°F and 36°C/97°F, draining off a third of the whey the first time and half of the remainder the second. It is then drained, scooped into moulds, and pressed for two and a half hours, which leaves it with enough moisture for the acidity to rise overnight. In the morning, it is unmoulded and brined for eight hours to three days according to size; it is matured for up to a year.

Gougère

This is traditionally made with Gruyère but works wonderfully with the powerful flavour of Teifi. Serve with Burgundy. The dough can be made up to twenty-four hours in advance.

Cooking time: 35–40 minutes
Makes 8 portions

125g/4¹/₂oz plain white flour
1 tsp dry mustard
¹/₂ tsp salt
generous grinding of pepper
55g/2oz butter
3 large free-range eggs, broken into separate bowls
20g/³/₄oz Parmesan, Cwmtawe (page 145), or other pecorino, finely grated
110g/nearly 4oz plain Teifi, finely grated

Sift together the first four ingredients. Chop up the butter and melt it over low heat in 220ml/just under 8fl oz water; raise the heat, and as soon as it is boiling vigorously, tip in the seasoned flour all at once. Remove the pan from the heat and beat with a tablespoon to a firm, smooth dough with no remaining pockets of flour: this will take 2–3 minutes. Return the pan to low heat and continue to beat for another 2 minutes, until it is shiny and leaves the sides of the pan in a smooth mass. Beat in the eggs one at a time; do not add another until the previous one is completely absorbed and the mixture is homogeneous. When all three eggs have been amalgamated, the mixture will be a stiff paste but not quite stiff enough to hold its shape. Stir in the Parmesan or pecorino and 80g/nearly 3oz of the Teifi, leaving the rest to sprinkle over the top. The dough can now be stored until needed.

To bake, set the oven to 190°C/375°F/Gas 5. Thoroughly butter a small baking sheet (unless it is thoroughly greased, the gougère will stick) and place tablespoonsfuls of the dough in a circle, each spoonful just touching the next. Sprinkle the tops thickly with the rest of the cheese and bake for 35 minutes without opening the oven door. The gougère will rise and turn golden, but if it is only pale gold, continue to bake it for another 5 minutes, until it is well browned and very crisp. The outside should be as crisp as a well-baked croissant but the inside slightly hollow and as soft as a soufflé. Serve hot or warm. Any portions left over are delicious heated up the next day: the hollow middles can be stuffed with soft cheese or butter.

CAERPHILLY AND REMARKABLE VALLEY

Bronze Medal, British Cheese Awards 1997 (Remarkable Valley)
A semi-hard or hard cheese, according to age; full-fat, unpasteurized milk; vegetarian
rennet. Caerphilly, 2.7–3.7kg/6–8lb; Remarkable Valley, 8kg/17½ lb

Like other Caerphillies, the cheese varies enormously at different ages. When very young, it is creamy; by about five months, it is mild and sweet, tasting of grass, flowers, and the soft Welsh water. At six months, it has begun to develop a tang; by eight, the tang is deep and lasting, although not strong. The same cheese made in a larger size becomes Remarkable Valley after maturing for over eight months.

The milk is heated to 31°C/88°F after the starter is added and renneted after thirty minutes. When set, the curd is heated to 35°C/95°F and cut over an hour; it is then drained and cut very small by hand rather than milled, which means that it retains a higher proportion of moisture. This is followed by moulding, pressing for twenty-four hours, and brining for up to twenty-four hours depending on size. At ten days, some of the smaller size are smoked; the rest are matured for up to fifteen months.

Pencarreg and Pencarreg Blue
RACHEL ROWLANDS, 36 GLANRAFON INDUSTRIAL ESTATE, ABERYSTWYTH, CARDIGAN. TEL: 01970 625805

The Pencarregs and T'yn Grug, which is now discontinued, used to be made by Dougal Campbell who, horrifyingly, was run over and killed by his own tractor in 1996: Rachel, who knew him well, gave me their early history. Dougal was a keen climber and first became interested in cheese when he saw it being made on a climbing holiday in the Austrian Alps. He was so fascinated that he stayed on a farm and learnt how to make it; as soon as he came back, he bought a couple of cows and 20ha/50 acres of land, which he set out to farm organically. While the herd increased, he built himself a dairy; then, for some years, he sold T'yn Grug from the farm gate. During that time, he met other members of the organic movement in Wales, including the organic market gardener Peter Seggars and Rachel's husband, Gareth; after discussing the development of a second cheese with Gareth, Dougal and Peter went to look for a suitable model in Brittany. The first result of this trip was a washed-rind cheese which Dougal discarded; however, because producing it meant that he needed extra milk, it convinced him that (as applied in the days before Milk Marque and regular testing) milk which was bought should always be pasteurized. In fact, early examples of Pencarreg were not: when he tried to market them, it became clear that he would not be able to sell them in this form in the supermarkets; the cheese has thus been pasteurized ever since.

Rachel, who is already well known for her organic butter, yoghurts, and cottage cheese, has now taken over the two Pencarregs; sadly, she is not able to continue T'yn Grug because at present her dairy is adapted only for soft cheese. She adds that T'yn Grug, much more than the soft cheeses, was very personal to Dougal and she doubts whether anyone else could maintain its individuality. Without ruling out the possibility of making some sort of hard cheese in the future, she emphasizes that for the time being she needs to concentrate on perfecting the Pencarregs.

PENCARREG AND PENCARREG BLUE

A soft organic cows' cheese with a white mould rind; full-fat, pasteurized milk; vegetarian rennet. Pencarreg 1.8kg/4lb rounds; Pencarreg Blue 300g/10 $\frac{1}{2}$oz rounds and 1.5kg/3lb 5oz rounds

In the recent past, Pencarreg has suffered from the fact that it is often sold under-ripe. Rachel assures me that this will happen no more, and the cheeses that I have tried since she took over bear her out. They did not flow like Camembert, but were rich and soft throughout, like extra thick cream. The taste is similarly creamy, with the soft herbal flavour which characterizes the cheeses from this part of Wales. At the time of going to press, Pencarreg Blue was not yet ready for marketing, but an advance sample had the same creamy texture and the promise of a piquant blue taste.

Penybont

ALAN AND KAREN REYNOLDS, MOUNTPLEASANT, PENYBONT, CAMARTHEN. TEL: 01994 484315

Last year, Alan and Karen were featured in a film about downshifting on Channel 4, *The Good Life*. Alan, who used to work for an employment agency, was first shown at his office desk and subsequently with Karen and their two small daughters, Alice and Katie, at an uproarious leaving party where he was presented with the conventional gold watch and, more to the point, a chain-saw. We then saw them drive up the M4 to Mountpleasant, a ramshackle farm in a charming but particularly remote spot, where they were confront-ed by a herd of goats on the look-out, as goats always are, for entertainment. Karen had taken a course on goat-keeping before they left, but neither of them had ever practised farming before and the only instruction they had received in cheesemaking had been squeezed into a hasty weekend with their predecessor. The film provoked a certain amount of negative comment: Polly Toynbee, uttering in dire tones, "'I know whereof I speak'", noted that it had been shot entirely in fine weather (which in the case of this part of the world is a fair point) and said that she did not think they would stay the course (*Radio Times*, 31 May–6 June 1997, p. 10).

We visited them three months later and felt that without question they will. The house had the comfortless, greenish-grey look of somewhere which had long been in need of redecoration, but was sound and efficiently equipped; similarly, the dairy was basic but adequate. Soon after they arrived, the goats stopped giving milk because of worms; this, however, was swiftly remedied. Besides the goats, they have half a dozen hens, two ducks, and two large white pigs, Ethel and Jointy, to whom Alan plans to add a pair of Gloucester Old Spots. Work is endless but to Alice and Katie life is a con-tinuous weekend because both their parents are at home all day (Alice, aged three and a half, could identify every goat by her face within two months: at this stage, her parents still only recognized them by their udders). Perhaps above all, Alan and Karen are lucky in having a sense of humour; also, they became hooked by cheese almost immediately, and by now have the benefit of both James Aldridge's and Eurwen Richards's advice.

PENYBONT

*A semi-hard goats' cheese; unpasteurized milk; vegetarian rennet. 1.6–2kg/3lb
8oz–4lb 6oz truckles in summer; slightly smaller in winter*

The original cheese, before Alan and Karen took over, had a slightly fudgy texture; the Reynolds' version is crumblier, with a nutty feel. The taste is a combination of lemon-like, herbal flavours and flowery overtones, very distinctive and positive, and remarkable for the complete absence of any suggestion of goat. Altogether, it is interesting, different, and I think extremely enjoyable. When heated, it retains its crumbly texture but becomes even sweeter and more flowery.

At the time of writing, their herd consists of forty-one goats in milk and fourteen out of a total of over seventy kids, fed organically although they are not at present registered with the Soil Association. They make the cheese every other day, taking it in turns, since they have decided to share every job equally (including looking after the children). Their starter comes from Sue Jones, a short distance away (page 150) and rennet from Rachel Roberts, who is now making Pencarreg (page 158). The milk of that and the previous day is mixed and heated to 30°C/86°F before the addition of starter; it is renneted half an hour later and the curd left to set for the usual forty to forty-five minutes. It is then cut into 2-cm/³/₄-inch cubes and scalded to 35°C/95°F over forty minutes, during which it is stirred continuously. After this, it is left to rest (pitched) for another forty minutes and drained. Thereafter, it is left in the vat for a further forty to forty-five minutes before being cut into blocks and piled once. Finally, after another ten-minute rest, it is milled coarsely, dry-salted, and moulded. The cheese can be eaten after ten days but is usually matured for six weeks.

Gorwydd Caerphilly

TODD TRETHOWEN, GORWYDD FARM, LLANDEWI BREFI,
TREGARON, CEREDIGLION SY25 6NY. TEL: 01570 493516

The Trethowens senior downshifted from Sussex eleven years ago, when Todd started at London University: his father, who had been a headmaster, decided to retire early, although he has now taken a job at Lampeter University. Nowhere makes downshifting look so tempting as Gorwydd. The house looks over the Teifi valley, facing west so that it catches the afternoon sun; in the front, the light is caught by flashes of soft pink and orange in the borders. The farm is a very old foundation: to one side of the present house is the original farmhouse, and on the other an enormous barn which will probably become Todd's cheese store. The walls of the buildings are 0.9 metres/3 feet thick, which creates the ideal conditions for cheese, since the temperature is kept cool and constant and humidity is over 90 per cent. In the smaller maturing room behind the dairy which he now uses, he says that even in very hot weather the temperature never rises by more than two degrees.

Todd's commitment to cheese originated at Neal's Yard Dairy, where he worked during vacations; when he went to Wales to stay with his parents, he helped Dougal Campbell, whose farm was only about 8km/5 miles away. After graduating, he took up a full-time job at the Dairy before training, first with Charlie Westhead (page 171), then with Chris Duckett (page 77), whose recipes for both the cheese and starter he now uses. At present, he makes cheese three or four days a week and delivers it on the other days; as the Trethowens do not keep animals, his milk comes via Milk Marque from two neighbouring farms. Every stage of the cheesemaking is carried out entirely by hand; a bulk milk-tank serves as a vat and his moulds, of the traditional cake tin-like shape, are made by the local blacksmith (where else in the UK could you still find a local blacksmith?). The maturing time on the farm is two months, but Neal's Yard matures the cheeses on for an extra month.

GORWYDD CAERPHILLY

Bronze Medal, British Cheese Awards 1996
A semi-hard cows' cheese; full-fat, unpasteurized milk; vegetarian rennet.
1.1kg/2lb 7oz, 1.8 kg/4lb, and 3.6kg/8lb truckles

The Trethowens gave us a two-month-old cheese which I tried directly and again after a week, having kept it from necessity rather too warm but in an atmosphere of high humidity. At first, the texture was open and slightly crumbly and the taste full, complex, and with just a hint of sharpness: it was quite different from Duckett's but had similar undertones to T'yn Grug (now defunct). A week later, it had already become much sweeter and creamier: the sharpness had completely disappeared. It was delicious both ways, but the riper version more so: in fact, at this stage it was so rewarding that as I write we have just ordered another (the Trethowens will send them to order, not by post but by twenty-four-hour dispatch). True to Welsh tradition, it is wonderful toasted, melting to a rich cream and becoming even sweeter.

Gorwydd Lemon Tart

To give contrast to the filling, these should be made with part-wholemeal or almond pastry: the almond pastry is delicious but breakable and tends to be sticky to roll. You can make either small tartlets or one large tart.

Cooking time: 12–15 minutes for tartlets or 20–25 for a large tart
Makes about 16 or enough to fill a 22-cm/8½-inch tart tin

short pastry (page 20) made with equal quantities of wholemeal and white flour *or* 100g/3½oz white flour, 50g/1¾oz wholemeal flour, and 50g/1¾oz ground almonds
75g/2¾oz Gorwydd Caerphilly or Wheems (page 252), finely grated
4 large free-range egg-yolks, beaten
zest of ½ large organic lemon
2 tbsp lemon juice
1 tbsp brandy
115g/4oz caster sugar
100ml/3½fl oz thick double cream

Roll out the pastry thinly: if using almonds, knead it slightly before use and dust with plenty of flour. Lightly butter and line the tart or patty-tins.

Mix together the cheese and egg yolks; wash the lemon and grate in the zest. Stir in all the other ingredients. Bake in a pre-heated oven at 190°C/375°F/Gas 5, 12 minutes for tartlets or, in the case of a large tart, 20 minutes or until the filling is firm and just beginning to bubble. Serve hot or warm with more thick cream.

Little Acorn Products

DON AND KAREN ROSS, MESEN FACH FARMHOUSE, BETHANIA, LLANON, CEREDIGION SY23 5NL. TEL: 01974 821348

Don and Karen moved from Manchester in search of the good life some fourteen years ago: Don formerly worked for a vending-machine company and Karen in a fashion boutique. Their transition was carefully planned: Don had already worked on a farm, both studied cheesemaking in Devon before they left, and they travelled all over Britain looking for the right place prior to choosing Mesen Fach. They nearly settled in Orkney, where they would have milked cows, but at the last moment had to abandon their plans because the milk quota was introduced just at this time, which put the initial outlay beyond their means. At Mesen Fach (the name means 'Acorn') they have 6ha/16 acres suitable for sheep on which they still keep a pedigree Friesland flock, although they now buy in their milk because they found that they did not have time to milk and make cheese. Even with a staff of four, their wide range of speciality cheeses means that they work almost round the clock.

They developed their first cheese, Acorn, slowly and patiently, trying out different variations on a standard recipe and test-marketing the results until they were satisfied that it was distinctive enough to be interesting but not too strong to be popular (to start with, it was stronger than most of their customers liked). After two or three years, they took over the recipe for a Caerphilly-style cheese marinated in mead which had been made on Skirrid, a mountain near Abergavenny. Eighteen months later, they introduced two more sheep's cheeses (both now discontinued), one smoked and the other flavoured with horseradish. They became increasingly fascinated by flavourings and began a series of experiments with spices, fruit, wine, and spirits and liqueurs as well as the more traditional herbs; however, the cost of the flavourings on top of sheep's milk (which is much more expensive than cows') encouraged them to produce a cows' cheese which they use as the basis of most of their flavoured products. These now include a total of ten flavoured Cheddar-style cheeses and the three described here.

ACORN

A semi-hard sheep's cheese; unpasteurized milk; vegetarian rennet. 2.3kg/5lb truckles

This is a distinctive, very unusual cheese with a soft, crumbly texture reminiscent of Wensleydale; the taste, however, could hardly be more different, since it has a pronounced herbal tang which strikes some of the same notes as Penybont (page 160). Sub-flavours include grass, nuts, and a hint of the sea, which is only about 11km/7 miles from the farm. The cheese is particularly good with hazlenuts or apple cheese (page 24), and excellent toasted, when it becomes mild, rich, and sweet.

SKIRRID

A semi-hard sheep's cheese; unpasteurized milk; vegetarian rennet. 2.5kg/5½lb truckles

Although made by a different method, the taste and texture are similar to Acorn but less pronounced: partly because the cheese has been marinated, the texture is softer and moister, and the mead imparts an overtone of honey which modifies the tang and accentuates its nutty character.

LADY LLANOVER

A saffron-flavoured semi-hard sheep's cheese; unpasteurized milk; vegetarian rennet. 2.3kg/5lb truckles

This is softer, smoother, and less crumbly than the other two, with sweet, flowery notes which mask the natural flavours; to my taste, less successful than Skirrid, but I gather that plenty of customers take the opposite view. It is named after the well-known Welsh cookery writer.

Caws Cenarth

GWYNFOR AND THELMA ADAMS, FFERM GLYNEITHINOG, ABERCYCH, NEAR NEWCASTLE EMLYN, DYFED SA37 0LH. TEL: 01239 710432

Thelma Adams's television appearances and the numerous articles about her in newspapers and magazines mean that she is probably already well known to many readers. While the Ducketts have made Caerphilly in Somerset for generations, she is the only remaining maker born to it in Wales. She learnt by watching her mother, and after marrying Gwynfor made it for her family for years before deciding to turn it into a business, largely, as with others, in response to the milk quota. Even now, however, despite her success (she has won dozens of awards), the Adamses run their farm primarily to produce liquid milk. They have just over 100 Friesian–

Holsteins and make cheese three times a week, using morning milk only, which means that the cheeses are relatively low in fat. Thelma has not had them analysed but reckons that, allowing for the shorter maturing time and higher retention of moisture, the fat content of her Caerphilly is about ten per cent lower than that of mature Cheddar.

Besides the plain Caerphilly for which they are chiefly known, the Adamses produce smoked and garlic and herb versions, and also a second, Cheddar-style cheese, Caws Mamgu. They are helped by their son and daughter but make the cheese without additional staff and entirely by hand. Like Leon Downey (page 151), they are happy to have an audience: on cheesemaking mornings, visitors can watch from a viewing gallery where there is also a small museum and shop.

CAWS CENARTH

A semi-hard cows' cheese; lower-fat, unpasteurized milk; vegetarian rennet. 225g/8oz, 450g/1lb, 900g/2lb, and 4–4.5kg/9–10lb rounds

Despite its lower-fat content, the cheese is notable for its deliciously rich, creamy feel: though not as soft as the Ducketts' after maturing, it is almost semi-soft rather than semi-hard, very smooth-textured, and slightly elastic. The taste is mild and sweet: the very gentlest herbal background is overlaid with delicate grassy and flowery flavours which very much bring to mind the countryside where it is made.

The milk is used while it is still warm from the cow: starter is added without further heating and the milk allowed to ripen for 1–1¾ hours. After renneting, it is left to set for another hour. For Caerphilly, the curd is cut with knives, stirred and scalded to 34.5°C/94°F over nearly a further hour, and left to settle before draining. It is then 'textured' by cutting into progressively smaller pieces until the right acidity is reached; salting, milling, and moulding follow, with turning after an hour. Finally, the cheeses are pressed overnight and brined; the maturing time is three to four weeks.

CAWS MAMGU

A hard cows' cheese; lower-fat, unpasteurized milk. Sizes as above

This is similarly sweet, mild, and gentle-tasting, with a slightly fudgy feel. Rather than a Cheddar-like tang, it develops a soft herbal, peppery edge in the mouth which leaves a gentle spicy aftertaste on the tongue.

CHAPTER 5

The Midlands

MALVERN CHEESEWRIGHTS

ANSTEYS OF WORCESTER

NEAL'S YARD CREAMERY

WOMERTON FARM

APPLEBY'S CHESHIRE

BERKSWELL

INNES

COLSTON BASSETT AND DISTRICT DAIRY

STAFFORDSHIRE ORGANIC

LINCOLNSHIRE POACHER

Malvern Cheesewrights

NICHOLAS HODGETTS, POND FARM CHURCH LANE,
WHITTINGTON, WORCS WR5 2RD. TEL: 01905 350744

I met Nicholas just a year after he had moved to Pond Farm, when he felt that he had still hardly settled in. From a cheesemaking point of view, the farm is ideal, since it is only 3km/2 miles from the M5 and has accommodation for animals and an enormous dairy with a correspondingly large drying room and storeroom and an office as big as a sitting room. He remarked that when he arrived, he had wondered if he would ever be able to fill so much space – but of course he has. He now makes six cheeses, all based on traditional recipes: Malvern, his first, which he launched ten years ago, when he was still milking his own sheep, Hereford Red and Hereford Hop, Worcester Gold, Buffalo, the first buffalo cheese to be made in Britain, and his newest, Whittington Organic. At the time of my visit, Whittington was not yet on sale, although there were rows of them maturing in the storeroom: after tasting several at different stages of maturity, I felt that it was probably the clearest example that I had yet encountered of the superiority of organic milk. At that time, the milk was from Ayrshires at Highgrove; this has been replaced by Friesian milk from Sherborne Farm, near Stow-on-the-Wold.

A large flock of sheep, some with very new lambs who spin their tails like propellers as they run to suckle, were grazing in the field next to the dairy; nevertheless, all Nicholas's milk is bought, including the sheep's, for the usual reason: he does not have the time or labour to milk the sheep as well as make the cheese. The cows' milk for the Hereford cheeses and Worcester Gold comes via Milk Marque from specified farms and the buffalo milk from a herd of 120 at Shipton-on-Stour.

MALVERN

Bronze Medal, British Cheese Awards 1996; Silver Medal, 1997
A hard sheep's cheese; unpasteurized milk; vegetarian rennet. 200g/7oz and
1.5kg/3lb 5oz truckles or 2.3kg/5lb wheels

Although a hard cheese, Malvern has a soft, moist, notably smooth texture and delicate, creamy taste overlaid with the sweetness of the milk and wild flowers. Its gentle flavours make it more suitable for the cheeseboard than cooking, but left-over pieces can be used in the same way as pecorino for grating over vegetable dishes.

To make Malvern, Nicholas uses an adaptation of a white Wensleydale recipe (Wensleydale was originally a sheep's cheese). Starter is added when the milk is at 20°C/68°F; it is heated to 31°C/88°F before the addition of a little rennet, left to set for half an hour, and cut into 1.25-cm/$^1/_2$-inch cubes. This is followed by scalding to 38°C/100°F over an hour, during which it is stirred continuously. The stirring is mechanical, but as the curd is very delicate, the rest of the process is carried out by hand. The curd is tipped on to a draining table and gently blocked and piled before being broken into walnut-sized pieces; it is then salted in three sessions, moulded, and piled into blocks of three to drain. Finally, it is re-moulded in cloths and pressed with increasing pressure for twenty-four hours. The maturing time is five months, with turning four times during the first week and once a week thereafter; the cheeses are also regularly rubbed to keep them free of mould.

HEREFORD HOP

> *Gold Medal and Best Speciality Cheese, British Cheese Awards 1995;*
> *Gold Medal, 1997*
> *A semi-hard cows' cheese; full-fat, unpasteurized milk; vegetarian rennet.*
> *1.8kg/4lb wheels*

The cheese derives its name from its thick coating of dried hops. It has a moist, slightly fudgy texture and a sweet taste of grass and flowers strongly impregnated with the flavour of the hops.

WORCESTER GOLD

> *A hard Jersey cheese; full-fat, unpasteurized milk; vegetarian rennet. 400g/14oz and*
> *1.5kg/3lb 5oz truckles or 2.5kg/5lb 8oz wheels*

Worcester Gold is made with the milk of cows who graze on the pastures of the former Cistercian Sandwell Priory. Its texture is rich and creamy, with a very mild taste which develops flowery and herbal flavours on the tongue.

WHITTINGTON ORGANIC

> *A hard cows' cheese; full-fat, unpasteurized milk; vegetarian rennet.*
> *3kg/6lb 10oz truckles*

The samples of Whittington that I tried in Nicholas's store-room differed considerably according to age. At two to three months, the cheese was fresh and creamy rather than sweet, tasting of herbage to a remarkable degree; when fully matured, it had a soft, melting texture and buttery rather than creamy taste, with quite a strong sweet/salty tang. Both were outstanding: most people would probably disagree, but I liked the immature version more.

Whittington is made to a very old recipe which Nicholas found in a museum. It was a spring cheese, made with milk drawn when the grass was new, just after calving, and sold at the autumn fairs. Nicholas has made no alterations except to use a little starter and vegetarian rennet and lard rather than the traditional animal versions. The milk is first left to ripen, unchilled, overnight; after the addition of a little starter, followed by rennet, it is scalded by one degree over an hour, until it has formed a soft curd. It is then tipped onto a draining table and gently broken up by hand. Salting, also carried out by hand, is in three sessions; thereafter, the cheese is moulded, pressed with increasing pressure for three days, and dried for another day in the drying room. Finally the surface is larded and bound with cloth and the cheeses are left to mature for six months.

BUFFALO

Gold Medal and Best New Cheese Award, British Cheese Awards 1996
A hard buffalo cheese; full-fat, unpasteurized milk; vegetarian rennet.
1.8kg/4lb wheels

The buffalo-milk cheese has a compact, slightly fudgy texture and the creamy taste that one might expect from the very rich milk: its chief characteristic, however, is a caramel-like sweetness which develops into a burnt orange aftertaste. It is quite unlike any other cheese made in Britain and I think totally delicious. A very good way of serving it is as a salad with hot or bitter leaves, e.g. mizuna, baby chard, or spinach.

Ansteys of Worcester

ALYSON AND COLIN ANSTEY, BROOMHALL FARM, BROOMHALL, WORCESTER WR5 2NT. TEL: 01905 820232

When Colin's grandfather bought Broomhall Farm in 1923, it was presumably well out into the country: it is now almost in Worcester, on the A38 to Tewkesbury. However, largely thanks to Alyson's initiative and energy, the Ansteys have gained considerably from their urban situation. Before they married, Colin produced only liquid milk, but Alyson, a trained cheesemaker, insisted that they needed 'a challenge', as she put it, and helped him to develop their first cheese, Old Worcester White – called 'White' because they had originally hoped to make a blue cheese, but the blue refused to grow. A second cheese was launched just after the birth of their second child (each of their three cheeses, they say, coincided with the birth of a child). This new cheese was Worcester Sauce, made by request because Lea & Perrins' factory is just down the road 'within smelling distance' when the wind is in the right direction. To start with they did not regard the cheese as a serious proposition, but it turned out to be exceptionally popular. By the time they had evolved the third cheese, Double Worcester, so many people were coming to buy cheese from the farm that they decided to take advantage of their position and start a shop, where they now sell not only about forty per cent of their own output but also a discriminating range of other British cheeses, accompaniments such as olives, and stiff, nubbly, not-too-sweet Worcestershire honey. As at Neal's Yard Dairy and Iain Meliss in Scotland, all the cheeses they sell are British and, because they are cheesemakers, invariably in perfect condition. Around Christmas, they may have homemade mince pies, but otherwise all their stock is connected with cheese except the honey, which is produced (though not by them) on the farm.

OLD WORCESTER WHITE

A hard cow's cheese; full-fat, unpasteurized milk; vegetarian rennet. 450g/1lb and 3.5kg/7lb 11oz truckles

The cheese has a hard-pressed, dryish but cohesive texture and creamy, nutty taste with a distinctive tang: as it matures, the taste deepens and the tang develops. At five months it is a pleasant all-purpose cheese; when more mature, it becomes surprisingly powerful.

All the cheeses are based on the Old Worcester White recipe. After adding starter and rennet and waiting for the curd to set, which takes about fifty minutes, the curd is cut into 1.25-cm/^{1}/$_2$-inch squares, scalded slightly, and blocked and piled. Draining, milling and salting follow; the cheeses are then pressed for twenty-four hours and dipped in hot water to encourage a crust to form. They are pressed for a further twenty-four hours, coated with lard to inhibit the growth of mould, and matured for a minimum of five months.

DOUBLE WORCESTER

An annattoed cow's cheese; full-fat, unpasteurized milk; vegetarian rennet. 450g/1lb and 3.5kg/7lb 11oz truckles

Double Worcester has a slightly crumbly texture and a deep, rich taste slightly mellowed by the annatto but with a sharp punchy tang: when well matured it is strong enough to serve on a cheeseboard in place of a blue cheese.

Double Worcester is called 'Double' because everything is doubled: the curd is cut smaller and scalded to a higher temperature, cut into blocks twice, and milled twice. The minimum maturing time is six months.

Neal's Yard Creamery
CHARLES WESTHEAD, CAPERTHY, ARTHURSTONE LANE, DORSTONE, NEAR HAY-ON-WYE, HEREFORDSHIRE HR3 6AX. TEL: 01981 500182; FAX: 01981 500395

Charles came to cheesemaking by instinct rather than design: one day when he was on the dole and wondering what to do next, he happened to pass Neal's Yard Dairy in London, went in, and in effect never emerged again. He served his apprenticeship, first behind the counter and then driving round the country collecting cheeses. His first dairy was on top of Ragstone Ridge in Kent, only a few minutes from the M25: you drove down an unremarkable wooded road, turned right – and there, without warning, was the Weald of Kent spread out before you. However, the dairy, perched on the hillside, was very small and it was no surprise to hear that he had moved. More surprising was where to: even after writing this book, I would have thought that it would be almost impossible to find a view to equal the one he has left – but he has succeeded, and now makes cheese on top of Dorstone Hill on the edge of the Black Mountains, overlooking the Golden Valley. Here, as before, he makes goats' curds (the equivalent of cows' curd cheese) and two goat cheeses, Perroche and Ragstone (called after the Ridge), plus cows' crème and fromage frais and two cows' cheeses, Wealden Round and Finn (he chose the name Finn, which means 'White Ancient One' in Irish, because the cheese is the only one he makes which is matured). The cows' milk comes from Milk Marque and the goats', which he collects himself in a refrigerated van, from a mixed herd near Market Drayton, whose milk, he says, is 'absolutely marvellous'. The cheeses have naturally changed as a result of the move, especially the goats', which are slightly fuller flavoured than before, but the particular quality which characterizes them all is the delicate texture produced by Charles's touch: perhaps more than anyone, he takes enormous care to treat both the goats' and cows' curds gently and handle them as little as possible.

NEAL'S YARD CREAMERY GOATS' CURD

Fresh curds; full-fat, unpasteurized milk; vegetarian rennet. Sold by weight; seasonal: March–December

The curd has a light, creamy consistency and mild, sweet taste crossed with just enough tartness to give it character. Like cows' curd cheese and fromage frais, it makes an excellent base for a wide range of dishes, including fools, ices, and cheesecake.

The same basic method is used for all the cheeses: the milk is heated to 30°C/86°F, starter and rennet are added more or less simultaneously, and the curd is left overnight. In the morning, except for Wealden, the curd is cut into 3-cm/1¼-inch squares with a steel ruler. For plain goats' curds, it is drained briefly and hung in a cloth until the next morning, when it is ready for use; for the other cheeses, it is transferred into moulds with a shovel rather than a ladle because a shovel has an open front and thus disturbs it less. I offered to help with moulding the Perroches and (in the nicest possible way) was rebuked for disturbing it by dragging the shovel over the surface. The moulds are topped up at intervals as the curd settles, left overnight, and brined.

Goats' Curd and Strawberry Fool with Maraschino

One way of serving goats' curd with strawberries is simply as an alternative to cream: to take the edge off its sharpness, beat it with 15g/¹/₂oz caster sugar per 250g/9oz curd or to taste (it should not, however, be sweet). Since the strawberries can be puréed the previous day, the fool is an excellent way of preventing berries picked in advance from going mouldy. To disguise its ever-so-pretty pale pink colour, pour a little extra purée over it before serving. A similar mixture makes a very rich, delicious ice.

For 6–8

125g/4¹/₂oz caster sugar
400g/14oz strawberries, hulled, washed, and left to dry
1 tablespoonful maraschino
400g/14oz goats' curd

Add 55g/2oz of the sugar to the strawberries, leave them to soften for 15–20 minutes, and pass them through a sieve, pressing as much pulp through the mesh as possible. Stir in the maraschino. Beat the curd with the rest of the sugar and gradually stir in as much of the strawberry purée as is necessary to give them a stiff, creamy texture. You will have about a quarter of the purée left over: pile the fool into the serving bowls and pour a little over each.

Strawberry Curd Ice

For 6

400g/14oz strawberries, hulled, washed, and dried, plus extra for serving
190g/generous 6¹/₂oz caster sugar
juice of ¹/₂ lime
200g/7oz goats' curd

Cover the berries with some of the sugar and leave them to soften for 15–20 minutes. Pass them through a sieve with the rest of the sugar, and add the lime juice. Beat the purée into the curd until smooth. Freeze for 2¹/₂–3 hours or until the ice has half-set; beat thoroughly and freeze for another 1–2 hours or until firm. Serve decorated with whole or half strawberries.

PERROCHE

Gold Medal, British Cheese Awards 1995; Silver Medal, 1996; Bronze Medal (Plain) and Gold Medal (Herbs), 1997
A fresh goats' cheese; full-fat, unpasteurized milk; vegetarian rennet. 150g/5¹/₄oz rounds; seasonal: March–December

Perroche has a wonderfully light, melting texture and a sweet, mild taste shot with hints of honey, herbs, and lemon. Some of the cheeses are flavoured with herbs (rosemary, tarragon, or dill).

The curd for Perroche and Ragstone is prepared in the same way as the goats' curd. The Perroches are piled in towers to drain so that the cheese is pressed lightly; after draining, they are brined and the flavoured cheeses rolled in herbs.

 ## Hot Chocolate Creams

The operative word here is rich rather than delicate; however, the background of goats' cheese gives the chocolate a surprisingly refreshing quality. The texture is actually almost cake-like. The creams can be prepared up to twenty-four hours in advance (store them in the refrigerator).

Cooking time: 25–30 minutes
For 6–7

100g/3¹/₂oz Valrhona cooking chocolate
200ml/7fl oz (¹/₃ pint) extra thick double cream, plus extra for serving
2 large free-range egg yolks, beaten
100g/3¹/₂oz Perroche or Innes Button (¹/₂ a Perroche or 2 Innes Buttons)
75g/2³/₄oz caster sugar
1 tbsp brandy

The chocolate comes in buttons or a solid block: cut the block into small pieces if you can or grate it coarsely. Set it with the cream over very low heat and stir gently until it is about two-thirds melted. Remove from the heat and continue stirring until the mixture is completely smooth.

Beat together the yolks, cheese, and sugar until smooth (the mixture will soften as you proceed). Stir in the brandy, then the chocolate. Heat the oven to 180°C/350°F/Gas 4; spoon the creams into ramekins and bake for 25–30 minutes, until they just begin to bubble. Serve hot covered with more cream.

RAGSTONE

Bronze Medal, British Cheese Awards 1996
A white mould rind goats' cheese log; full-fat, unpasteurized milk; vegetarian rennet.
200g/7oz; seasonal: March–December

Again, the texture is deliciously light and smooth; the taste, which has become more distinctive since Charles moved, includes a flash of lemon and quite a strong infusion of honey. As it is now, it is one of the subtlest, sweetest goats' cheeses made in Britain. In one way, it seems a pity to use it for cooking, but it is particularly outstanding grilled.

Ragstone is moulded in tall pipes which are set on end, the cheese inside being pressed by its own weight. The maturing time is two to three weeks. The cheese is at its lightest if eaten promptly but can be kept for at least another two weeks.

WEALDEN ROUND

Silver Medal, British Cheese Awards 1996
A flavoured, fresh cows' cheese; full-fat, unpasteurized milk; vegetarian rennet.
200g/7oz rounds

Of all Charles's cheeses, Wealden is the most remarkable for its texture, which is as light, moist, and delicate as a baked egg custard. The mild taste is strengthened by a choice of flavourings (tarragon, chives, parsley and garlic, or spring onion).

For Wealden, the curd is not cut but left as a solid block floating in the whey and placed in the moulds in layers, between which the flavourings are sprinkled. The fresh herbs are snipped very finely and evenly by Charles's wife.

FINN

An unpressed, white mould rind cows' cheese; full-fat, unpasteurized milk with 10%
cream added; vegetarian rennet. 200g/7oz rounds

Finn is soft but firm and compact rather than runny; the taste is sweet and nutty, with a mild but distinctive, slightly salty tang.

For Finn, which is a cream cheese, ten per cent of cream and penicillin mould for the rind are added to the milk with the starter and the cheeses are matured for a fortnight while the rind develops.

Finn and Watercress Soup

This is very quick to prepare and cook, and can be made the previous day.

Cooking-time: 15–17 minutes
For 4–5

1 large or 2 small onions (150g/5^1/$_4$oz), peeled and finely chopped
1 tbsp oil
25g/1oz butter
2 cloves garlic, peeled and finely chopped
150g/5^1/$_4$oz watercress, washed, and roughly chopped (keep the stems)
850ml/1^1/$_2$ pints vegetable (page 22) or strong, fresh chicken stock (page 21)
salt and pepper
3 tbsp extra thick double cream
100g/3^1/$_2$oz Finn, chopped very small, including the rind

Fry the onion in the oil and butter over low heat for about 2 minutes; add the garlic and continue to fry for another 5 minutes or until the onion is soft but not brown. Add the cress and stir until it is thoroughly coated with oil. Add the stock, 1 teaspoonful of salt, and a moderate grinding of pepper and bring it to a simmer; simmer, covered, for 4–5 minutes. Liquidize the soup, allow it to cool, and chill until needed. When you are ready to serve, re-heat it over fairly high heat; when just simmering, stir in the cream and cheese. Remove from the heat and stir until the rind of the cheese has melted: return to the heat very briefly if necessary. Serve at once.

Womerton Farm

RUTH LAWRENCE, WOMERTON FARM, ALL STRETTON, NEAR CHURCH STRETTON, SHROPSHIRE SY6 6LJ. TEL: 01694 751260

You could spend a lifetime searching for somewhere with a situation like this: Ruth, however, did not have to look, since she inherited the farm from her parents and was brought up here. It is nearly 300 metres/1,000 feet up on the Long Mynd, an isolated outcrop of hills just south of Shrewsbury, with a view over Shropshire to the east and sheep-cropped slopes dropping into steep, bracken-covered valleys to the north and west. It was and still is primarily a sheep farm, but Ruth's father raised a few beef cattle, and Ruth keeps goats, two red-haired Tamworth pigs, hens, guinea-pigs, rabbits, and a duck (there were two but one was eaten by a fox: the other now lives very happily with the rabbits). The goats are crossed Anglo-Nubian, which means that the milk is very rich milk: its quality is evident from her soft cheese, St Francis, but was also immediately obvious to us when she gave us tea. The tea itself was perfectly ordinary but so transformed by the creamy milk, only a few hours old and full of sweet flavours, that it was a revelation. Until recently, she was milking a herd of ninety: now, however, in order to leave more time to make the cheese, she has sold all but ten and buys in the rest of the milk, much of which still comes from her own former goats.

WOMERTON

A hard goats' cheese; full-fat, unpasteurized milk; vegetarian rennet. 1.4kg/3lb and 4.5kg/10lb truckles

The texture is slightly fudge-like; the taste is mild, with a mixture of earthy and herbal flavours. A smoked version is also available. Womerton is based on a Cheddar-type recipe and I think does not do Ruth's goats' milk justice, as St Francis certainly does: when I put this to her, she replied that she is not particularly satisfied with it either, and is already planning to replace it with a new hard cheese.

ST FRANCIS

A soft white mould rind goats' cheese; full-fat, unpasteurized milk; vegetarian rennet. Various sizes, ranging from 55g/2oz buttons to 675g/1lb 8oz logs

The texture of the cheese is like very thick cream but much lighter; the taste is a blend of clear, delicate, refreshing flowery flavours. If there is any trace of goat, it is in a slight undercurrent of lemon. Altogether, the cheese is a rare delight – I say rare because at the moment it is difficult to find in the south. Like James Aldridge's version (page 38), it is delicious instead of cream with fruit and can be used as a filling for pies and tarts.

Only the richer evening milk is used: it is taken directly after milking and cooled to 20°C/68°F. Starter, rennet, and penicillin for the rind are added simultaneously and the curd is left to incubate overnight. The next day, it is drained in baskets for an hour and a half, moulded, and left, still at 20°C/68°F, until the following day, or for a shorter period for the small sizes; finally, it is brined and set to ripen for a fortnight while the rind develops.

Appleby's Cheshire

EDWARD APPLEBY, HAWKSTONE ABBEY FARM, WESTON-
UNDER-REDCASTLE, SHREWSBURY, SHROPSHIRE SY4 5LN.
TEL: 01948 840221/01948 840387

The salty/sweet tang associated with Cheshire, and which certainly characterizes the Appleby's, is said to be due to the salt under the soil not only in Cheshire, but also parts of Lancashire, Staffordshire, and Shropshire: Hawkstone, at the edge of the Dee and Mersey basin, lies at the southern end of the area. The country is lush, with thick hedges, spreading trees, and rich grazing.

The first building to catch the eye as you approach the farm is a long black and white Tudor barn, which faces the back of the house and the cheese-room. The house, which was also originally Tudor but rebuilt on a larger, grander scale, seems unremarkable until seen from the front, when it is revealed as a particularly fine, tall, four-square, eighteenth-century Shropshire manor house. It faces a lawn bounded by shrubs and banks of foxgloves, lupins, larkspur, and delphiniums; at one end is an orchard and vegetable garden fruitful (in June) with ripe strawberries and nascent apples, gooseberries, and raspberries. Here we met Mr Appleby, or so we deduced. When I said, 'How do you do? Are you Mr Appleby?', he replied with dry humour, 'You may presume so. I am just the gardener.' These days (he is eighty-nine), his main interest is the garden; Mrs Appleby, however, who comes from a farming family and has made cheese all her life, is still as preoccupied with it as ever, although the actual work is now carried out by a cheesemaker and three assistants.

Although not on the scale of Quicke's (page 101), the Applebys are one of the largest cheese-farms in the country, keeping a closed herd of 290 Friesians or part-Friesians and handling an average of 3,600 litres/790 gallons of milk a day. The milk vat is as large as a small swimming-pool; of necessity, the curd is stirred and broken after scalding by machinery. The most impressive piece of machinery connected with the cheese, however, is not in the dairy but a slowly revolving carousel which replaces a conventional milking parlour. It is one of only two so far installed in this country and the only one for cows (the other is for sheep). To reduce the amount of power needed and the noise, which might upset the cows, it floats on a bed of water; the cows took about a year to get used to it but now queue up to board it as willingly as others come when they are called. Each chews a feed of concentrates calculated by computer to meet her individual needs as she goes round; the milking apparatus falls off when she is dry, her yield is automatically registered, and the milk piped directly to the dairy.

The whey is separated, pasteurized, and used for particularly excellent whey-butter; the Applebys also make ordinary butter, small quantities of smoked Cheshire, and Double Gloucester instead of Cheshire once a week.

APPLEBY'S CHESHIRE

Gold Medal (coloured), Silver Medal (white), British Cheese Awards 1997
A hard cows' cheese; full-fat, unpasteurized milk; vegetarian and traditional rennet.
1.25kg/2lb 12oz, 2.3kg/5lb, 9kg/20lb, and a few 28kg/62lb Traditionals

The white and coloured cheeses are exactly the same except that the white ones are made without annatto. The texture is short, light, and crumbly; when young, the taste is mild and mellow, giving only a promise of the lively flavours of the mature version. After six months or more (in the case of the larger sizes), they become rich, piquant, deep-tasting, and surprisingly powerful, with a sharp sweetness offset by an almost smoky tang; occasionally, they may have a few veins of green under the rind which are an assurance of age and enhance flavour. The cheese is not only superb on the cheeseboard, but also excellent for cooking (before the days of creamery-made Cheddar, Cheshire was the standard cheese recommended for flavouring).

The cheese is made with morning and evening milk; a home-cultured starter with annatto for the coloured cheeses is added and the milk is left to ripen for two hours before renneting. When it has set, which takes the usual forty minutes, the curd is stirred and scalded very slightly, and stirring continued until the correct acidity is reached; it is then cut into blocks and turned and broken rather than blocked and piled, as for Cheddar. Salting, milling, and moulding follow, after which the cheeses are pressed overnight; finally, they are turned and pressed again, briefly for the small sizes or for another day in the case of the 28kg/62lb size. The maturing times are a minimum of six weeks for the smallest size and from two to ten months for the largest, with twice-weekly turning and wiping throughout.

Over tea with homemade lemon cake, Mrs Appleby recalled that her father ate the cheese with raspberry jam – which is unexpectedly good, perhaps because the two flavours have a similar richness. A deep, rich six- to ten-month-old cheese also goes well with gooseberry jam.

Cheshire Rarebit with Whisky

There is nothing traditional about whisky with Cheshire; however, the taste of whisky has an affinity with the matured cheese which makes this the most interesting and successful rarebit mixture that I have tried.

For 2

slice from a large loaf
butter
2 level tsp plain white flour
salt
Cayenne pepper
$^3/_4$ tsp Dijon mustard
2 tbsp whisky
150g/5$^1/_4$oz mature Applebys' Cheshire, finely grated

If you like, trim the crust from the bread; butter it, cut it in half, and bake it (page 22). Mix together the flour, a pinch of salt, and a generous pinch of Cayenne. Put 15g/$^1/_2$oz butter into a small saucepan over low heat until it melts; remove the pan from the heat and stir in the seasoned flour. Return it to the heat and add the mustard, whisky, and 2 tablespoonsful of water. Cook for 1–2 minutes, stirring continuously, until the mixture is very thick but not too stiff to mix with the cheese. Stir in the cheese off the heat: it should just melt but no more. If necessary, return it to the heat for a second or two, but be careful only to warm it gently. Pile the cheese mixture over the pieces of toast, making sure that it covers them completely: any exposed edges will burn. Place the rarebit under a hot grill until it turns pale brown and serve at once.

APPLEBYS' DOUBLE GLOUCESTER

A hard cows' cheese; full-fat, unpasteurized milk; vegetarian and traditional rennet.
1.8kg/4lb, 6.8kg/15lb, and 13.5kg/30lb wheels

The Double Gloucester has a similar salty/sweet tang to the Cheshire but the texture is crumblier and the taste milder, mellower, and smokier. It leaves quite a strong, rich, smoky aftertaste.

Applebys' Jerusalem Artichoke Soup

You can make this with either Cheshire or Double Gloucester: Cheshire is livelier and tangier, Double Gloucester deeper and richer.

Cooking time: just under 1 hour
For 4

1 tbsp oil
15g/¹/₂oz butter
125g/4¹/₂oz (1 small) onion, peeled and diced
2 cloves garlic, peeled and diced
1 small leek, finely sliced, washed, and dried
250g/9oz carrots, peeled and finely sliced
salt and pepper
150ml/¹/₄ pint dry white wine
250g/9oz floury potato, peeled and sliced
450g/1lb Jerusalem artichokes, peeled and sliced
1 litre/1³/₄ pints vegetable (page 22) or fresh chicken stock (page 21)
2 tbsp double cream
a little milk for thinning if needed
at least 125g/4¹/₂oz Applebys' Cheshire or Double Gloucester, finely grated

Warm the oil and butter in a large saucepan or wok and fry the onion over low heat for 4–5 minutes; add the garlic and fry for another 4–5 minutes or until the onion is soft but not brown. Add the leek and carrots, season with 1 teaspoonful of salt and a moderate grinding of pepper, and turn for about 2 minutes. Pour in the wine; raise the heat, and boil it away. Add the potato, artichokes, and stock, bring to the boil, and simmer for 25–30 minutes or until the carrot is soft. Liquidize the soup until it is very smooth; return it to the pan and heat it very gently until simmering. Stir in the cream. If it is very thick, add a little milk. Remove from the heat and add half the cheese: sprinkle the rest over each serving.

Berkswell

STEPHEN AND TESSA FLETCHER, RAM HALL DAIRY SHEEP, RAM HALL, BERKSWELL, COVENTRY, WEST MIDLANDS CV7 7BD. TEL: 01676 532203

Ram Hall is of ancient origin: the Fletchers are not sure how long a farm has been on the site, but the present farmhouse is sixteenth century and as little altered as you could hope to find. You go in through a deeply weathered, iron-studded wooden side-door to the former kitchen, where a huge, curving brick flue leads from where the bread-oven used to be up through the rafters. An original staircase, complete with banisters, is in the main part of the house, as is the room (still labelled) which was used for maturing cheeses. In Cheshire this was usually an attic, but in the Warwickshire area the maturing room was often on the first floor, with another storey above, as was the case here. The cheesemaking room was directly underneath and below that a cellar which may also have been used for maturing. It was almost certainly used for cheese at some point, since it is connected to a nearby pond so that the atmosphere could be kept moist by flooding.

Originally, the Fletchers milked cows, selling the milk direct; in the late 1980s they decided to keep sheep as well, although at first without any thought of making cheese. Milk sales started well but fell off; then a goats'-cheesemaker who supplied the local farmshop gave up and the shop asked them for sheep's cheese instead. Although Stephen did not know how to make cheese, he seems to have a talent for collecting willing helpers: first, he found Sally, a trained cheesemaker, who produced a cheese based on a Caerphilly recipe; then his mother took a short cheesemaking course. Soon afterwards, they were joined by Tessa, who is now Stephen's wife. When Sally left, Tessa took over, and now makes Berkswell with a full-time and several part-time assistants. In summer, when there is plenty of milk, Stephen's mother also sometimes makes soft cheese (which is sold only locally).

For some time, the Fletchers continued to keep both cows and sheep: however, the cows were sold two years ago. At the time of my visit, they had 250 Frieslands, who took three hours twice a day to milk; by now, there will be 350. The cheese is made two or three times a week to a recipe which no longer bears any significant resemblance to Caerphilly, but involves cutting and working the curd and then scalding it and allowing it to free-drain. The cheeses are finished with cheese-paint to ensure that they have firm but thin rinds; the maturing time is four to eight months.

BERKSWELL

Gold Medal, British Cheese Awards 1994 and 1995; Bronze Medal, 1997
A hard sheep's cheese; unpasteurized milk; vegetarian rennet.
3–4kg/6lb 10oz–8lb 13oz baskets

At eight months, Berkswell is close-textured, silky and yet slightly crystalline, and as hard as a mature pecorino; however, instead of being salty and smoky, it is full, rich, and sweet, with exceptional power and layers of taste which unfold on the tongue by degrees. The flavours are unmistakably of the rich grass and herbage of Middle England: eating it seems almost like eating distilled meadow. It is wonderful on the cheeseboard and for sprinkling. In particular, its sweetness brings out the flavour of sweet vegetables.

Spaghetti with Berkswell, Basil, and Courgettes

Cooking time: under 30 minutes
For 2

400g/14oz medium to small courgettes, washed and trimmed
fine salt
250g/9oz fresh or dried spaghetti
1 small clove garlic, peeled and roughly chopped
about 24 basil leaves, washed and dried
$2^1/_2$ tbsp oil
pepper
2 large cloves garlic, washed and finely chopped
25g/1oz pine-nuts
70g/$2^1/_2$oz 8-month-old Berkswell, finely grated

Cut the courgettes into slices about 8mm/$^1/_3$ inch thick, sprinkle with salt, and leave them to sweat for 20 minutes. Rinse and blot them dry.

Set a large pan of water to boil for the spaghetti. Start cooking dried pasta if you are using it: when the water is boiling vigorously, add a little salt (about 1 teaspoonful per litre/$1^3/_4$ pint) and the pasta, bring back to the boil, and stir. Cook for the shortest time given on the packet.

Crush the small clove of garlic in a mortar. Roughly chop, add, and crush the basil; moisten the paste with about a $^1/_2$ tablespoonful of oil.

If you are using fresh pasta, start cooking it, which takes about 5 minutes, and warm the rest of the oil over medium to high heat in a large frying pan. With dried spaghetti, heat the oil 5 minutes before you think the pasta will be ready. Add the courgettes to the oil, season lightly with pepper, and fry until they begin to change colour. Add the garlic and fry, turning constantly, until the garlic and courgettes are a light gold. Add the nuts, stir-fry for a few seconds, and remove from the heat. Stir in the garlic and basil paste.

Drain the pasta as soon as it is *al dente*. Toss with half the cheese. Serve with the basil, courgettes, and the rest of the cheese on top.

MARLOW

A fresh sheep's cheese; unpasteurized milk; vegetarian rennet.
225–450g/8oz–1lb; basket-shaped

Marlow has a moist but notably light, frothy texture and a mild, sweet taste. The top half of the cheese is lightly coloured with annatto, which gives its sweetness a mellow quality and contrasts with the fresher tasting, uncoloured cheese underneath. It goes particularly well with low-sugar digestive biscuits.

 # *Innes*

STELLA BENNET, HIGHFIELDS, CLIFTON LANE, STATFOLD, TAMWORTH, STAFFS B79 0AQ. TEL: 01827 830197

Innes became famous in 1994 when it won the Supreme Championship at the first British Cheese Awards. It was started by Hugh Lillingston, heir to Thorpe Park, as part of his strategy to make enough money for the upkeep of the house; having launched Innes cheeses, he went on to found a partner venture in the form of a bakery. Some of the bread, like the cheese, was made in Staffordshire, but he also had a large bakery under London Bridge Station, where, looking faintly incongruous with his white baker's coat covering a velvet jacket and handmade shoes, he told me that his original ambition was to be a musician (he was sacked from Eton because of the time he spent playing with rock groups). Music is still very important to him: hence his experiments with it on his goats, whom he found give ten per cent more milk if they are entertained by Mozart on rainy afternoons.

He originally chose goats because he rented Highfields from his father 'on the usual terms – no favours' and did not have enough land for cows or sheep. He went to Angoulême to study cheesemaking but never made the cheese himself commercially because, apart from his other commitments, he feels that he is too impatient. To make good cheese, he says, you need a passive, quiet temperament so that you can fill in the intervals while the curd sets or the acidity rises with thought. Instead, he found a local cheesemaker, Stella Bennet, who has made it ever since. When Hugh withdrew, she bought the business herself, and now carries it on independently.

The particular quality of the cheese is due partly to her almost obsessive concern for hygiene, to the fact that the milk is used literally within twenty minutes of leaving the udder, and her extraordinarily light touch. The goats are part-organically reared, since the Highfields land is organic, but they are given non-organic concentrates. The freshness of the milk is assured by the fact that either the cheese is made twice a day or the afternoon's milking is sold in liquid form. Before he sold out, Hugh's plans included branching out into yoghurt. At the time of writing, Stella was not yet sure whether she will follow this through: for the moment, she is simply concerned to maintain the quality of the cheese.

INNES CURD CHEESE

A soft goats' curd cheese; full-fat, unpasteurized milk; vegetarian rennet.
175g/6oz pots or 1.8kg/4lb tubs

As with all the Innes cheeses, the texture is so light and delicate that it floats down the throat like air. The taste is similarly delicate, with the sweetness of the absolutely fresh milk and virtually no hint of goat. The version I tried was flavoured with garlic and chives but, as with the Button, the sweetness of the cheese means that the plain version would go excellently with fruit.

INNES BUTTON

Gold Medal and Supreme Champion, British Cheese Awards 1994;
Bronze Medal, 1996
A fresh goats' cheese; full-fat, unpasteurized milk; vegetarian rennet.
40g/1¹/₂oz buttons or 170g/6oz rounds

This is the lightest and most soufflé-like cheese that I have ever tried, except possibly the Crundwells' fresh sheep's cheeses (page 55). To enjoy it at its lightest, buy and eat it as soon as possible after it has been made. Like the curd cheese (above), the flavour is very mild, with the sweetness of fresh milk: some of the cheeses are rolled in flavourings, including ginger, caraway seeds, and peppercorns.

Grilled Innes Button with Cherries in Brandy

This can also be made with peaches. The fruit benefits from being soaked in the brandy overnight.

Grilling time: 4–5 minutes
For 2

75g/2³/₄oz red or black cherries, washed, dried, halved, and stoned
or 1 large peach, sliced
1 tbsp brandy
1 tbsp demerara sugar (for cherries) *or* caster sugar (for peach)
4 tbsp double cream
2 Innes Buttons

If possible, soak the fruit in the brandy and sugar overnight; beat together the cream and cheese. Place the fruit, cut-side up, in two individual ramekins or similar ovenproof dishes, pour the juices over them, and cover with the cheese mixture. Place under a hot grill for 4–5 minutes, or until lightly browned. Serve at once.

INNES LOG

A goats' cheese with an ash coating covered with a white mould rind; full-fat, unpasteurized milk; vegetarian rennet. 175g/6oz log

Like the other Innes cheeses, the log has an exceptionally fine, light texture. It tastes mild and sweet, with flavours of nuts and mushrooms and virtually no trace of goat. It is delicious toasted, when the nutty flavour is intensified and it melts to a creamy consistency.

BOSWORTH AND CLIFTON LEAF

White mould rind, Camembert-style goats' cheeses; full-fat, unpasteurized milk; vegetarian rennet. Bosworth, 150g/5¹/₄oz rounds; Clifton Leaf, 70g/2¹/₂oz rounds

The cheeses flow slightly; the taste is mild and sweet, with overtones of mushrooms and nuts, as before. The leaf, which is sweet chestnut, emphasizes the sweet, nutty flavour.

Colston Bassett and District Dairy

RICHARD ROWLETT, COLSTON BASSETT AND DISTRICT DAIRY,
HARBY LANE, COLSTON BASSETT, NOTTINGHAMSHIRE NG12
3FN. TEL: 01949 81322

The country around Colston Bassett is very open, predominantly flat, but punctuated at intervals with small hills or wolds. You pass woods, but I did not notice a single ploughed field: the entire area seems to be grazing, which perhaps is as one would expect in a region famous for cheese for two and a half centuries. As with other cheeses, the distinctive taste of Stilton is associated with a particular type of soil: the most northerly Stilton dairy is at Hartington, near Matlock in Derbyshire, and those furthest south at Melton Mowbray, Leicestershire.

No farmhouse Stilton has been made since before the war; Colston Bassett, however, is the smallest of the creameries. Colston Bassett itself is a village in the proper sense of the word, with an old-fashioned post office-cum-shop and large church, designed to accommodate all the families on the surrounding farms. The creamery is professional and workmanlike, with a small shop, which was empty on the day of my visit but, as I was assured, becomes extremely busy in the autumn, when people are stocking up on Stilton for Christmas.

I went just before Ernest Wagstaff retired after being the manager for thirty-five years (the creamery has only had one other manager since it was founded in 1920). Two relatively recent changes introduced during his time were pasteurization and the use of the genetically engineered rennet, Chymosin. Remarkably, he held out against pasteurization until the listeria scare six or seven years ago: with only memory to serve as a comparison, I cannot judge its effect on the cheese. Chymosin is used at present only for Shropshire Blue, which Ernest feels that it positively improves, and a few Stiltons produced for vegetarians. When I tried two Stiltons of nearly the same age, one made with Chymosin and the other with traditional rennet, I marginally preferred the Chymosin version, which I thought had a creamier taste; however, the difference could have been due to other factors, such as the weather. According to Ernest, Stilton is especially sensitive to weather, or more particularly, humidity: 'Anybody can make Stilton cheese in September when it is dry outside.'

COLSTON BASSETT STILTON

Gold Medal, British Cheese Awards 1996; Silver Medal, 1997
A blue cows' cheese; full-fat, pasteurized milk; vegetarian and traditional rennet.
2.3kg/5lb cylinders and 7.2kg/16lb

The texture is creamy but not so moist as to be semi-soft, the blue deep and powerful, and (despite pasteurization) the cheese itself distinctive, with a strong herbal, almost spicy flavour: the herbal flavour lingers on the tongue as an aromatic aftertaste. As well as being a splendid cheese for the table, it keeps its flavour perfectly when heated and is exceptionally adaptable for cooking. It also freezes perfectly.

The milk comes from five farms in the district and is left to stand for twenty-four hours before pasteurization. Starter and *Penicillium roqueforti* are added when it has cooled to 30°C/86°F; after renneting, the curd is left to set for seventy minutes before being cut and left to settle for a further three hours. Whey is then drawn from the top of the vat and the curd ladled into cooling trays by hand – by hand because Ernest, like others, is emphatic about the importance of disturbing it as little as possible. It remains in the trays until the next morning; milling, salting, and moulding in tall moulds lined with 'bits' (cloths) at the bottom follow. For the next five days, it is turned and the 'bits' are renewed daily, after which the sides of the cheeses are smoothed by hand and left to dry further, with turning every day, for another three weeks: at this stage, the smoothed cheeses are deep butter-yellow, with a skin which looks like a thick coat of paint, and still contain sixteen per cent more moisture (which is needed by the mould) than after they have matured. Piercing to supply the mould with extra air, which is repeated once and if necessary twice, is carried out at five to seven weeks, depending on acidity level; thereafter, the cheeses become covered with a film of calcium, which is drawn out as the pH rises and causes them to become progressively softer and creamier. Subsequently, they develop a crusty, almost rocky-looking brownish-gold rind. The maturing time is twelve weeks from when they are made: before being sent out, every cheese is ironed, i.e. a small piece is removed from the middle, to test for quality. Shropshire Blue is made in exactly the same way but with vegetarian rennet only and annatto, which gives it a deep marigold colour and mellower, slightly earthy flavour.

Stilton Mashed Potato

You might not think of serving mashed potato as a first course, but the following is quite interesting enough to stand on its own. It can be prepared ahead of time.

Cooking times: 1 hour for the potato; 20 minutes to brown
For 3–4

450g/1lb baking potato or potatoes, e.g. Estima, Cara, King Edward
1 tbsp red wine vinegar
2 generous tbsp low-fat fromage frais
$1^1/_2$ tsp Dijon mustard
salt and pepper
140–150g/5–5$^1/_4$oz Colston Bassett Stilton, crumbled or finely grated
watercress or chicory to garnish

Pre-heat the oven to 200°C/400°F/Gas 6. Wash the potatoes if they are muddy, prick them as a precaution against bursting, and bake for 1 hour, until they are soft all the way through. (Baking, although it takes longer, gives a lighter, drier result than boiling.) Halve and scoop out the flesh while the potato is still warm. Add the vinegar, fromage frais, mustard, about $^1/_3$ teaspoonful of salt, and a generous grinding of pepper, and mash the potato thoroughly; finally, mash in 100g/3$^1/_2$oz of the Stilton.

If the dish is prepared ahead of time, allow it to cool before chilling it; when needed, reset the oven to 200°C/400°F/Gas 6. Transfer the potatoes to individual ramekins or similar ovenware dishes and sprinkle the rest of the Stilton on top. Bake for 20 minutes or until brown. Serve surrounded with watercress or chicory.

Staffordshire Organic

Betty, Michael and David Deaville, New House Farm, Acton, Newcastle-under-Lyme, Staffs, ST5 4EE. Tel: 01782 680366

Acton is about 5km/3 miles to the west of the M6; directly opposite on the other side of the motorway are Newcastle-under-Lyme and Stoke-on-Trent. The motorway is effectually a green-belt boundary: Acton is small and rural, although prosperous and obviously a dormitory village, and New House Farm is surrounded by hills and woods. So far as I was concerned, the farm marked another boundary: Ulceby Grange in Lincolnshire (page 192) is in fact further north, but New House was the last I visited in England where a Cheddar-style cheese is made: after this, open-textured cheeses such as Cheshire, Lancashire, and Wensleydale prevail until one reaches Scotland.

When Betty married Michael, he did not farm organically but kept a dairy herd; he sold it soon afterwards, preferring to concentrate on meat, but kept a few 'house cows' for their own use. Some years later, when they became interested in converting to organic, Betty began to experiment with cheese as an added-value product, using milk from the house cows; never having made it before, she taught herself from books and did not attempt commercial production for some time. In 1984, however, they bought more cows, bringing the total to a dozen, and she went into business in a small way. The next year, they doubled the number of cows; in the third year, they started buying in milk and thereafter, like many others, gave up the herd in favour of the cheese. After a time David, who had been studying music, finished his course and joined them: he turned out to be a first-class cheesemaker and now, eight years later, has entirely taken over, leaving his mother to grow the herbs for the cheese and run their farmshop where, besides the hard cheese, they sell their own curd and cottage cheeses, delicious eggs (which are not registered as organic), meat, including occasional Gloucester Old Spot pork, and a range of organic wines.

The cheese is made once or twice a week with milk from an organic Friesian herd at Oswestry; the entire process is carried out by hand, which accounts for the fine, delicate texture of the cheese, but is extremely hard work. David said that if he made it every day, he would need an assistant.

At the time of my visit, he had just been offered a supply of organic sheep's milk: and was planning a weekend with James Aldridge to decidewhat sort of cheese to make with it: as a result, he is now producing one of the very few hard organic sheep's cheeses made in Britain and Ireland (others are Duddleswell and Orla: pages 42 and 141).

STAFFORDSHIRE ORGANIC

Bronze Medal, British Cheese Awards 1997
An organic cows' cheese; full-fat, unpasteurized milk; vegetarian rennet. 1.4kg/3lb,
9kg/20lb and 18kg/40lb truckles

The cheese is distinguished by its fine-grained, velvet-like texture: at three months, when it is still fairly moist, it is mild and sweet, tasting of butter and a wide range of herbage, with a soft, fairly discrete tang; at six months the tang is more developed. At either age, it is an outstanding all-purpose table cheese, just as good for a quick lunch as on the cheeseboard.

As well as plain, it is made flavoured with wild garlic, chives, or apple-mint grown by Betty, or mixed dried organic herbs. Usually, I find that I prefer the plain version of a really good cheese such as this, but the flavourings are so beautifully balanced and suit the cheese so well that I can heartily recommend them all: particularly good are the mixed herbs and apple-mint (apple-mint is softer and sweeter than the usual spearmint). A smoked version, which is similarly smoked just enough to bring out the natural flavours of the cheese, is also available.

After adding starter and rennet, David cuts the curd to the size of peas and stirs and scalds it over thirty minutes to 40°C/104°F, or a few degrees lower in winter, when the cows are living on dried fodder and the curd is correspondingly drier. Stirring continues for another fifteen minutes before pitching (leaving to rest) and draining; blocking and piling follow. For this, David cuts the curd first into 25-cm/10-inch squares, then into 5-cm/2-inch strips which he piles eight or ten times: this takes about two hours. Salt is added during the final piling: he uses relatively little because his aim is only to bring out the natural flavours in the cheese rather than produce a salty tang. The curd is then put through a fine mill, moulded, and pressed at increasing pressure overnight, after which it is capped in muslin and pressed overnight again. On the third day the cheeses are wrapped entirely in muslin and left at 12–14°C/54–57°F for two weeks; finally they are moved to a cooler store and matured for a further three to six months.

STAFFORDSHIRE ORGANIC SHEEP'S CHEESE

A hard sheep's cheese; unpasteurized organic milk; vegetarian rennet.
About 1.8kg/4lb truckles

The cheese I tried just before going to press was experimental and may not have been typical of it as it is now; however, it was superb, and a particularly clear example of the superior qualities of organic milk. It had a deliciously gritty, slightly crystalline texture and combined a strong tang with the unmistakable flavour of grass and flowers. Like Orla (page 00), it was excellent for grating, although the taste is lighter and sunnier; it was also effective as a flavouring for sauce.

Lincolnshire Poacher

SIMON AND JEANETTE JONES, ULCEBY GRANGE, ALFORD,
LINCOLNSHIRE LN13 0HE. TEL: 01507 462407

Lincolnshire Poacher is remarkable for several reasons: besides winning the Supreme Championship at the 1996 British Cheese Awards, it is the only cheese made in Lincolnshire, part of which is fen and most of which, like the counties further south, is arable – and in fact, milk production at Ulceby is partnered by a large arable acreage. The farm, however, is at the southern tip of the Lincolnshire Wolds, where the country is undulating rather than flat and the soil lies over chalk, yielding milk with an enviable range of flavours; less satisfactory for dairying purposes is the low rainfall, which means that the grass tends to dry out in the summer. Simon counters this by reversing the usual pattern and making cheese throughout the winter instead of the summer: from June to September, when relatively little milk is produced, he sells it directly to Milk Marque. As was pointed out by his father, who used to sell all the milk in liquid form, a reduced yield in summer is economically advantageous because milk prices are then at their highest.

Another interesting feature of the cheese is that Simon was taught to make it by the late Dougal Campbell, which means that it is in effect the sibling of T'yn Grug (now discontinued). To start with, Simon spent a week at Dougal's farm in Wales; later, Dougal came to make cheese with him at Ulceby. In between, he continued to act as Simon's mentor: 'He was always at the end of the telephone. It was really Dougal who inspired us and got us going.' As well as commitment to cheese, Simon shared Dougal's belief in organic farming: at present, he has converted only 9.6ha/24 acres, but plans to extend the area by degrees, which means that the taste of the cheese may become even better.

Everything except the initial cutting of the curd is carried out by hand: Simon works with a full-time cheesemaker, Richard Tagg, an assistant who comes three days a week, and Jeanette, who makes cheese on Mondays. The cheese is made four days a week: Wednesday is given over to preparing the cheeses for sale, which involves scrubbing off the mould – a pity from an aesthetic point of view, since it grows in the most artistic black and white patterns.

LINCOLNSHIRE POACHER

Gold Medal and Supreme Champion, British Cheese Awards 1996; Gold Medal, 1997
A Cheddar-style cows' cheese; full-fat, unpasteurized milk; vegetarian and traditional rennet. 2.3kg/5lb 'Babies' and 18kg/40lb truckles

A full-sized, eleven-month-old Poacher (the small ones mature more quickly) and a two-year-old Vintage Poacher are almost different cheeses. In the younger, the taste of milk and herbage is still very much to the fore, balanced but not overwhelmed by a sweet, clean tang; the older has a much more pronounced tang, but the milky flavour is overlaid. I took away a year-old 'Baby', unironed and chosen by me solely for its mould pattern. If the cheese which won the Championship was like this one – well, it deserved its success. It was not only a beautiful cheese, but had that indescribable soft, earthy overtone which sometimes characterizes matured cheeses and, I think, makes them exceptional. It made us happy for several weeks: I still mourn its passing.

The evening and morning milk, which is used while still warm from the udder, are mixed, starter is added, and the milk is left to ripen for an hour before renneting. When the curd has set, it is cut to the size of baked beans over fifteen minutes: this is followed by scalding to 40°C/104°F and stirring for one and a half to two hours, 'until the curd is springy and squeaks between the teeth'. After pitching (leaving it to rest) and draining, the curd is blocked and piled three times at half-hourly intervals; it is then simultaneously milled and salted. The salt is rubbed in three times, which is the hardest part of the whole process and demands a team of three. This is followed by moulding, pressing for over forty-eight hours, and finally coating the cheeses with a plastic cheese coating, which protects them until they have grown their own firm rind. The maturing time is eleven to twelve months for ordinary Poachers, and up to two years for the Vintage cheeses.

The North of England

Kirkhams Lancashire

JOHN AND RUTH KIRKHAM, BEESLEY FARM, GOOSNARGH, PRESTON, LANCASHIRE. TEL: 01772 865335

There are some who maintain that plants need to be loved, even talked to, if they are to flourish: Ruth Kirkham loves her cheeses, along with her cows and the plants in the meadows where they graze. John sells the bullocks for beef but she has never been persuaded to eat any of them. Occasionally, to enhance the taste of the cheese, she goes out to plant extra meadowsweet; she also encourages dandelions and clover (rather than daisies, which she does not think add to flavour).

The country round Goosnargh is green and lush, not picturesque but surprisingly unspoilt, given that it is only about 6km/4 miles out of Preston and less than 3km/2 miles from the motorway. Beesley Farm is by no means as large as the fame of the cheese might lead one to expect: unlike the Applebys (page 178) or the large Cheddar-makers in the south, the Kirkhams have a modest herd of thirty-eight Friesians, who supply all their milk and, apart from the calves, are the only livestock they now keep. In today's economic climate, only the cheeses enables them to survive. They employ no help: John looks after the cows and Ruth makes the cheese in a tiny but immaculately clean dairy. Every day, seven days a week, Christmas Day included, she processes an average of 450 litres/100 gallons of milk, yielding 52kg/114lb of cheese, which works out at two large cheeses and two small.

The storeroom smells of cheese and meadowsweet. As is often the case with Kirkham's Lancashire, all the mature cheeses were sold at the time of my visit, but I bought an 11kg/24lb, ten-week-old one to give to a relative in Shropshire as a wedding present. Having nowhere to mature it myself, I took it straight to his house, which has a large cellar. He stored it in a basket, and manfully turned it twice a week until, nearly three months later, it was cut and served at the wedding reception. Even amateur maturing had not spoilt it: it was superb.

KIRKHAM'S LANCASHIRE

Gold Medal and Supreme Champion, British Cheese Awards 1995; Gold Medal, 1996 and 1997
A semi-hard cows' cheese; full-fat, unpasteurized milk; traditional and vegetarian rennet. 1.4kg/3lb, 1.8kg/4lb, 2.7kg/6lb, 11kg/24lb, and 20.3kg/45lb truckles

Traditional Lancashire, known for its pale colour, crumbly texture, and excellent toasting properties, is made partly or entirely with curds that have been prepared one or more days previously: partly because of the crumbly result, this method of production has never been adopted by creameries, so that mass-produced Lancashire bears virtually no relation to the farmhouse original. The texture of Ruth Kirkham's is melting and delicate as well as crumbly; the taste is mild, flowery, and above all buttery, with no hint of sharpness or acidity. It is wonderful toasted or added to the pastry cream underneath the apples on a tart, or, as Ruth suggests, slipped under the lid of an apple pie.

She makes her Lancashire in exactly the same way as her mother and grand-mother before her, using curd made on the previous two days. The first part of the morning's work is to prepare that day's curd. The morning and evening milk are mixed, heated to 29.5°C/85°F, and a very little cultured starter and rennet added. When the curd has set, after about an hour, it is cut into cubes and left to stand for another hour; the whey is then drained off and the curd scooped into a drainer lined with a cloth, where it is crumbled by hand three times, with half an hour between each session. This completes its preparation: it is then covered and set aside until the next day, when some of it is added to the previous day's curd.

The rest of the cheesemaking process is straightforward. The mixed two- and three-day-old curds are milled and salted, with sea-salt when available (the Kirkhams have difficulty in buying large amounts). At this stage, the curd is a mass of little white bobbles which already taste deliciously of cheese. Moulding and pressing follow; halfway through the pressing, the cheeses are covered in muslin with a drawstring top. Two or three days later, when the rinds are dry enough, they are sealed by rubbing them with melted butter. The maturing time is usually four to six months, although Neal's Yard Dairy sometimes keep them for up to eight.

J. J. Sandham Ltd

CHRIS SANDHAM, ROSTOCK DAIRY, GARSTANG ROAD, BARTON, PRESTON, LANCS PR3 5AA. TEL: 01995 640247

Rostock Dairy is about 6km/4 miles from Beesley Farm (page 195) and Park Head at Inglewhite (page 199). As you realize as soon as you leave the main roads, this is the main dairying area of the north-west: both Beesley and Park Head are impossible to find without foolproof directions because the entire landscape is chequered with dairy farms (even with directions, I went to several before finding the right ones). Several generations ago, the Sandham family were farmers, and almost certainly made cheese; however, the present dairy was founded by Chris's grandparents in 1930, using milk produced on farms nearby. As the Milk Marketing Board had not yet been formed, the milk was brought by private contract which, because the quantities were inflexible, led on occasion to over-production: Chris described how surplus cheeses were piled two deep at the sides of the staircase in the house and, when the staircase was fully stacked, in the sitting room; finally, if sales did not catch up with supply before they became too mature to keep, they were buried in the field at the back.

Chris continues the family tradition, using milk delivered by Milk Marque from farms within a 1.6-km/1-mile radius. As he does not produce the milk himself, he pasteurizes; apart from this and the use of vegetarian rennet, he uses the same recipe as his grandparents. It is not unlike Ruth Kirkham's but differs in three important respects: the curd is only two- rather than three-day, the cheeses are matured in wax, and the maturing times are four to five weeks for the mild or about fourteen for the 'Tasty' version.

SANDHAM'S LANCASHIRE

A semi-hard cow's cheese; wax rind; full-fat, pasteurized milk; vegetarian rennet.
450g/1lb, 1kg/2lb 4oz, 6.3kg/14lb, 9.9–10.4kg/22–23lb, and 18kg/40lb truckles

The mild version is very moist, with a fairly smooth, soft, creamy texture, to the point that it is almost semi-soft: the taste is warm and mellow but with a slight peppery tang which develops in the mouth and leaves a gentle after-taste. 'Tasty' is drier and crumblier, with a more noticeable tang, although it is still warm and mellow rather than sharp. It melts smoothly and is delicious toasted, when its sweetness intensifies but the tang disappears: add a little crushed rather than ground pepper.

For the curd, the milk is 'flash' pasteurized (72°C/162°F for fifteen seconds), a traditional starter made and cultured at the dairy added, and the milk allowed to stand for 'as long as is needed', which is usually about fifteen minutes; rennet is stirred in for another fifteen minutes, and the curd is left to set for about fifty minutes. When sufficiently formed, the curd is cut to the size of baked beans, stirred and rested briefly, and drained; Chris and his assistants then divide it into two and break it by hand in six sessions at twenty-minute intervals. The half for use the next day is set aside and kept at 21°C/70°F: this dries it slightly and protects it from off-flavours. The half for immediate use is mixed with the previous day's curd, milled and salted, milled again, and moulded, after which it is pressed at increasing pressure for twenty-four hours (sudden strong pressure would cause uneven moisture distribution). Next day, the cheeses are turned out, bound in muslin, and briefly pressed again; finally they are dried in a drying room and waxed. All are turned daily during the maturing period, including the 'Tasties', which are kept for fourteen weeks.

As well as his regular Lancashire, Chris makes an organic version from Jersey milk and 'Crumbly', a quickly produced variation which is enormously popular: I had the impression that he did not expect me to like it, but I found it pleasantly mild and refreshing. The Jersey cheese, which he introduced last autumn, is made by the same method as his other Lancashires; for Crumbly, he uses a relatively enormous amount of starter, adds rennet and cuts the curd as before, and breaks it twice. It is then left at 21°C/70°F overnight; thereafter, it is milled and salted, pressed, and finally bound and waxed for consumption within twelve days.

Carron Lodge

ADRIAN RHODES, PARK HEAD FARM, CARRON LODGE,
INGLEWHITE, LANCS TEL: 01995 640352

As he himself admitted, Adrian could talk about cheese for days on end; however, the two points he emphasized in a shorter space of time were that his first priority is the quality of the milk and his second pleasing his customers, which he puts far above selling to prestigious shops or even winning at shows (although he has so many award certificates, kept in a large box, that finding the ones for the British Cheese Awards proved to be impossible).

Milk quality is taken care of by his herd of 250 elegant, high-yielding Friesian–Holsteins, built up and cherished by his father over the years. Pleasing his customers has led him into wholesaling as well as making cheese: in consequence, his storerooms are a wonderland of cheeses of every kind, ranging from his own double-curd Lancashires to Ribblesdale (page 202), imported smoked Brie, Wensleydale with blackberries, and a striped composition of cheeses of different kinds: 'very useful when people can't make up their minds which to choose'. Altogether, he makes fourteen different kinds, including several variations of Lancashire, Wensleydale, Sage Derby, Caerphilly, and a Cheshire which won the Championship at the Cheshire Show despite not being made within the prescribed area.

He is not sure how far cheese goes back in his family but his great-grandmother, grandmother, and mother all made it; nor is he the only only member of the family to keep up the tradition, since the Singletons, also well-known makers of Lancashire, are relations. Initially, he tried to avoid cheese by going to university, and subsequently tried to strike out in a new direction by taking courses in ice-cream and soft cheesemaking; however, instinct prevailed. He started his present business eleven years ago and was spectacularly successful right from the start. A helpful factor was that his father managed the farm and cows, leaving him free to concentrate on the cheese, until he retired three years ago and sold the farm to Adrian – for a fair price: muttering that he does not believe in inheritance, Adrian stressed that he did not take it on special terms but bought it just like anyone else.

The Lancashire is made according to the family recipe, which he preferred not to divulge; however, as he observed, its quality is due to many factors, including the cows, the rich, mixed soil on which the farm is situated, and in particular the fact that the cheese is not hurried. The total cheesemaking process is spread over five to six days: 'We take longer than anyone else. It is a low-acid cheese with a steady build-up which can't be rushed – that's what gives it its rich, creamy texture.'

CARRON LODGE LANCASHIRE

Gold Medal, British Cheese Awards 1994
A semi-hard cows' cheese (natural rind); full-fat, unpasteurized milk; vegetarian
rennet. 450g/1lb, 900g/2lb, and 10kg/22lb truckles; also 20kg/44lb 'Traditionals'

The cheese has a soft, light, nutty texture; the taste, like Sandham's, develops in the mouth. To start with, it seems innocuously mellow and mild, but as you eat it becomes full, fruity, and complex, with earthy undertones and quite a pronounced peppery tang. The overall effect is not exactly strong but vigorous and robust. It is totally different from Kirkham's but just as delicious in a more muscular way: it is a pity that it is not more widely available in the south.

MRS RHODES' FARMHOUSE TOASTER

A hard cows' cheese; full-fat, pasteurized milk; vegetarian rennet.
20kg/44lb 'Traditionals'

You could say that this is the opposite of Chris Sandham's 'Crumbly' (page 198). 'Toaster' originated with cheese which was over-mature and had developed a strong, sharp tang: to start with, it was sold at a discount, but, perhaps because a little went a long way, soon became popular in its own right. Adrian has revived an old recipe: raw, the cheese has an earthy rather than acidic tang; heated, it becomes much sweeter but retains a strong distinctive flavour.

Ribblesdale Cheesemakers

CHRIS AND IAIN HILL, ASHES FARM, HORTON-IN-RIBBLESDALE,
SETTLE, NORTH YORKSHIRE. TEL: 01729 860231

Ashes Farm is high up in the Dales, an oasis of trees and (in August) flowers on the bare moors, with a skyline of hills rising from the Ribble valley in both directions. It is small and in parts very old: the back of the farmhouse, where a hard buttermilk cheese called Old Whangby was once made, dates from about 1660. The rooms are still used for cheese by the Hills, but because of lack of space and the situation of the farm in the Dales National Park, which means that further building is prohibited, the actual making is now carried out further down the Ribble, at Longridge, near Preston (in fact, it is quite near the Kirkhams: page 195). However, every single cheese is sent to the farmhouse for inspection, waxing, and maturing before sale.

Iain is an engineer, and has also worked in retailing, which he found intensely dispiriting but is useful to him now. Cheesemaking was a hobby, which he would almost certainly never have developed further had it not been for one of his sons, force of need, and Chris. The son announced that he wanted to go into farming and make cheese: as part of setting him up, Iain invested in a herd of 300 goats. The son then changed his plans, leaving the goats and the disposal of the milk to Iain (who, until then, had been planning to retire). Iain first tried to sell the milk in liquid form, but because of competition succeeded only in the winter, when many of the rival herds were dry. Next, he tried yoghurt, but found himself delivering absurdly small orders enormous distances. The situation became so serious that 'we were down to only one car' (which if you live in a place like this has more meaning than to the rest of us). By then, however, he had married Chris, who is a cheese-maker: as they were warned that, again because of competition, very mild goats' cheese would be difficult to sell, she invented the recipe for Ribblesdale Original, which is relatively strong but with a smoky tang rather than the flavour of goat. This was followed by Ribblesdale Superior, plus smoked versions of both. To start with, Iain's other son, Adrian, smoked them himself over a mixture of oak and beech; although Adrian is no longer involved, the same mixture is still used. Iain's contributions are Ribblesdale Original Dairy Cheese, based on a Wensleydale recipe, and a buffalo cheese.

Part of the reason for the distinctive character of the goats' cheeses is the starter, which, like the rest of the recipe, is Chris's own; special care is also taken over applying the wax rinds with which they are coated. A crucial point about waxing is the moisture content of the cheese: traditionally, this was judged by placing the cheese on absorbent paper to see how much liquid was released. The goats' milk comes from St Helen's Farm in Yorkshire, the cows' from the Longridge area, and the buffalo milk from Warwickshire.

RIBBLESDALE ORIGINAL GOAT CHEESE

Bronze Medal, British Cheese Awards 1996
A hard goats' cheese; yellow wax rind; full-fat, pasteurized milk; vegetarian rennet.
1.8kg/4lb wheels

Ribblesdale Original has a hard, dryish, slightly grained texture; the taste is of smoke and peat, with a tang which makes it almost the goat equivalent of matured pecorino. The taste of goat is scarcely noticeable as such but adds to the strength of flavour. Altogether it is an interesting, punchy, and different cheese – very much an original. The smoked version is also very successful, chiefly because the taste, which is delicate and slightly charcoal-like, echoes the natural smokiness of the cheese.

RIBBLESDALE SUPERIOR GOAT CHEESE

A hard but moist goats' cheese; yellow wax rind; full-fat, pasteurized milk; vegetarian rennet. 1kg/2lb 4oz half-wheels or 2kg/4lb 6oz wheels

The Superior Goat has a notably smooth, soft, creamy texture; it is much milder than the Original, with (given pasteurization) a surprisingly wide range of herbal flavours. It is delicious with fruit or nut breads, e.g. apricot or hazelnut. The smokiness of the smoked version is more in evidence than with the Original because the cheese itself is milder.

RIBBLESDALE ORIGINAL DAIRY CHEESE

A semi-hard cows' cheese; yellow wax rind; full-fat, pasteurized milk; vegetarian rennet. 2kg/4lb 6oz wheels

The cows' cheese has a very delicate, crumbly texture with a mild, sweet, creamy taste. Like white Wensleydale, its sweetness makes it suitable for cheesecake, apple tart, and similar dishes.

Ribblesdale Lemon Cheesecake

This is as light and luscious as mousse: for the best texture, however, you need a curd cheese sufficiently drained to hold its shape.

Cooking time: 7–8 minutes; allow at least 2 hours for setting and chilling
For 6–10

55g/2oz butter, chopped
100g/3^1/$_2$oz low-sugar digestive biscuits, finely crushed
25g/1oz hazelnuts, crushed
^{1}/$_2$ tsp ground ginger
150g/5^1/$_4$oz caster sugar
nutmeg
225g/8oz curd cheese
1 lemon, preferably organic (you need the zest)
125g/4^1/$_2$oz Ribblesdale Original Dairy cheese, finely grated
200ml/7fl oz (^{1}/$_3$ pint) whipping cream
1 tbsp brandy
9g/^{1}/$_3$oz gelatine

Pre-heat the oven to 200°C/400°F/Gas 6. Melt the butter over low heat and mix it with the biscuits, nuts, ginger, 25g/1oz (1 tablespoonful) of the sugar, and a little freshly grated nutmeg. Spread the mixture over the base of a 22-cm/8^1/$_2$-inch tart dish, pack it down firmly, and smooth the surface with the back of a spoon. Crisp the base in the oven for 7–8 minutes, when you should be able to smell the spices. Allow it to cool completely.

Beat the curd cheese and the rest of the sugar until smooth. Wash the lemon and finely grate about half the zest into the cheese mixture; then add 2 tablespoonsful of the juice. Stir in the Ribblesdale.

Put 3 tablespoonsful of the cream and the brandy into a small saucepan and heat almost to boiling. Sprinkle in the gelatine, remove from the heat, and stir until it has dissolved completely. Allow it to cool a little before stirring it very thoroughly into the cheese mixture.

Whip the rest of the cream until it is very stiff and fold it gently into the cheese and gelatine. Spread the mixture evenly over the base and chill for at least 2 hours.

RIBBLESDALE BUFFALO CHEESE

A hard buffalo cheese; white wax rind; full-fat, pasteurized milk; vegetarian rennet.
1.8kg/4lb wheels

I tried two samples of the cheese, at four and eleven months old. The older one was rich and nutty, with a robust, grassy tang; the younger, which I preferred, has a wonderfully light, silky feel and is mild and creamy. It was excellent with fruit bread but would also go well with oatcakes.

Wensleydale Dairy Products Ltd
WENSLEYDALE CREAMERY, GAYLE LANE, HAWES, NORTH
YORKSHIRE DL8 3RN. TEL: 01969 667664

The story of the Creamery is given in more detail in its own brochure than is possible here. In brief, however, it was effectually founded by a corn and cheese merchant called Edward Chapman, who delivered flour and corn to the local farms in return for cheese. Some of the cheese was so badly made that in 1897 he started to take milk instead and made the cheese himself, first in his flour mill, then in a converted woollen mill in Hawes. The creamery came to play a central role in the area, since the farmers at that end of the Dale were assured of an outlet for their milk and housewives, who might not be able to afford meat, could be confident of the quality of the cheese.

The creamery flourished until the Depression of the 1930s, when it ran into debt: it was almost bought by the Milk Marketing Board but was rescued by a farmer called Kit Calvert, who managed it successfully for over thirty years; he also bought up a number of dairies further east, including the original Fountains Dairy. As the time approached for him to retire, the Milk Marketing Board made a second offer and purchased both the dairies; Fountains regained its independence by means of a management takeover in 1987 and Hawes followed suit five years later. It is now not only successful in economic terms but has turned itself into a quite astonishingly popular tourist attraction. Visitors are catered for with a shop, coffee-shop, restaurant, and museum; a video illustrates the cheesemaking process, which can also be watched from a corridor with windows facing into the dairy. On a Saturday in August, the video-room was constantly packed and the windows overlooking the cheesemaking room lined with an audience two or three deep. As at Leon Downey's in Wales (page 151), everyone was enthralled.

The staff at the Creamery have themselves been surprised at the response: originally, they say, they decided to open to the public simply in order to boost confidence in the product. 'People are so worried now about food: we thought that the best way to convince them that the cheese is exactly what it is supposed to be was to let them see it being made for themselves.'

Besides blue and white Wensleydale, the creamery produces flavoured versions of the white (waxed rinds: chives and onion, blueberry, cranberry, apricot, ginger, and fruit and nut), smoked, white cows' and sheep's combined, and small amounts of Red Leicester.

WHITE WENSLEYDALE (TRADITIONAL AND MATURE)

Bronze Medal (Mature), British Cheese Awards 1997
A semi-hard cows' cheese; full-fat, pasteurized milk; vegetarian rennet.
Traditional: waxed rind, 250g/9oz truckles; cloth-bound, 400g/14oz, 500g/1lb 2oz,
900g/2lb, 2kg/4lb 6oz, 4kg/8lb 13oz, 4.5kg/10lb, and 6kg/13lb truckles;
Mature: cloth-bound, 2.5kg/5lb 8oz and 4.5kg/10lb truckles

The Traditional is moist and open-textured, with a very mild, fresh taste; the Mature is light and crumbly, with the sweet flavour which is characteristic of the area.

The milk comes from forty-three farms, all within 16km/10 miles of Hawes, and is pasteurized quickly (72°C/162°F for fifteen seconds). When the milk has cooled, a cultured starter made at the Creamery is added and the milk left to ripen for one and a half hours; after renneting, the curd is left to set for forty to forty-five minutes, to a 'semi-soft junket', and cut to the size of baked beans. This is followed by scalding slightly, stirring until the acidity has reached the desired level, and 'pitching', i.e. leaving the curd to settle. Next, the curds are drained, blocked and moved to the sides of the vat to release further whey; then comes 'cutting and ripping', which is crucial to the texture of the cheese and consists of slicing the curd into small squares with knives. The squares are forked over, salted and milled, moulded, and lightly pressed for twenty-four to seventy-two hours depending on size. Directly after unmoulding, all the cheeses except the smallest size of Traditional are wrapped in muslin, which is stuck to them with flour paste; finally, they are dried and turned daily for four or five days in a drying room. Traditional are matured for four to six weeks, Mature for twelve.

Wensleydale and Whisky Walnut Cake

The Yorkshire custom of eating Wensleydale (blue or white) with fruit cake has been followed up by Hawes with fruit and nut flavoured Wensleydale: I have turned this the other way round by using the cheese in a fruit and nut cake.

Like the cheese, the cake has a light, slightly crumbly texture; for maximum lightness, bake it in a 23-cm/9-inch tin. You can also use the mixture for small cakes.

Cooking time: 35–40 minutes for a large or 20–25 for small cakes

150g/5$\frac{1}{4}$oz butter, softened
200g/7oz caster sugar
2 large free-range eggs
zest of 1 lemon
1 tbsp whisky
150g/5$\frac{1}{4}$oz Traditional or Mature Wensleydale, finely grated
150g/5$\frac{1}{4}$oz walnuts, roughly chopped or crushed
100g/3$\frac{1}{2}$oz raisins
100g/3$\frac{1}{2}$oz sultanas
200g/7oz plain white flour
2 tsp bicarbonate of soda

Cream together the butter and sugar and beat in the eggs; continue to beat until the mixture is homogeneous. Stir in first the lemon zest and whisky, then the cheese, nuts, and fruit. Sift together the flour and bicarbonate of soda, add the sifted ingredients to the mixture, and stir thoroughly.

Pre-heat the oven to 150°C/300°F/Gas 2, butter the cake tin (use cake-papers for small cakes), and bake until the cake turns a deep brown and a knife inserted into the centre comes out clean. The cake is particularly enjoyable while still warm.

BLUE WENSLEYDALE

Silver Medal, British Cheese Awards 1996 and 1997
A blue cows' cheese; full-fat, pasteurized milk; vegetarian rennet. 2kg/4lb 6oz,
4kg/8lb 13oz and 8kg/17lb 10oz truckles

The Blue Wensleydale has a firm, slightly crumbly texture, a soft, sweet, aromatic flavour, and a moderately strong, deep rather than salty blue taste.

The cheese is made by a method about halfway between those used for the white version and Stilton. *Penicillium roqueforti* for the blue is added a little while after the starter; like Stilton, the curds and whey are left undrained for some hours but, unlike Stilton, the cheeses are lightly pressed. Piercing is carried out at about five weeks; the maturing time is four months or more.

WENSLEYDALE EWES' AND COWS' (WHITE)

A semi-hard combined sheep's and cows' cheese; full-fat, pasteurized milk; vegetarian rennet. 500g/1lb 2oz, 2.5kg/5lb 8oz, and 5kg/11lb truckles

The texture is short, open, and slightly crumbly; the taste is mild and flowery, with a soft, lemon-like tang and definite undertone of the moors: a delicious cheese.

Fortmayne Farm Dairy

SUZANNE STIRKE, FORTMAYNE COTTAGE, NEWTON-LE-WILLOWS, BEDALE, NORTH YORKSHIRE DL8 1SL. TEL: 01677 450660

Almost the first thing Suzanne said to me was 'I'd rather be described as a business woman than a cheesemaker. I'm here to make money, I'm not here to make cheese.' That she might choose cheesemaking as her way of making 'just a little' money is natural enough, since she is a farmer's daughter and a farmer's wife; however, she did not start just because the milk was there (which it was not in the usual sense) but because she had already become fascinated by the history and social significance of cheese. This has led her to become a popular speaker, giving lectures locally and appearing from time to time on TV.

She decided to follow up her academic interest by actually making cheese when she realized that Wensleydale was originally made with sheep's milk, which on the face of it suited her because her husband and brother raise sheep. The sheep had never been milked, and the flock did not include the higher-yielding breeds (e.g. Frieslands), but were divided into two groups, one for early lambing from whom the lambs were taken before the mothers were dry. She tried milking some of these, which with the untrained ewes was extremely hard, slow work, and after persisting for two years still found that milking took so long that there was no time left to make the cheese. She therefore abandoned the idea of using the sheep and instead bought milk from the farm next door, where she was (and is) able to take as much as often as she liked. Determined not to let cheesemaking dominate her whole life, she now makes cheese twice a week, using 500 litres/110 gallons of milk at a time. Besides a Wensleydale, which she calls King Richard III (confusingly, in that it is white whereas in Richard's day it would have been blue), she makes two versions of York soft cheese, Yorvik and Jervaulx (Yorvik is the Viking name for York and the site of Jervaulx Abbey is only about 6.5km/4 miles away; the Wensleydale is named after Richard III because he was brought up at Middleham Castle, which is also very near).

KING RICHARD III WENSLEYDALE

A semi-hard cows' cheese; full-fat, unpasteurized milk; vegetarian rennet.
500g/1lb 2oz and 2.3–2.7kg/5–6lb truckles

Like the double-curd Lancashires, this is a cheese truly described by the term 'semi-hard': it is moist, crumbly, and nutty yet creamy in texture, almost like a moist, rich but light cake. The taste is a blend of gentle flavours which includes a distinct hint of the local limestone soil. It steals on you rather than rushes at you: even those with a preference for strong cheeses acknowledge its quiet, low-key appeal.

Suzanne adds rennet an hour after the starter, leaves the milk for another hour to set, and chops the curd coarsely; she then stirs it for fifteen minutes, leaves it to settle for about forty-five, and runs off the whey. Next, she blocks and piles it to assist draining and leaves it to rest again for about half an hour. This is followed by milling, salting, and breaking up the curd by hand before moulding (without cloths). After moulding the cheese for the first time, she washes up the cheesemaking equipment before turning and remoulding them (still without cloths). The next day, she turns and moulds them in cloths; on the third day she turns them again, and on the fourth brines them briefly and wraps them in muslin, using an edible, starch-based glue which inhibits the growth of mould. The usual maturing time is three weeks, but some of the cheeses are made for storing longer: to ensure that they stay moist, Suzanne does not block and pile the curd for these but mills it directly after draining. Similarly, she encourages the development of a harder, 'bloomy' rind by extending brining from a brief dip to two days.

JERVAULX

A soft cows' cheese; full-fat, unpasteurized milk; vegetarian rennet. 450g/1lb rounds

Jervaulx is rich and creamy, with a nutty feel; it tastes of a mixture of herbs, flowers, and the soil. The herbal tones are quite strong, but the overall effect is light, sweet, and very individual. I thought it was delicious. At present, it is available only from the farm or (in cool weather) by post.

The soft cheeses, like the Padmores' (page 75), are made to a traditional recipe which is in effect a version of the Coulommiers method. The curd is left to set for two hours after the addition of rennet, moulded directly, and left to free-drain: whereas the Padmores' cheeses have penicillin rinds, Suzanne coats hers with wax.

YORVIK

A cows' cheese with chives, annatto and a wax rind; full-fat, unpasteurized milk; vegetarian rennet. 450g/1lb rounds

Like York (page 77), the taste is influenced indirectly rather than directly by the addition of herbs and is quite strong; the strip of annattoed curd in the middle adds a mellow overtone. Originally, the annatto in the middle used to be cream, which was turned orange by the acid in the cheese. Like Jervaulx, it is sold only from the farm or by mail order.

Shepherd's Purse

JUDY BELL, LEACHFIELD GRANGE, NEWSHAM, THIRSK,
NORTH YORKSHIRE YO7 4DL. TEL: 01845 587220;
FAX: 01845 587717

In the nine years since Judy went into business, Shepherd's Purse has gone from strength to strength. Aside from the cheeses themselves, there are obvious reasons for its success, one of which is Judy's vigorous and imaginative approach to marketing. The need for it was obvious to her from the beginning, since when she started out, in 1989 (the year of the Festival of Food and Farming in Hyde Park), prejudice against sheep's products was still very marked. When she took her cheeses to shows, 'everything went swimmingly *until* people noticed the pictures of sheep with the cheese – then all at once they would stop and look horrified. They equated it with goat and were convinced that it would be horrible. They thought that they only liked cows' cheese.' The change that has taken place over the last six or seven years she describes as 'incredible', but easier sales have produced other problems, notably how to ensure that her cheeses are properly treated in supermarkets. The policy she has adopted gives pleasure all round. She invites the staff, in parties of not more than fifteen, to come to the dairy and watch the cheese being made, gives them a tasting of all the kinds produced, and inspires them with her own enthusiasm; only the Tesco staff, she says, are fairly well primed because of the efforts of Juliet Harbutt, whose help in this and other ways she very freely acknowledges.

In fact, it was customers' needs which originally pointed her towards cheese. Ever since working at a chemist's before she married, she has believed in holistic medicine rather than drugs; then, when her youngest child went to nursery school, she took a job as receptionist at an osteopath's and was struck by the number of people who are allergic to cows' milk. Initially, she saw sheep's products as mainly for this market, and sold not only cheese but also yoghurt and (as she still does) milk. As her husband is a farmer and was used to managing sheep, raising a milking flock presented no difficulties: she bought forty British Friesland lambs plus eight lactating ewes and spent the summer practising milking the ewes. As she did not know how to make cheese, she used some of the milk to help out her Rhodesian Ridgeback bitch, who had eleven puppies, and froze the rest.

The next summer, like Suzanne Stirke (page 207), she discovered that it is almost impossible for one person alone to milk and make cheese: she therefore froze her entire output until the winter, when the sheep were dry. After taking a cheesemaking course in Devon, she experimented intensively all through the winter, during which, like everyone else, she became hooked; however, still feeling 'in a bit of a fog', she joined a food and drink producers' group called the Yorkshire Pantry, where she met the late Les Lambut, then the cheesemaking director at Fountains Dairy. He gave her three pieces of advice: to revive the original sheep's Wensleydale; to produce a range of cheeses rather than just one; and to go to shows so that she became known and could gauge customers' reactions at first hand.

The range she has developed includes not only white sheep's Wensleydale but two blue cheeses, a sheep's and a cows', which were effectually revivals too, since at that time blue as opposed to white Wensleydale had similarly lapsed: she can thus fairly be said to have reinvented the original Wensleydale (until the end of the last century, Wensleydale was always blue). She also makes a Cheddar-style cheese called Yorkshire Lowlands, feta, and plain and flavoured versions of a fresh sheep's cheese, Olde York. She says that Olde York was often made in the 1920s and '30s, but only for domestic use or local sale because of its perishability: she overcomes this by waxing, which increases its shelf-life from ten days to six weeks. For four or five years she produced her own milk, but partly because of bereavement she dispersed her flock in 1994 and now buys milk from wherever it is available, which in turn has led her to pasteurize. She works with her son and husband, who keeps the accounts, a cheesemaker called Mark whose grandfather used to be the chief cheesemaker at Fountains, and an assistant: in 1996 they processed 4,500 litres/nearly 1,000 gallons of milk a week and have recently won two Gold Medals at the British Cheese Awards.

THE ORIGINAL FARMHOUSE WENSLEYDALE

A semi-hard sheep's cheese; wax rind; pasteurized milk; vegetarian rennet.
250g/9oz and 1.5kg/3lb 5oz rounds

The Original Wensleydale has a moist, flaky, open texture and is very mild; the sweetness of the milk is offset by a gentle, lemon-like tang.

After the addition of starter and rennet, the curd is cut fairly coarsely (sheep's milk tends to dry out if cut finely); it is then stirred and left to settle, the acidity checked, and all but enough of the whey to bring the acidity to the correct level run off. When the right acidity is reached, the curd is milled and salted, moulded, and lightly pressed overnight. The maturing time for most of the cheeses is two months, but a longer-matured version is also made which is constantly turned rather than pressed.

YORKSHIRE BLUE (COWS')

Bronze Medal, British Cheese Awards 1996 and 1997
A soft cows' cheese; full-fat, pasteurized milk; vegetarian rennet. 3kg/6lb 10oz rounds

Yorkshire Blue has a soft, creamy texture; its medium strong, slightly salty blue taste contrasts with the sweetness of the cheese itself, which is typical of the area. The effect is rich but fresh, delicate, and altogether softer and lighter than either Stilton or the stronger sheep's version.

As the sweetness of the cheese suggests, the milk, although not produced by the Bells themselves, comes from nearby. Neither of the Shepherd's Purse blue cheeses is called Wensleydale because the farm is not in the Dale but the Vale of York (besides the fact that the sheep's milk is no longer from the area); also, Judy had a problem over the method. As no blue Wensleydale had been made for some time, she could not find a local recipe: after experimenting on her own, she ended up with a few 'brilliant' failures, and therefore adopted the Roquefort method (from which Wensleydale is in fact descended). For both the cows' and sheep's version, *Penicillium roqueforti* is added to the milk with the starter; after renneting, the curd is left to set for an hour, cut, and allowed to stand until the acidity starts to rise. It is then ladled directly into tall, chimney-pot moulds (which are actually pieces of drainpipe) and turned three times on the first day and twice on the second. The cheeses are then unmoulded, rubbed with salt, and left in a drying room until piercing four or five days later: Judy now has a machine, but until two years ago they were stuck with skewers in the old-fashioned way. Four weeks later they are wrapped in foil to inhibit further blueing; the total maturing time is about three months.

YORKSHIRE BLUE (SHEEP'S)

Bronze Medal, British Cheese Awards 1996; Gold Medal, 1997
A blue sheep's cheese; pasteurized milk; vegetarian rennet. 3kg/6lb 10oz rounds

In the past, the cheese was sometimes seriously strong, but recently Judy has achieved the perfect balance between the blue and the actual cheese, which is gloriously rich, creamy, and sweet. It is now as good a blue as you will find anywhere, both for the cheeseboard and for cooking.

Yorkshire Blue and Chicken Mousse with Watercress

The mousse has a frothy, melting texture which is achieved entirely by means of whipping cream, without raw egg white. You can use pre-cooked chicken (e.g. from that used for the stock), but freshly poached breasts will give a smoother texture.

Cooking time: 30 minutes; allow 3–4 hours for the mousse to set
For 6–8 as a first course

150g/5¼oz skinned chicken breasts, washed
600ml/1 pint strong chicken stock (page 21)
salt
200ml/7fl oz (⅓ pint) dry white wine
½ tsp Cayenne pepper
15g/½oz (1 sachet) gelatine
225ml/8fl oz whipping cream
50g/1¾oz watercress, washed, left to dry, and shredded, plus a little extra
for garnishing
2 or 3 spears dill, washed and finely chopped
6 spring onions, peeled and finely sliced
100g/3½oz Yorkshire Blue sheep's cheese, finely grated

Poach the chicken in the stock with a pinch of salt for 25–35 minutes or until it is tender and no pink liquid emerges when it is pierced in the thickest part. Keep it covered as it cooks and allow the stock to simmer only very gently (if the chicken is boiled instead of simmered, it will be tough). Leave the chicken to cool; keep the stock to hand.

In another pan, reduce the wine to about a third of its original volume. Add the stock with 1 teaspoonful of salt and the Cayenne. Bring it to the boil, allow it to cool for a moment or two, and sprinkle in the gelatine: stir until it has dissolved. Leave the mixture to become cold and chill it for 2–2½ hours, until it has half-set.

Stiffly whip the cream and keep it chilled until needed. Dice the chicken as finely as possible. Mix together the watercress, dill, onions, and cheese and stir in the half-set stock; gently fold in the cream. Chill the mousse for at least another hour and serve it decorated with extra watercress.

YORKSHIRE LOWLANDS

A hard sheep's cheese, either wrapped in muslin or with a red wax rind; pasteurized milk; vegetarian rennet. 280–350g/10–12oz and 1.4–1.8kg/3–4lb rounds

Yorkshire Lowlands is a moist cheese with a satisfyingly nutty, slightly gritty texture. The taste is sweet and similarly nutty, freshened with a faint citrus tang.

The milk is left for an hour after the addition of starter and fifty to ninety minutes (depending on the weather) after renneting. The curd is cut moderately finely, stirred and scalded by about 7°C/45°F (9°C/48°F for muslin-wrapping), and most of the whey drained off; the rest is removed when the acidity has risen sufficiently. It is then blocked and piled at the sides of the vat, milled, salted, moulded, and pressed hard overnight; finally, the cheeses are wrapped or coated with wax, and matured for six months.

YORKSHIRE FETA

Gold Medal, British Cheese Awards 1996
A soft sheep's cheese with a green/natural wax rind; pasteurized milk; vegetarian rennet. 300g/10½oz and 1.8kg/4lb rounds

The cheese is soft, rough, and nutty, with a pleasantly sharp, citrus taste; unlike traditional feta, it is not particularly salty and can be served or used for cooking directly, without soaking. It is excellent for salads and dishes such as stuffed aubergine, spinach pie, or on top of roast vegetables.

Feta is customarily preserved in brine, which was (and still is) convenient in a hot climate: instead Judy's is rubbed twice with dry salt and, like the other non-blue Shepherd's Purse cheeses, preserved by waxing. Starter and rennet are added and the curd left to set for fifty or more minutes: it is then cut, stirred, and allowed to settle. Thereafter, it is moulded and left to drain for thirty-six hours before being salted and waxed.

OLDE YORK

Silver Medal, British Cheese Awards 1996 and (Garlic) 1997
A fresh, soft sheep's cheese; wax rind; pasteurized milk; vegetarian rennet. 450g/1lb rounds

Olde York is very light but, like Judy's Feta, with a slightly textured, nutty feel. It comes plain or flavoured with green peppercorns, chives, parsley and garlic, or mint. The plain is mild but with a herbal tang just strong enough to give it interest; peppercorns add zest, and chives strengthen the flavour considerably. It develops quite a strong lemon-like tang when heated and is delicious fried in egg and breadcrumbs (page 23): serve the plain version with redcurrant jelly or the herb flavours with salad.

The cheese is made very simply by the free-draining Coulommiers method. After the addition of starter and rennet, the curd is left to set for fifty minutes or longer, according to the weather, and ladled directly into the moulds. The cheeses are then turned three times on both that and the following day, rubbed with salt, and left to absorb it for two hours at room temperature before being chilled, shaped, and waxed.

Swaledale Cheese Co.

DAVID REED, SWALEDALE CHEESE CO., MERCURY ROAD,
RICHMOND DL10 4TQ. TEL: 01748 824932

Like Judy Bell (page 210), David's success with Swaledale has been remarkable. He puts it down to luck, although others attribute it to hard work; either way, it was only by coincidence that he came to make cheese at all. Interestingly to me, he started out as a chef: after training, he went to the Black Bull Inn at Moulton (about equally known for seafood and a dining room in a stranded Pullman railway carriage). After five years, feeling that it was time to move on, he left and took a job as development chef with a large company; by then, he had also married. Four days before his first child was due, he was made redundant: thus when he stopped at the Black Bull on the way home from the hospital to tell the staff that he had a daughter, he was 'rather desperately' wondering what to do.

Aside from fish, one of the specialities of the Black Bull was Swaledale cheese, which was so popular that customers who ordered it often ended up buying whole cheeses to take away. Until that time, it had been made by a Mrs Wagstaff and her husband; however, it so happened that Mr Wagstaff had just died and his widow, feeling unable to continue with it alone, had given up. David went to see her and persuaded her to give him the recipe.

His training as a chef perhaps helped him to master the cheese quickly; however, he puts special emphasis on the fact that he took it over at exactly the right time. 'We started making Swaledale just when there was a cheese boom, 1986–7, when gourmets and cheese-sellers were touring Britain looking for native cheeses.' Randolph Hodgson of Neal's Yard Dairy seized on it at once: 'We were made.' Within eighteen months, David was able to buy the unit in Richmond where his dairy still is. He now makes Swaledale not only with cows' and sheep's milk but also with goats', plus smoked and flavoured versions, and Beamish, a crumbly cheese made at the Beamish Open Air Museum near Chester-le-Street, a little further north, where the dairy is open to the public. He is also hoping to make a new soft cheese, Farmdale, but to date has not been as lucky with his plans as previously. The milk for the others is bought, but for a soft cheese, when the quality of the milk is particularly important, he feels that it is essential to produce it himself. When I visited him, he was living in rented accommodation because he had made an offer for a suitable farm and sold his house, but the deal had fallen through: he has now bought another house, but without a farm, so for the time being Farmdale is on hold.

SWALEDALE COWS'

A semi-hard cows' cheese; full-fat, pasteurized milk; vegetarian rennet. 225g/8oz, 450g/1lb, and 2–2.5kg/4lb 6oz–5lb 8oz truckles; Richmond Peculiar: 450g/1lb and 6kg/13lb 3oz truckles; Richmond Smoked: 450g/1lb and 1.6kg/3lb 8oz truckles

Swaledale Cows' has a moist, soft, deliciously melting texture: it dissolves to cream on the tongue. The taste is mild but with a gentle herbal sharpness and definite overtone of the moors. The flavoured versions are garlic and herbs, apple-mint, and Richmond Peculiar (with a black rind), for which the curd is soaked in Theakston's Old Peculiar Ale: the mint is subtle and delicate, the garlic and herbs stronger, and the Old Peculiar Ale definitely evident. The smoked version, Richmond Smoked (red wax rind) is smoked over oak and applewood: the taste is mild and the texture pleasantly moist and nutty.

The milk comes from Milk Marque but is local; the recipe, like Cotherstone (page 218) is similar to Wensleydale. The gentle, melting texture of the cheese, which is part of its particular attraction, can only be achieved by making it entirely by hand. About eighty per cent of the plain and herb-flavoured cheeses have natural rinds, but David waxes a few to protect them from storage at the wrong temperature (some customers also favour wax because it avoids wastage when cutting off the rind).

SWALEDALE EWES'

Silver Medal, British Cheese Awards 1997
A semi-hard sheep's cheese; pasteurized milk; vegetarian rennet. 225g/8oz, 450g/1lb, and 2–2.5kg/4lb 6oz–5lb 8oz truckles

Like the cows', the sheep's version of the cheese has a soft, moist texture; the mild but beautifully balanced taste is just salty enough to offset a gentle herbal tang. The milk is not necessarily local but apparently comes from moorland areas: three samples bought at different times and places tasted unmistakeably of heather.

SWALEDALE GOATS'

A hard goats' cheese; full-fat, pasteurized milk; vegetarian rennet. 225g/8oz, 450g/1lb, and 2–2.5kg/4lb 6oz–5lb 8oz truckles

In contrast to the other two, the goats' cheese has a compact, almost grainy, satisfyingly nutty texture. It tastes subtly of flowers and the moors, with a suggestion of peat. I think it is delicious.

BEAMISH

A semi-hard cows' cheese; natural rind; full-fat, pasteurized milk; vegetarian rennet. 450g/1lb truckles

Beamish is moist and crumbly rather than creamy, with a mild, sweet, flowery taste: in fact, it very like a handmade white Wensleydale. It goes well with fruit, e.g. bananas.

Cotherstone

JOAN CROSS, QUARRY HOUSE, MARWOOD, BARNARD CASTLE, CO.
DURHAM DL12 9QL. TEL: 01833 650351

As you drive north from Richmond, the country becomes larger-scale, with long ranges of hills spaced by wide valleys. Quarry Farm is in a stunning situation, nearly 300m/1,000 feet up on the edge of a dramatic drop overlooking a view south towards the Dales. The farm is quite small but orderly and as clean as if it had just been vacuumed, which Joan said is because they have given up their dairy herd and now raise stock only for meat, so that the cows no longer come in twice a day for milking. The other particularly striking feature about it was the garden, which glowed with pinks, oranges, and reds worthy of David Hockney.

Like Mrs Appleby and Ruth Kirkham (pages 178 and 195), Joan was brought up to cheesemaking and, although she did not practice it for a time after she married, has produced a steady supply of Cotherstone for over twenty-five years. Everyone in the area (as in the Dales) used to keep a cow and make cheese, including Joan's mother, who took it for granted that as long as Joan was living at home, she would help. When she married, Joan thought, 'Thank goodness I won't have to make cheese any more' – but, as her husband is a farmer, she naturally went back to it rather than see surplus milk go to waste. She used their own milk for many years but now buys it from a particular farm via Milk Marque – who have surprised her. 'The MMB [Milk Marketing Board] were dreadful: they bullied you and told you what you must have or do whereas Milk Marque are actually nice to people and give customers what they want.' She does not make cheese continuously but in bursts, whenever the storeroom looks empty: at the time of our visit, she had just finished a ten-day run.

Except for the use of starter and vegetarian rather than natural rennet, she makes the cheese in exactly the same way as her mother. As with Swaledale, the recipe is similar to that for Wensleydale and depends for its texture on being completely handmade. Next to her dairy is a long room, or barn, containing twenty-two cheese-presses, all local and all at least 100 years old, many of which, after her recent run, were in use. In the storeroom, since she has no humidity control, the cheeses are kept moist by wrapping them in damp cloths. The cooler the weather, she says, the better the cheese: 'Mind you, we don't get many heat waves up here, so it isn't a problem.'

COTHERSTONE

A semi-hard cows' cheese; wax or natural rind; full-fat, unpasteurized milk; vegetarian rennet. 450g/1lb, 900g/2lb, and 2.7kg/6lb rounds

Like Swaledale, the texture is irresistibly moist, soft, and creamy, melting in the mouth like mousse or the very finest shortbread. The taste is mild and sunny, with a fresh, gentle tang and hints of grass, flowers, and herbs. With recipes in mind, I bought the largest size while I was there; however, we were going on to stay with friends in Scotland, and before I had had time to think about cooking, every delicious crumb was gone.

Northumberland Cheese Co.

MARK ROBERTSON, MAKE ME RICH FARM, BLAGDON, SEATON BURN, NORTHUMBERLAND, NE13 6BZ. TEL: 01670 789798

In the face of all the advantages of Make Me Rich over his previous farm, Mark stresses that he did not choose the name: it originated at least a century ago from the fact that the soil is sandy loam, which was easily worked with a horse-drawn plough and yielded early harvests. Before moving there, he had made cheese for twelve years at Soppitt Farm, only 24km/15 miles from the Scottish border: Make Me Rich is less than 16km/10 miles from Newcastle upon Tyne. The new dairy is four times as big as the old; there is a shop with windows overlooking the cheesemaking area, a coffee-shop, and in the future Mark is hoping to open a restaurant where dishes made with his cheeses will be served. The dairy was converted at a cost of £15,000, with the aid of grants from the Department of Trade and Industry and the Ministry of Agriculture, Fisheries, and Food: the second of these was to enable him to recruit a board of non-executive directors, which he especially values because it means that instead of being alone, he has the support of a group of people with an interest in the business. The scheme has parallels with the co-operative formed by Plaw Hatch and Tablehurst Farms (page 39).

Originally Mark was a sheep farmer; he was tempted into cheese by Olivia Mills's book (page 32), and, like others, eventually gave up the sheep in favour of the cheese. At the time of writing, all his milk is bought, but he was planning to use a herd of Friesians at Make Me Rich for his cows' cheeses by this summer. Last autumn, he employed five full-time cheesemakers; by now he expected that there would be eight or nine. Altogether, he makes six cheeses: Elsdon, a goats' cheese; Redesdale, a sheep's cheese; an eighty per cent cows'/twenty per cent sheep's white Wensleydale; and three cows' cheese, Northumberland, Coquetdale, and a washed-curd cheese which he introduced when his new dairy was completed last year. The earlier cheeses have changed slightly as a result of the move but, to use Mark's description, not more than wine from a different slope of the same vineyard.

REDESDALE

A hard sheep's cheese; pasteurized milk; vegetarian rennet.

Redesdale has a velvety texture with a few small holes. The taste is beautifully balanced and strong enough to be bracing, like the invigorating Northumbrian air, with quite a strong, salty tang and slightly peppery aftertaste. It is excellent for cooking, since it keeps its flavour when hot and can be used as an alternative to pecorino for sprinkling. It also comes flavoured with herbs.

Cod and Redesdale Fish Cakes with Chives

The cakes can be made a day in advance. Serve with a tomato sauce.

Cooking time: 1 hour (potato only)
Makes 8–9 cakes

250g/9oz (1 small) baking potato, e.g. Estima, Cara, Marfona, washed
250g/9oz cod, washed, skinned, and boned
salt and pepper
1 large, or 2 small (85g/3oz) shallot/s, peeled and very finely chopped
1 small handful chives, washed and very finely snipped
175g/6oz Redesdale, finely grated
25–30g/1–1$^1/_4$oz white flour
1 large free-range egg, beaten
55g/2oz finely grated fresh breadcrumbs
oil for frying

Pre-heat the oven to 200°C/400°F/Gas 6. Prick and bake the potato for an hour, until it is soft all the way through. As soon as it is cool enough to handle, peel it or scoop out the inside, discarding the hardened flesh next to the skin.

Season the fish lightly with salt and pepper and wrap it in a parcel of cooking foil. Bake the fish at the same temperature as the potato for

12 minutes or until it flakes easily with a fork and is opaque all the way through. Thoroughly drain and mash it with the potato, a little salt, and rather more pepper. Stir in first the shallot and chives, then the cheese.

Spread the flour over a plate and season it moderately with salt and pepper. Crack an egg into a bowl or saucer and season it. Spread the breadcrumbs over another plate. Form the fish mixture into cakes and coat them very thoroughly with the flour, egg, and crumbs, making sure that the entire surface is covered but shaking off any surplus. Warm the oil over fairly high heat and fry the cakes until golden on both sides. Serve at once.

ELSDON

Bronze Medal, British Cheese Awards 1997
A hard goats' cheese; full-fat, pasteurized milk; vegetarian rennet. 850g/1lb 14oz and 3kg/6lb 10oz truckles

Elsdon has a deliciously smooth, soft, sometimes almost semi-soft texture; the taste is mild and creamy, with virtually no trace of goat.

NORTHUMBERLAND

Bronze Medal, British Cheese Awards 1997 (Smoked)
A hard cows' cheese; full-fat, pasteurized milk; vegetarian rennet. 450g/1lb, 1kg/2lb 4oz, 3kg/6lb 10oz and 10kg/22lb truckles

Like Elsdon, part of the attraction of Northumberland is its smooth, creamy, melting texture, which contrasts interestingly with a pronounced herbal flavour and crisp, bracing northern tang. It comes plain, smoked, or flavoured with nettles or chives: necessarily, the herb-flavoured versions have a slightly less smooth, creamy feel than the original and although apparently more popular, I think are less successful.

Northumberland Potato Omelette

This omelette is quick rather than elegant, but it is totally delicious, mainly because of the cheese.

Cooking time: about 15 minutes
For 2

1 medium onion (about 150g/5¼oz), peeled and thinly sliced
150g/5¼oz waxy new potatoes (e.g. Charlotte), scrubbed or peeled and very thinly sliced; if peeled, use slightly more
2 tbsp virgin olive oil
salt and pepper
3 cloves garlic, peeled and thinly sliced
1 green pepper, washed, cored and with seeds removed, cut into thin half-rings
3 large free-range eggs, beaten and seasoned moderately with salt and pepper
100g/3½oz plain Northumberland cheese, very thinly sliced
hot brown bread for serving

Put the onion and potatoes into a large wok or frying pan with the oil, season moderately with salt and pepper, and fry over medium heat, turning constantly, for about 2 minutes. Add the garlic and green pepper and fry for about another minute; then reduce the heat to very low. Cover and cook for 8–10 minutes or until all the vegetables are soft, turning them from time to time. Raise the heat a little and continue to cook the vegetables until the potato and onion begin to show traces of gold. Beat and pour in the eggs; raise the heat a little more, tilt the pan, and push back the egg as it sets so that the part which is still liquid runs to the bottom. When most of it has set, spread the cheese on top. Continue to cook until the bottom is firm and golden and the top has just set; cut the omelette in half, fold it gently (it is very thick but folds easily) and serve it with hot brown bread.

COQUETDALE

Bronze Medal, British Cheese Awards 1997
A hard cows' cheese; full-fat, pasteurized milk; vegetarian rennet.
650g/1lb 7oz and 2kg/4lb 6oz truckles

Coquetdale has a similar creamy, melting texture to Northumberland, but instead of the fairly robust tang of both Northumberland and Redesdale, a mild, fresh taste of grass and herbs.

WENSLEYDALE (WHITE)

A semi-hard, mixed cows' and sheep's cheese; full-fat, pasteurized milk; vegetarian rennet. 850g/1lb 14oz and 3kg/6lb 10oz truckles

The cheese has a soft, open, fairly dry texture, with a mild, grassy taste. It is slightly tart and does not have the sweetness of the cheeses made in the Dale but is very pleasant in its own right.

MAKE ME RICH

A semi-soft cow's cheese; full-fat, pasteurized milk; vegetarian rennet. 2.25kg/5lb rounds

Again like Northumberland, the cheese has a soft, melting texture which is actually somewhere between semi-soft and hard. The effect of washing the curd is to modify the tang and soften the flavour, so that it tastes relatively mild and creamy. Its creaminess and soft texture mean that it goes especially well with rough brown bread and oatcakes.

North Doddington Farm
NEILL MAXWELL, NORTH DODDINGTON FARM, WOOLER, NORTHUMBERLAND NE71 6AN. TEL: 01668 282081

North Doddington is a very large mixed farm: the need for specialization is not felt here. Neill and his family raise cereals as well as livestock and, besides sheep, have a small beef herd and a dairy herd of 250 Friesians and Normandies. The Normandies are especially suitable for cheese because their milk is higher in protein than Friesian, but not proportionately fattier, and coagulates very easily. The cows are managed by one of Neill's two brothers, Robert, whose feelings for them extend not only to knowing each one individually but also to giving them names. When I remarked that thinking of so many names must be difficult, Neill replied, 'Oh, he's called them after all his girlfriends.' (Later Robert said, 'Yes, it's an odd thing: I mean it as a compliment, but they don't always see it that way.') The herd has been with the family since before the war: it was brought to Doddington in 1944, but before that was kept by Neill's parents in Dumfries. The farm is now run jointly by Neill, his two brothers and sister, and their mother, whose parents were dairy-farmers in Ayrshire, traditionally Scotland's main dairying area.

She remarked that whereas early in the century everyone there made cheese, as in Yorkshire, cheesemaking had been eroded by the easier transport of milk in the period between the wars, and finally killed by the establishment of the Milk Marketing Board.

Neill's enthusiasm for cheese is electric. He started making it six years ago, initially experimenting, like everyone else, with a bucket and spoon in the kitchen; he then took a cheesemaking course and when we visited him had just returned from studying how to make farmhouse Gouda in the Netherlands. He has evolved three cheeses: the first, Doddington, is of the open-textured, Leicester type; the second, Berwick Edge, of the Gouda type; and the third, St Cuthbert's Cave, based on a Caerphilly recipe. St Cuthbert's Cave is named after a local cave said to have been used by the saint as a resting-place but is always referred to by Neill as 'Cuddy's Cave'. To achieve the creamy, semi-hard texture for which it is notable, he makes it with milk taken only at the beginning and end of lactation, when the yield is low but the fat content relatively high. For all the cheeses, he uses half as much starter as usual and leaves the milk to ripen for twice as long, which may help to account for their distinctive flavour.

DODDINGTON

A semi-hard cows' cheese; full-fat, unpasteurized milk; traditional rennet.
2kg/4lb 6oz, 5kg/11lb and 20kg/44lb truckles

Though of different types, Neill's three cheeses share an exceptionally light, melting texture and bold, interesting, totally unique flavour, combined in the case of the first two with a herbal, almost spicy tang. Doddington is fairly dry and almost but not quite crumbly, with flavours suggestive of the earth, grass, and sea air (the sea is about 19km/12 miles away). The tang is fairly strong when the cheese is younger, and powerful by the time it reaches nine months. Altogether, it is different and memorable. Toasted, it is delicious in a different way, since the tang is subdued and the cheese becomes much sweeter.

BERWICK EDGE

A hard cows' cheese; full-fat, unpasteurized milk; traditional rennet.
2.5kg/5lb 8oz and 5kg/11lb

At seven to eight months, this has an airy, insubstantial, lace-like texture, with small holes; at a year, it becomes more compact and creamier. Like Doddington, the younger cheese tastes of earth and grass, with a moderately strong tang; when older, the tang becomes deep, mellow, and vigorous, almost hot, as if seasoned with chilli. I served the older version to guests on Christmas Day and everyone agreed that it was quite exceptional.

ST CUTHBERT'S CAVE (CUDDY'S CAVE)

A semi-hard cows' cheese; full-fat, unpasteurized milk; traditional rennet.
1.5kg/3lb 5oz and 4kg/8lb 13oz

Cuddy's Cave is semi-hard verging on semi-soft, light, melting, mousse-like, and above all creamy. The creaminess carries through to the taste, making it milder than the other cheeses but with an interesting range of grassy and herbal flavours and background hints of both spiciness and flowers. It is possibly my favourite of the three. If it is not already very soft, store it at room temperature covered by a dish to keep it moist.

Scotland

Easter Weens Enterprises

JOHN AND CHRISTIAN CURTIS, EASTER WEENS FARM,
BONCHESTER BRIDGE, HAWICK, BORDERS TD9 8JQ.
TEL: 01450 860635

In June, the Easter Weens' borders glowed with carnations and pinks as well
as columbine and piercingly blue Himalayan poppies; at the end of the garden is a stream flanked by a thick, dark hedge of rhododendrons. The stream
separates the house from the farm and dairy; on the other side the cows graze
peacefully in idyllically green fields shaded by enormous trees.

John and Christian were among the first in Britain and Ireland to make
a soft, mould-ripened cow's cheese: they started in 1980, soon after Veronica
Steele (page 130), not so much because it seemed a good commercial proposition as simply because they liked the soft cheeses that they ate on
holiday in France. As well as Bonchester, their first and best known cheese,
they now make Belle d'Ecosse and Teviotdale, which are respectively twice
and four times as thick and lightly pressed. For most of the year, with the
help of a cheesemaker and two assistants, they make 150 full-sized cheeses
and sixty 'babies' every day, seven days a week: the difficulty of finding
suitable staff plus the expense of increasing the milk quota make expansion
impossible, at least for the moment.

The milk is supplied by twenty-five Jerseys, all with names, who come
into the milking-parlour in turn as they are called. Before and after milking,
the udders of each one are gently but thoroughly wiped and disinfected:
since the cheese is soft and the milk unpasteurized, hygiene precautions are
particularly stringent at all points of the production process.

BONCHESTER

Bronze Medal, British Cheese Awards 1996
A Camembert-style Jersey cheese; full-fat, unpasteurized milk; traditional rennet.
100g/3¹/₂oz and 280g/10oz rounds

Bonchester is soft and flowing, with a crisp penicillin rind. The Jersey milk
produces a richer, thicker texture than Camembert; the taste is buttery, with
pronounced flowery flavours which vary according to the time of year. Of all
British cheeses, this is one of the warmest, sweetest, and most luxurious. If it
is still hard when you buy it, leave it at room temperature for a few days or
in the refrigerator for up to six weeks. When used for cooking, it loses some

of its floweriness, but is nevertheless delicious fried in breadcrumbs (page 23); partly because of the Jersey milk, it is also the best British or Irish cheese to use for a pie, when it melts to a creamy, golden sauce.

The cheeses are made by the Coulommiers method: as elsewhere, enormous care is taken throughout to disturb the curd as little as possible. The morning and evening milk are mixed and warmed, starter and penicillin mould added, and the milk left to ripen for an hour and a half. As for Bath Soft (page 76), the milk is transferred into buckets before renneting to ensure even setting without stirring (although unusual here, this is a common practice in France). After about an hour, the curd is cut into 2.5-cm/1-inch 'columns' and left to stand for another twenty minutes. It is then ladled very gently into the moulds; Belles d'Ecosse and Teviotdales are unmoulded and set under pressure in the evening, while Bonchesters are turned again that evening and the following morning. Finally, the cheeses are brined and matured for sixteen days before wrapping and labelling.

Bonchester Pie

The other cheeses recommended for pies (Somerset Camembert, St Killian, and Cooleeney: pages 95, 121, and 122) call for only a half-quantity of pastry: however, as Bonchester is bigger, you will need slightly more.

For a tidy pie, the cheese must be chilled when you start so that it is firm when you shape the pastry. The pie is very rich: serve it with frisee or other crisp or bitter leaves.

Cooking time: 15 minutes
For 6–8

$^2/_3$ quantity puff pastry (140g/5oz each flour and butter)
1 ripe Bonchester (280g/10oz) straight out of the refrigerator
a little flour for rolling
egg or milk for glazing (optional)

Roll out the pastry to about 4-mm/less than $^1/_4$-inch thick and cut two circles from it, one large enough to cover the bottom and sides of the cheese plus 2cm/$^3/_4$ inch, and the other the size of the top plus 1cm/$^1/_2$ inch. Place the cheese in the middle of the larger circle and put the smaller one on top. Draw the pastry at the bottom up the sides of the cheese, moisten both edges, and pinch them firmly together round the top, making a rim. Stamp the pastry with a blunt knife, decorate it with pastry leaves, and make an air-hole in the middle. Set the oven to 210°C/410°F/Gas 6–7; leave the cheese to warm at room temperature while it heats.

Glaze the pie if you wish and bake it until it has puffed up and turned golden. Keep an eye on it for the last minute or so and remove it from the oven if there is any sign of cheese oozing from the bottom. Serve it at once.

BELLE D'ECOSSE AND TEVIOTDALE

Soft cows' cheeses; full-fat, unpasteurized milk; traditional rennet. Belle d'Ecosse: 550g/1lb 4oz rounds; Teviotdale: 1.1kg/2lb 7oz rounds; scarce January–April

These cheeses are similar to Bonchester but firmer: they are softer than semi-soft but will not flow. The taste is a little more herbal and concentrated.

Loch Arthur Creamery
BARRY GRAHAM, CAMPHILL VILLAGE TRUST, BEESWING, DUMFRIES DG2 8JQ. TEL: 01387 760296

The Camphill Village Trust is part of the Camphill Movement, which was founded by an Austrian paediatrician, Dr Karl König, to provide education and a family environment for children with learning difficulties. The Village Trust extends his ideas to adults: there are six village communities in England, one in Ireland, and two in Scotland, where the other is at Newton Dee, near Aberdeen. Residents with learning difficulties live in family houses with co-workers and their children, sharing domestic life and types of work which vary according to location and circumstance. At Loch Arthur there is a weaving workshop, bakery, and two farms: on one beef-cattle, sheep, and pigs are reared, and the other has a market garden and a herd of twenty-four Ayrshires, who supply the milk for the Creamery. We visited the bakery just as trays of little oat biscuits scented with honey were being taken from the oven; in the market garden we could see every kind of vegetable, soft fruit including raspberries and strawberries, and huge clumps of herbs, all interspersed with the bright colours of marigolds and nasturtiums. The movement holds Rudolf Steiner's ideas 'in special respect': thus a school for the younger children is run on his principles and the farms are bio-dynamic.

When Barry and his wife joined the Community, two years after it was founded in 1984, a dairy for making butter and soft cheese had already been set up by a Trust worker called Vivian, chiefly to provide employment for a Community member who was paralysed from the waist down but could churn butter; however, Vivian left soon after Barry arrived, leaving him as her obvious successor. In response to the general feeling of the community, he set about reorganizing the dairy to make hard cheese, and gradually built up a team which now consists of four co-workers and six members with learning difficulties. Watching them working together, I was deeply impressed by their commitment and efficiency; I was also astonished at the confidence and maturity of a group of Community children who joined them for tea. They seemed to prove the value of early contact with adult occupations and, perhaps even more, of having both parents near to hand for most of the day, although their Steiner schooling perhaps deserves some of the credit.

For some years, Barry concentrated on the hard cheese, for which most of the milk is still used; however, he also continued Vivian's soft cheese, and recently, feeling that it could be improved, asked Iain Mellis in Edinburgh for advice (although he now sells rather than makes cheese, Iain used to be a cheesemaker). Between them, they devised a semi-soft version which Barry had only just perfected at the time of my visit, although it has now been on sale (in limited quantities) for some time. The Creamery also makes yoghurt and a rich, flowery-tasting curd cheese which is ideal for cooking.

LOCH ARTHUR ORGANIC FARMHOUSE CHEESE

Silver Medal, British Cheese Awards 1995; Bronze Medal, 1996
A Cheddar-style cheese; full-fat, unpasteurized organic milk; vegetarian rennet.
9kg/20lb truckles; smaller sizes also available

At six months, which I consider to be its optimum age, this cheese is moist, mild, rich, and wonderfully multi-flavoured, with a creamy background against which herbal and flowery tastes are evenly balanced. Its varying tones and subtleties mean that you could eat it every day for years without being bored. At a year, it is drier and has developed a tang, but to some extent at the expense of the sub-flavours, which become subordinate and less lively.

It is made according to a Cheddar recipe and bound with cloth which is stuck on by 'burning' or scalding rather than with lard or flour-paste. The maturing time is six to twelve months. For the soft cheese, Crannog, some of the curd is scooped off before being cut for the hard cheese and left to free-drain: it then is ripened for two to three weeks. The new cheese, Criffel, is made similarly, but rind-washed in brine and matured for at least a month.

 ## Loch Arthur Potatoes

This can be made with almost any Cheddar-type (and other) cheese, but Loch Arthur gives a gentle flavour which does not overwhelm the taste of the potatoes. Waxy potatoes that will not disintegrate are essential; it is also important to slice them thinly, partly to reduce the time they take to cook. If you are in a hurry, the slices can be boiled in water, which takes 4–5 minutes, rather than simmered in the sauce; however, the result will not have quite the same richness and unity. The dish can be prepared in advance up to baking.

Cooking times: 18–25 minutes for the potatoes in sauce; 20–25 minutes for baking
For 2–3 as a main course or 4–6 as a vegetable

450ml/16fl oz milk
salt and pepper
400g/14oz preferably organic waxy new potatoes, e.g. Charlotte or Jersey
Royal, scrubbed and very thinly sliced
125g/4^1/$_2$oz shallots, preferably organic, peeled and finely chopped
20g/^{3}/$_4$oz butter
20g/^{3}/$_4$oz white flour, preferably organic
1 tsp Dijon mustard
150g/5^1/$_4$oz Loch Arthur Organic Farmhouse Cheddar, finely grated
nutmeg

Heat but do not boil the milk; season the potatoes moderately with salt and pepper. Fry the shallots in the butter over medium to low heat – if possible in a non-stick pan – for 2–3 minutes or until they are soft but not brown; add the potatoes, stir-fry for about half a minute to coat them with oil, and stir in the flour gently but thoroughly off the heat. The pan will be very dry, but because of the cheese the finished dish might become greasy if more butter is used. Pour in the milk gradually, stirring continuously; return the pan to the heat and stir until the sauce has thickened. Lower the heat to a simmer, season lightly with salt and a little more generously with pepper, and cook until the potatoes are just tender, turning them often to ensure that they do not stick to the pan. Gently stir in the mustard; allow the potatoes to cool briefly before adding and stirring in the cheese.

Turn the potatoes into a lightly greased soufflé or other baking dish and grate a little nutmeg over the top. Bake the potatoes at 190°C/375°F/Gas 5 for 20–25 minutes, until they are lightly browned. Serve at once.

CRIFFEL

A semi-soft cows' cheese; full-fat, unpasteurized organic milk; vegetarian rennet. 25–30-cm/10–12-inch discs

Criffel has a smooth, consistent texture not quite soft enough to flow. The taste is fairly strong, tangy yet sweet, with a wide range of flavours among which butter and wild flowers predominate. It is a lovely cheese, but at present regrettably scarce.

CRANNOG

Bronze Medal, British Cheese Awards 1996
A fresh, wax-coated cows' cheese; full-fat, unpasteurized organic milk; vegetarian rennet. 280g/10oz rounds

Crannog has a firm, compact, nutty texture. Thanks to the organic Ayrshire milk, the taste is surprisingly distinctive, with flavours of grass and wild herbs combined with an earthy, almost mushroom-like sweetness. It comes plain or flavoured with organic herbs (mixed) or green peppercorns.

Galloway Farmhouse Cheese
ALLAN BROWN, MILLAIRIES FARM, NEWTON STEWART,
WIGTOWNSHIRE DG8 8AL. TEL: 0198 885 0224

Allan Brown illustrates the difficulty of both milking sheep and making cheese single-handedly: more than anyone else I have met, he needs a carousel (page 235). He has a flock of 400 Frieslands or Friesland crosses, of whom he milks 100 for eight months of the year: during that time, he makes 112kg/250lb of cheese a week and is 100% busy all and every day. The fact that we arrived at Millairies (the name means watermill) on Bank Holiday Monday was irrelevant to him. We talked in the dairy while he made the cheese, for which he barely has time after the day's milking.

He originally decided to keep Frieslands partly as a result of reading Olivia Mills's book (page 32) and, like Ann Dorward (page 237), started out simply intending to sell the milk in liquid form. However, incredible as it may now seem in England, where the shortage of sheep's milk is acute, neither of them could find a market. Initially Allan, entering the field several years after Ann, froze his milk and took it to her dairy, where she made cheese for him; he then began making his own from a recipe in *The Small-holder*. At present, he makes only the one kind, although with four variations; however, he has just installed his own smokery and opened a shop selling a range of products connected with sheep, From Ewe to You, with a window overlooking the dairy so that visitors can watch the cheese being made. As well as aiming to milk twice as many sheep (which will mean employing an assistant), his future plans include making ricotta and a cows' cheese while the sheep are dry in the winter.

We did not discuss all the details of his recipe; however, an aspect of his procedure which I found particularly interesting is that he matures all his cheeses in vacuum-packs, which considerably retards the ripening process. After six months, some cheeses are left plain and coated with wax, some are flavoured with peppercorns or smoked before waxing, and some matured on for another four months. By then, the cheese has formed a natural rind with brownish mould, which, combined with a drier texture and the extra maturing time, effectually transforms it into a different cheese.

CAIRNSMORE (NATURAL RIND)

Bronze Medal, British Cheese Awards 1996; Silver Medal, 1997 (Smoked)
A hard sheep's cheese; unpasteurized milk; vegetarian rennet. 900g/2lb and
1.8–2.3kg/4–5lb truckles

The ten-month-old cheese is pure delight, with a soft but pronounced sweet, creamy taste and undertones of nuts and earth. It is not in the least like the more usual pecorino-style sheep's cheeses: the sweetness, which also distinguishes Ann Dorward and Humphrey Errington's cheeses, seems to be characteristic of the area. The wax-rinded version is much less distinctive but is excellent fried in red wine or cider batter (page 66).

H. J. Errington
BRAEHEAD FARM, WALSTON, OGSCASTLE, CARNWATH,
STRATHCLYDE ML11 8NF. TEL: 01899 870266

By now, BSE and the American attempt to persuade the European Union to adopt compulsory pasteurization have pushed the Errington case into history, but three years ago cheeselovers all over Britain joined in a campaign to help Humphrey Errington to save his sheep's cheese, Lanark Blue, from extinction. Humphrey has already given his own account of what happened in *Lanark Blue: a Brief History of the Battle*, available from the Specialist Cheesemakers' Association. Very briefly, however, he was asked by the local council to recall all the cheese on the market from sale and cease trading because a sample test showed that it was so heavily contaminated with *Listeria monocytogenes* that it could have caused 'a UK-wide outbreak ... with a possible fatality rate of 40%'. (*Lanark Blue*, p. 4) Astonished and appalled, Humphrey of course complied and waited with dread for the predicted reports of illness. None came, and independent tests on the cheese showed that it was perfectly normal (it was later alleged that a patient had died of listeria which could have been transmitted by it, but the claim was shown to be false). After several months, Humphrey informed the council that he proposed to start trading again. The ensuing series of hearings lasted a year, with a final judgement in his favour. He says that he could never have sustained the strain of the legal proceedings without the tremendous public support he received, which in cash terms totalled £35,000.

Two points proved by the case were that it is possible for a small producer to challenge the authorities and win, and that consumers really value good cheese: 'If anyone needs convincing that in Britain there is an enormous desire for artisan cheese, despite the best attempts of the regulatory authorities to frustrate that desire, he has only to study the case of Lanark Blue...'. (*Lanark Blue*, p. 14) A further point which emerged was that unpasteurized cheese contains natural controls which can make it safer than pasteurized. Humphrey says: 'Fresh raw milk contains "bacteriostats", i.e. substances which prevent the growth of pathogens during the critical stage when the milk is warm in the vat but before starter activity has begun. There are no bacteriostats in pasteurized milk. Also, many raw milk cheese processes include the production of various organic acids in addition to lactic acid: for example, acetic acid, well known as an effective agent against pathogens, is often present. Thirdly, the microflora present in raw milk cheese after it has been made (and absent in pasteurized cheese) will include significant populations of organisms such as enterococci, which are highly inhibitory to invading pathogens.'

The farm which gave rise to the drama is in a sternly beautiful situation in the Pentland Hills; battle-scars remain in the form of large notices at either end of the cheesemaking area forbidding the entry of unauthorized persons for reasons of hygiene (Lanark Blue is now also sold with a sticker warning pregnant women and those who are immuno-compromised not to eat blue cheese – which, with equal justification, should be on every cheese matured for less than four months). At present, Humphrey has 300 Friesland sheep, but aims at 500: the problem of the time it takes to milk them, which haunts Allan Brown and Ann Dorward (pages 233 and 237) simply does not exist here. The shepherd, Walter Robertson, showed me the item of equipment which every sheep-cheesemaker needs: a carousel, or revolving milking-parlour. It does not float on water, like the Applebys', and is fairly noisy, but the sheep apparently do not mind. Twenty-five can be accommodated at once and the total milking time is reduced to thirty or forty minutes in the morning and thirty minutes in the afternoon. The milk for the cows' cheese, Dunsyre Blue, comes from a herd of Ayrshires on the farm next door.

LANARK BLUE

A blue sheep's cheese; unpasteurized milk; vegetarian rennet. 1.4–1.8kg/3–4lb rounds; seasonal: available April–Christmas

I am told that the cheese can be fairly strong, but the examples I have tried have been moderate, with blue which does not overpower the gentler tastes of sheep, grass, herbs, and somewhere in the background a slightly smoky suggestion of peat. It is particularly good with plums or pears; it is also excellent for adding a subtle piquancy to cooked dishes.

Marrow Rings Stuffed with Plums and Lanark Blue

This is a brilliant way of finishing up remains of the cheese, since you only need 40g/1½oz: the result is quite surprisingly full and rich-tasting.

Cooking time: 35–40 minutes
For 2 as a light main dish or 4 as a vegetable

400–450g/14oz–1lb piece of a small or long, thin marrow, washed
salt
1½ tbsp oil
150g/5¼oz (1 medium) onion, peeled, quartered, and finely sliced
100g/3½oz (2) red plums, washed and diced
1 fairly sharp eating apple, peeled and diced
2–3 sage leaves, washed and finely chopped
40g/1½oz walnuts, crushed or chopped
½ tsp Dijon mustard
4 tbsp whipping cream
40g/1½oz Lanark Blue, finely grated

Chop the marrow into slices 2.5cm/1 inch thick, barely cover them with slightly salted water, and boil for 9–10 minutes, until the marrow is tender but still firm. Drain the slices and leave them on a plate to drain further.

Warm the oil over low heat and fry the onion for 8–10 minutes or until it is soft and starting to change colour. Add the plums and apple and fry them for 4–5 minutes; add the sage and cook for about another minute; add the nuts, turn up the heat slightly, and stir for a few seconds. Add the mustard and cream and stir gently until the liquid is slightly reduced. Remove the pan from the heat.

Cut the fibrous centres, with the seeds, from the slices of marrow. Lay the slices in a baking dish and fill the holes with the plum stuffing. Cover the stuffing with the cheese and bake in a pre-heated oven at 200°C/400°F/Gas 6 for 9–12 minutes or until the cheese is melted and golden. Serve at once.

DUNSYRE BLUE

A blue cows' cheese; full-fat, unpasteurized milk; vegetarian rennet. 1.4–1.8kg/3–4lb rounds

Dunsyre Blue is milder, sweeter, and creamier-tasting than the Lanark; probably partly because of the Ayrshire milk, it has an unusually wide range of rich, grassy flavours. On a cheeseboard, it is particularly well partnered by Bonnet (hard goat: page 238) or Cairnsmore (sheep: page 234): the background tastes of both harmonize with it beautifully.

Dunlop Dairy Products
ANN DORWARD, WEST CLERKLAND FARM, STEWARTON, STRATHCLYDE KA3 5LP. TEL: 01560 482494

The drive up to West Clerkland Farm leads past very, very green fields, with kids in one and lambs in the next, all adolescent and quite large but still looking as perfectly white and clean as when they were born. At present, Ann keeps seventy milking Saanen goats and sixty Friesland sheep, and besides a goats' and sheep's cheese makes a farmhouse Dunlop which at the time of writing was the only one I had tasted in Scotland; she also has a shop where she sells the cheese, and a three-year-old son. Her husband manages his own farm next door; her parents live with them at West Clerklands, which obviously helps to ease her situation, and she has a part-time student assistant, but she acknowledges that she has far too much to do. Like Allan Brown (page 233), she started out with the intention simply of selling liquid sheep's milk but found that there was no demand; having embarked, first on sheep's, then on goat's cheese made with milk from a neighbour, she decided to keep goats only when two successive suppliers let her down. 'Often, oh often, I wish I hadn't – they're so lively, and I haven't time to entertain them!'

If only from necessity, her approach to cheesemaking is relaxed. When someone needs serving in the shop, the cheese has to wait; she is not concerned about 'touch' (she does not need to be) and is pragmatic about pasteurization. When she started, eleven years ago, she pasteurized all her cheese because she was told not only that the authorities preferred it but also that unpasteurized products would soon be made illegal – whereas in fact, as she said, feeling has gone the other way. She now makes all her cheeses in a pasteurized and unpasteurized version; the former are matured in vacuum-packs and rindless and the unpasteurized ones (with rinds) are matured normally. As is traditional, she uses Ayrshire milk for the Dunlop, delivered by Scottish Milk, who also supply local Marks & Spencers (where I bought some and was astonished by the flavour).

SWINZIE (WITH RIND)

A hard sheep's cheese; full-fat, unpasteurized milk; vegetarian rennet.
2.5kg/5lb 8oz truckles

Swinzie is sweet and rich-tasting, with a predominantly nutty flavour: like Cairnsmore (page 234), it is completely different from pecorino, although if matured for a long time, it acquires a smoky tang. Ann's cheesemaking may sometimes have to take its turn, but instinct and judgement compensate: this is a wonderful cheese. She won first prize with it at Nantwich in 1992, and first prize with Bonnet (below) for three consecutive years, but has never entered for the British Cheese Awards: she should. The pasteurized version (rindless) is milder and less distinctive.

All the cheeses are made by the Dunlop method, which is similar to Cheddar but the curd is cut larger and scalded to a slightly lower temperature, which gives a moister result. After starter and rennet have been added, the curd is cut into 1.5-cm/^{1}/$_2$-inch squares; it is then scalded to 38°C/100°F and stirred 'for a wee while' before being left to settle. Draining and piling in blocks follow, as for Cheddar, until the acidity has risen; finally, it is milled and salted, moulded, and pressed. The unpasteurized cheeses are wrapped and matured in muslin: except for the larger Dunlops, which need longer, the maturing time is a minimum of six months.

BONNET (WITH RIND)

A hard goats' cheese; full-fat, unpasteurized milk; vegetarian rennet.
2.5kg/5lb 8oz truckles

This has virtually no flavour of goat, but tastes of blossom and herbs, with a soft lemon-like tang: it is very unusual and utterly delicious. When matured beyond six months, it becomes dryish and, like Swinzie, acquires a soft, smoky tang. The name originates from the local craft of making bonnets for Scottish regiments. As with Swinzie, the rindless pasteurized version is much milder.

DUNLOP (WITH RIND)

A hard cow's cheese; full-fat, unpasteurized milk; vegetarian rennet. 2.5kg/5lb 8oz and 50kg/110lb truckles; pasteurized 2.5kg/5lb 8oz truckles only

The cheese has a slightly fudgy, cohesive texture and mild but deep taste, predominantly of nuts but with earthy tones and a hint of smokiness; unlike Cheddar, it has virtually no salty tang.

The pasteurized version is almost unrecognizably different, with a silky texture and fresh, grassy flavour; if matured for over six months, it develops a caramel-like overtone faintly reminiscent of Emmental.

Isle of Mull Traditional Farmhouse Cheese

CHRIS AND JEFF READE, SGRIOB-RUADH FARM, TOBERMORY, ISLE OF MULL PA75 6QD. TEL: 01688 302235

We crossed to Mull on the small Lochaline ferry, which operates without fuss or formality: you simply drive to the water's edge and pay on the way over. The road to Tobermory is a 'major road with passing-places': on one side were woods carpeted with fern and on the other the Sound, with the silhouette of the mountains stretching northwards like the teeth of a saw, their peaks echoed by a magnificent cloudscape above. The Reades' farm is on a hill with a view not only of the mountains but south over the island to Ben More, from the top of which you can see as far as Ireland. In front of the house is a curiously shaped tall, gabled conservatory filled with hanging baskets and urns of flowers, which is used as a shop and tearoom; besides the flowers, it is furnished with a cheese-dale, or cheese storage-dresser, now used as the counter, and an old turning-dale for turning cheeses. The reason for its pointed shape is that it was the framework of the local village hall, transported up the hill and filled in with glass instead of boards.

Jeff and Chris were dairy-farmers in Somerset, producing milk only until, like Mike Davies (page 85), they became discouraged by the size of the milk lake: cheese was an obvious possibility, but competition in Somerset is harsh. As they were then approaching forty, 'the age when you start saying,

"If I don't do it now, I never will'", they decided to fulfil a long-standing wish and set up a cheese-farm in Scotland. They bought Sgriob-ruadh (the name means 'red furrow') on sight, even though it had been unoccupied for sixteen years and was almost a ruin: as the house had no roof, they began by living, with all four sons, in a caravan. By degrees, with the sons' help, they renovated it entirely themselves. Their final achievement has been to dig an underground cheese-store, the nearest possible equivalent to a cave; when we were there it was visible as a patch of concrete in the grass, but they were planning to turf it over, not only for aesthetic reasons but also to increase the humidity. Another imaginative touch, inspired by the need to keep the cows indoors for seven months of the year, is their four-star luxury cow-shed. The floor is covered with a six-inch-thick rubber carpet which is as springy and comfortable as a mattress; on top of this, instead of straw, is a colourful layer of shredded recycled paper, collected from all over the island.

They now have a closed herd of 100, mainly Friesians, but with a sprinkling of coffee-coloured Swiss cows, plus the odd Jersey and Ayrshire. As Jeff is the only dairy-farmer on Mull, they sell liquid milk as well as cheese, half the herd being used for each. Chris took lessons in Cheddar-making before leaving Somerset and makes the cheese, working entirely by herself, to a conventional Cheddar recipe. She is one of the only two cheesemakers I have met who prefers using winter to summer milk: she says that in winter, when she has complete control over the cows' diet, the quality is predictable, but when the cows are out at grass the taste can vary considerably. One year, she said, when they had just been let out to eat the new grass in May, the curd was unusable: she has never been able to work out exactly why. As well as large truckles, she makes a few small ones coated with wax called Tobermory Truckles, some of which are flavoured; the large cheeses are cloth-bound and matured for ten to twelve months.

ISLE OF MULL

A hard cows' cheese; full-fat, unpasteurized milk; traditional rennet.
22kg/48lb truckles

The Reades do not call their cheese Cheddar because it is not made in the traditional area and therefore tastes different from the Somerset version; however, it is sufficiently Cheddar-like to have been included in a tasting of six Cheddars organized by the Specialist Cheesemakers Association. It is paler than the West Country cheeses and distinguishable for a clean, light feel and flavours of the sea: the tang, which is strong, is correspondingly salty. It often has blue veins, especially under the rind: rather than being undesirable, these are a sign of maturity. Mail order is welcomed.

Wester Lawrenceton Cheeses

PAM AND NICK RODWAY, WESTER LAWRENCETON, BY FORRES, MORAY IV36 ORL. TEL: 01309 676566

I first heard about the Rodways' venture through a friend, Jane Heape, who used to make goats' cheeses but recently gave up and sold some of her goats to Pam. At the time of my visit, the dairy was still being converted, although sufficiently advanced to show that it would be spacious and well planned, with a milking-parlour for cows at one end and the goats' down the side. As she could not yet use it, Pam was making soft cows' and goats' cheeses in the kitchen which, because of the other food prepared there, she had (very rightly) pasteurized. Much to my surprise, I found that they were nevertheless quite exceptional, with a very unusual taste and varied subflavours. Later in the year, after her dairy was finished, she came to London with samples of the two matured cheeses she is now making, a hard goats' cheese and a cows' cheese which she had originally intended to mature for longer; however, it was so good as it was, at seven weeks old, that she had decided to sell at least some of it at that age.

The Rodways are deeply committed to organic principles: Nick has been a member of the Soil Association for thirty years and Pam has already made cheese on two organic farms. On one of the farms, near Edinburgh, she worked with ex-prisoners, drug abusers, and others in need of rehabilitation: 'Working on an organic farm turned around the lives of some of them quite dramatically,' she remarked. On the other, in Devon, she taught for the Yarner Trust and made a cheese called Welcome Barton. At Wester Lawrenceton, she and Nick have a flock of nearly 300 very free-ranging hens, the goats, of whom last summer there were twenty-four in milk and by now will be thirty-seven, and (last summer) four Ayrshires and a Jersey. To help finance the cows, they have launched a cow-share scheme by which ten families have bought a £500 share and in return receive £50-worth of products a year: for the moment, this means cheese, but eventually Pam will also make butter and yoghurt. (It should be added that the farm is ideally placed, since the organic community at Findhorn is only a few miles away.)

WESTER LAWRENCETON FRESH CHEESES

Fresh cows' and goats' cheeses; full-fat, organic pasteurized milk; vegetarian rennet.
Sold by weight in tubs

Both cheeses are smooth, fine-textured, and of a slightly firmer consistency than thick cream. The goats' in particular is remarkable for its subtle but distinctive taste, which includes virtually no trace of goat and is utterly different from the lemon-like tang of the cheeses further north: rather, it is short, cool, almost sweet, with a slight hint of nuts and a strong infusion of herbs. It is excellent on its own but is also delicious with fruit. I have tried to find an alternative available in the south for the recipes below but have failed: other soft goats' cheeses give either actively unpleasant or nondescript results. The cows' cheese is similar but milder and richer.

Wester Lawrenceton Blueberry Fool or Ice-Cream

This tastes wonderfully creamy yet intense, and could hardly be simpler to make: you do not even have to purée the fruit, which adds interest to the texture. It also makes excellent ice-cream. Blackberries can also be used but should be puréed: for the same amount of cheese and cream, you will need 225g/8oz berries and 75g/generous 2½oz caster sugar.

Cooking time: 5 minutes; 1½–2 hours to chill fool or at least 3½ to freeze ice-cream
For 3–4

100g/3½oz blueberries, washed
50g/1¾oz caster sugar
75ml/2½fl oz whipping cream, whipped stiff
100g/3½oz Wester Lawrenceton goats' cheese

Put the berries and sugar into a small saucepan and set it over very low heat until the berries are submerged in juice. Remove the pan from the heat and leave the berries until they are cold. Fold the cream into the cheese; then stir in the blueberries very gently. Chill the fool for 1½–2 hours.

For ice-cream, freeze it for 2¼–2½ hours, until it is frozen stiff round the edges but is still liquid in the middle. Beat quickly with a fork until it is homogenous but still stiff and re-freeze it for 1–1½ hours or until needed.

WESTER LAWRENCETON SWEET-MILK

A Dunlop-style semi-soft cows' cheese; full-fat, organic unpasteurized milk; vegetarian rennet. 1.6–4kg/3lb 8oz–8lb 13oz truckles

At seven weeks old, the cheese has the most delicious moist, semi-soft texture and a mild, pure, sweet taste with flavours of cream, butter, and wild flowers; by five months, it was hard, although moist, with a predominantly buttery taste and the promise of flowers to come. Older samples were not available at the time of writing: of the two I tried, I preferred the first.

WESTER LAWRENCETON GOATS' CHEESE

A hard goats' cheese; full-fat, organic unpasteurized milk; vegetarian rennet. 1.6–4kg/3lb 8oz–8lb 13oz truckles

The cheese has a pleasantly soft, smooth texture and, like the fresh goats' cheese, an unusual herbal tang with a hint of nuts. At five weeks, it is very mild; again, older samples were not available at the time of writing, but it can be expected to gain strength with age.

Highland Fine Cheeses Ltd
SUSANNAH STONE, KNOCKBRECK, TAIN, ROSS & CROMARTY.
TEL: 01862 892034

We drove to Tain from Ballater in late August, when the heather was just coming out and the moors, instead of blazing with colour, were a soft greenish purple. The hills were dotted with the white bodies and black faces of sheep; here and there were dark fir plantations which on the one hand interrupt the natural flow of the landscape, but on the other add contrast and scale. We crossed the Moray Firth at Inverness, and the Cromarty Firth via a long, low bridge like a causeway which makes you feel almost as if you are skimming the water. Knockbreck is a house to die for, large enough to seem spacious but small enough to be comfortable, with a view over a wide lawn and low-set double bow windows to make the most of the sun. Susannah told us that it is a sixteenth-century foundation, but had been devastated by raids and rebuilt around 1790 by her husband's ancestors. Later, they sold it, and it was eventually bought back by her father: she inherited it just at the point when she and her husband needed more space for the cheese (and, to begin with, privacy from the prying eye of the authorities).

Her account of how she started to make cheese was so racy that I wished I had brought a tape-recorder and could transcribe it verbatim. Before the war, everyone in the Highlands, including her mother-in-law, had made crowdie or, to give it its local name, 'gruth'; afterwards, mainly because of the Milk Marketing Board, it disappeared. However, her husband had a nostalgic longing for it and asked her to make some. She knew how because she had watched her mother-in-law, but had never actually tried, and started by buying a churn of 45 litres/10 gallons of milk, which she almost immediately realized was far too much. It was supposed to be left to sour naturally in the sun or by the fire: instead, she stood it in warm water in the bath. After two days it showed no sign of curdling; on the third, her husband, fed up with not being able to use the bath, went to the chemist and bought a packet of lactophyllic acid pills (normally used for babies), which curdled it very effectively. The next stage is to cook the curds to the consistency of scrambled eggs: Susannah achieved this by simply running in the hottest possible bath water. Finally, she hung up the curds to drain in a pillowcase. The result was delicious, but even her husband could not eat it all: they therefore took the surplus to the local grocer, who was very scathing, remarking that nobody liked crowdie any more. It sold out immediately, so the Stones, who were chronically short of money, made more, first with two churns and 90 litres/20 gallons of milk, then with three.

However, as its popularity grew, so did the Stones' worry about the local sanitary inspector. Soon after graduating to three churns, they moved to Knockbreck, where, unable to afford a proper dairy, they made the cheese in the secrecy of the cellar and, as a further precaution, took to working at night. Even after they built a dairy, their troubles were not over, chiefly because, while it was under construction, the sanitary inspector asked the builder where the drains would be, and the builder jokingly replied that there were not going to be any. This seemed to confirm the inspector's worst suspicions, and thereafter he harassed them on every possible occasion. They were also threatened with competition from the Milk Marketing Board, which began to manufacture a rival brand of crowdie, but this turned out to be to their advantage, since the Board's version went mouldy and they were able to pick up all its customers.

Susannah now has an impeccable modern dairy, a staff of ten (part-time so that mothers can look after their children), and makes five varieties of cheese: crowdie, two cheeses flavoured with garlic, Hramsa and Galic, and two cream cheeses, Gruth Dhu and Caboc. She pasteurizes because the milk is bought, but compensates by using a custom-made starter designed to give the traditional flavour of the cheese by reintroducing specific local bacteria. The crowdies are still made to her mother-in-law's recipe, with a jacketed vat to replace a fire or the bath, and Caboc to a recipe said to have been used in the sixteenth century by her ancestor Mariota de Ile, daughter of The Macdonald, Lord of the Isles.

HIGHLAND CROWDIE (LOW-FAT)

A soft, fresh cows' cheese; low-fat, pasteurized milk; rennet-free. 140g/5oz pots and 2kg/4lb 6oz tubs

Crowdie is made with skimmed milk to which enough cream has been returned to bring the fat content to the equivalent of hand-skimmed milk. The texture is as light, mousse-like, and melting as fresh sheep's cheese; presumably thanks to the starter, the taste includes not only the lemon-like tang which is characteristic of the northern Highlands and Orkney, but also undertones of earth and flowers. It is a delight, and invaluable to anyone watching fat intake or calories. The traditional partner to crowdie is oatcakes; alternatively, eat it with Susannah's herb biscuits (page 18), specially designed to go with it. The cooked, low-fat curds are unsuitable for heating but can be mixed into excellent creams or pâtés.

At the time of going to press, a full-fat version which is pleasantly creamy but much milder was being considered but had not yet been put into production.

Highland Whisky Cream

For 4

125g/4¹/₂oz low-fat Highland Crowdie
100g/3¹/₂oz icing sugar
142ml/¹/₄ pint whipping cream, stiffly whipped
1 tbsp freshly squeezed lemon juice
1 tbsp whisky

Beat the cheese and sugar together: the mixture will seem very stiff at first but will become moist as mixing proceeds. Fold in the cream; then stir in the lemon juice and whisky. Chill for 2 hours or more before serving.

HRAMSA AND GALIC

A soft, fresh cows' cheese flavoured with wild garlic; full-fat, pasteurized milk; rennet-free. 140g/5oz pots or 1kg/2lb 4oz logs; Galic: 110g/3³/₄oz or 1kg/2lb 4oz logs

The garlic comes from Black Rock Gorge, near Evanton (the name 'Hramsa' is the Saxon word for wild garlic). The texture of the cheese is again deliciously light and frothy; the flavour of the garlic, although quite strong, is soft and aromatic.

Galic is similar to Hramsa but is rolled in toasted hazlenuts: the name is derived from 'garlic' and 'Gaelic'.

GRUTH DHU

A soft, fresh cows' cheese; 50%-fat, pasteurized milk; rennet-free. 110g/3³/₄oz or 1kg/2lb 4oz logs

Gruth Dhu is made of two-thirds Crowdie and one-third double cream, and rolled in pin-head oatmeal and peppercorns. It has an exceptionally light texture and rich taste, with a faint lemon tang and strong earthy undertones.

CABOC

A soft, fresh double-cream cows' cheese rolled in toasted oatmeal; full-fat, pasteurized milk; rennet-free. 110g/3³/₄oz or 1kg/2lb 4oz logs

Caboc has a light, melting texture like the other cheeses, but with a sharp lemon tang. It is particularly good with digestive biscuits.

The story associated with this cheese is that the heiress Mariota de Ile was hidden under a cheese-barrel at the age of twelve in the attempt to save her from a rival family, the Campbells, who planned to abduct and marry her for the sake of her castle and lands. The Campbells found her and carried her off to Cawdor Castle but it seems that she had the last word, since she outlived her first husband and married again, this time perhaps according to her own choice.

Seator's Orkney

HILDA SEATOR, GRIMBISTER FARM, GRIMBISTER, FINNSTOWN,
KIRKWALL, ORKNEY KW15 1TT. TEL: 01856 761318

The east coast of Scotland above Tain is relatively flat, although higher-lying than it seems, as one realizes from the periodic descent of the road into steep, wooded estuary valleys; except in the shelter of the valleys, trees become sparser the further north you go. Leaving the coast, the country is featureless bog and grassland, relieved only by the blackened area of a peat farm and the silhouette of a group of hills to the west. The ferry to Stromness, in contrast, takes you close to the nearest Orkney island, Hoy, which has a volcanic-looking mountain and extraordinary red sandstone cliffs horizontally seamed and worn into pillars and milk-bottle shapes reminiscent of the rock formations in the Painted Desert: most eye-catching of all is a gigantic pillar standing alone in the sea, the Old Man of Hoy, which looks like some grand, prehistoric monument.

Grimbister Farm is on the main island about halfway between Stromness and Kirkwall, standing on the side of a hill overlooking the sea and a vista of islands which includes Garsay, Shapinsay, and two tiny ones in the bay below, one of which is uninhabited. Only Hoy is mountainous; the rest of Orkney is rolling or flat, and almost completely treeless. Once you have become used to it, you realize that treelessness is the essential ingredient in the openness and sense of space which is the islands' peculiar charm. At one time, there were more trees than today, but early settlers who migrated from mainland Scotland were attracted by the fact that they could graze their animals without having to clear the land of forest.

The Seators keep a herd of Charolais and Aberdeen Angus cattle for beef and fourteen Friesians for the cheese; they also have two handsome chestnut horses, ridden by Hilda, and grow barley. The dairy herd is kept to fourteen, with calving in rotation, because she could not handle more milk without an assistant. She has made the cheese every day for twenty-seven years, using a traditional recipe absolutely unchanged except for the replacement of animal rennet, which she can no longer buy, with the genetically engineered equivalent, Chymosin. Neither she nor the other Orcadian cheesemakers given here use starter, which helps to account for the unusually distinctive local taste of their cheeses: in her case, the acidity is given plenty of time to develop by the fact that cheesemaking is spread over twenty-four hours.

SEATOR'S ORKNEY

A fresh cows' cheese; unpasteurized; vegetarian rennet.
675g–3.2kg/1½–7lb truckles

Seator's Orkney is crumbly and fairly moist, especially when just made. When new, it is gentle and delicate, tasting mainly of milk, but after a few days it develops the lemon-like tang characteristic both of crowdie and the other Orkney cheeses. The one I bought on the day of my visit was relatively mild, even at two weeks old, but others I have tasted have been surprisingly deep and powerful, with a taste like a mixture of lemon zest and the sea shot with the sweetness of honey and wild flowers. The plain version, particularly when mature, is delicious accompanied by bananas. As the cheeses are sent to Neal's Yard by post, they are not available from July to early September because of the weather.

Chymosin is added while the milk is still warm from the cow and the curd is left to set for three to four hours; it is then broken by hand and allowed to stand for another three to four hours before being drained and left overnight. Next morning, it is broken by hand again and salted; flavouring is also added when required (flavourings include chives, garlic, caraway, walnut, and pineapple). Moulding and pressing follow, after which the cheeses can be eaten straight away or kept for up to two weeks. Most are sold locally; the rest (plain only) go to Neal's Yard Dairy in London.

Lairobell Goats

JOCK AND HATTY BELL, EAST LAIRO, SHAPINSAY, ORKNEY KW17
2DZ. TEL: 01856 711341

The quay at Balfour, on Shapinsay, has to be one of the prettiest in Britain: just a couple of old houses overshadowed (figuratively speaking) by the incongruous but splendidly romantic castle, built by the Balfour family in 1848 and now run as a hotel. The rest of the village consists of not much more than a few hundred metres/yards of street, the school, and one of the two shops on the island. To reach East Lairo, we drove up tiny roads through a hinterland of continuous green; the farm is small, with only 2.4ha/6 acres, but every yard and stone is lovingly cherished, although the Bells' priority is clear: their own needs are incidental beside the welfare of their goats.

Jock spent most of his earlier life in the police force, ending up as a chief detective-inspector; however, his father was a racehorse trainer and he grew up with a love of dogs as well as horses. His attention was first attracted to Hatty by the fact that she had a German Shepherd dog with a leg in plaster. 'He didn't marry me. He married the dog,' said Hatty cheerfully. He retired early after breaking his back; they decided to move to Orkney as a result of seeing a property advertisement in a newspaper. Hatty had always wanted to keep goats; he planned 'you know, to do a little writing and painting.' They started off modestly with a couple of mixed-breed goats, giving the surplus milk to pigs: making cheese did not occur to them until, again as a result of seeing an advertisement, Jock bought Hatty a pure-bred Toggenburg called Kelly for Christmas. Kelly had star quality: she completely captivated Jock, won a string of shows, filling their sitting room with rosettes, and, because they felt that the goats on Orkney were too inbred, impelled them to buy their first billy. Soon, the increase in the herd prompted Hatty to take a cheesemaking course and evolve Lairobell, which she continued to make until arthritis intervened; Jock then took over the cheesemaking and she now looks after and entertains the goats. In particular, she is in sole charge of the billies, since during the rutting season they will fight any male of any species on sight, including Jock (it seems that in nature, survival of the fittest means that billies in a herd will fight until only one or two are left).

Although not registered as such, the farm is organic, not on preconceived principle but because when they arrived Jock was repelled by the 'oily gunge', caused by heavy use of fertilizer, which squelched over his Wellingtons every time it rained. It was years before it disappeared, but he was eventually rewarded by its replacement with good, clean mud. Besides the varied herbage in their fields, the goats are fed on home-grown hay, rationed portions of home-grown nettles and kale, homemade concentrate, and afternoon snacks of peanuts, carrot-chips, and cooking apples.

LAIROBELL

A semi-hard goats' cheese; unpasteurized; vegetarian rennet. 1.1kg/2lb 7oz, 1.4kg/3lb, 1.6kg/3lb 8oz, and 1.8kg/4lb truckles

It is a tribute perhaps above all to Hatty's scrupulous housework on behalf of the goats, whose quarters she cleans out completely every other day, that the cheese truly does not taste of goat at all. When young, it has a lemon-like Highland tartness combined with a taste of grass and the sweetness of wild flowers, which grow freely in the goats' fields; by five or six weeks, the tartness has given way to a gentle, citrus tang. In particular, the lemon taste is wonderfully complemented by olive bread.

The cheese is made every day earlier in the season but by the time of our visit, in late July, only every other day; as this suggests, there is no milk in the winter, but Jock makes a longer-matured cheese in the autumn so that he has something to sell throughout the year. The dairy is equipped with a de-humidifier because of high humidity and wide variations in temperature; Jock also avoids stainless steel, which would encourage condensation.

Like Hilda Seator, he does not use starter: the milk is warmed to 28–29°C/82–84°F before the addition of rennet, left to set for half an hour, and the curd cut into 2.5-cm/1-inch cubes. After another half-hour, it is scalded and stirred gently and left to rest for a further thirty minutes; it is then drained and left briefly again before being cut into blocks and, instead of piling, merely turned at intervals over two hours. When it is 'nice and ready', it is broken by hand almost to a powder and salted; this is followed by moulding in cloths moistened with hot water and light initial pressing. Finally, the cheeses are remoulded, trimmed, and pressed at increasing pressure for a total of fourteen hours. All are requisitioned in advance: a few small ones go to local shops and restaurants and the rest to Iain Mellis in Edinburgh and Glasgow.

Wheems

CHRISTINA SARGENT AND MIKE ROBERTS, WHEEMS, EASTSIDE, SOUTH RONALDSAY, ORKNEY KW17 2TJ. TEL: 01856 831537

Mike and Christina are among the very few who carry on the pre-industrial tradition of making cheese with the surplus milk of just one household cow, although in fact they have two so that they have milk all the year round. Less because of small output than Mike's principles, which dictate that food should be produced and eaten locally if possible, the cheese is only to be had in Orkney: we tasted it at the Creel Inn, St Margaret's Hope, where the cooking is equalled only by the excellence of the ingredients (I can testify to the perfectly fresh fish, full-flavoured Orkney steak served that night with slices of black pudding, and not only local cheeses but strawberries which actually had flavour).

Before coming to Wheems, Mike and Christina tried communal organic farming in Devon and considered settling in Shetland, but were attracted to Orkney by the survival of the custom of mixing different activities together and the lively atmosphere it creates. There is not much demand here for landscape architecture, which is Mike's original profession; however, Christina, as both artist and musician, generates a string of commissions and concert and teaching engagements: 'I'm afraid it's all very rushed here – overflowing with vegetables and now school has restarted and I have to think flutes and clarinets when I haven't finished felt commissions and the shops are running out of cards...'. Most of Mike's time is devoted to looking after a large market garden and organizing a vegetable box scheme: extra help is supplied by WWOOFers (Willing Workers On Organic Farms), who come to the islands from all over the world. This, in turn, means that, along with her other commitments, Christina necessarily runs a hostel.

They also keep ducks and hens, and, until lack of time forced them to give up, milked and made cheeses from sheep. Christina fell in love with the first cow, Gretel, a Jersey, twelve years ago and gave her to Mike as a birthday present; the second, Gelda, is Gretel's daughter. Christina makes the cheese daily in summer and two or three times a week in winter from one milking; the other milking is used for drinking, yoghurt, and butter.

WHEEMS

An organic, semi-hard Jersey cheese; unpasteurized milk; vegetarian rennet.
1.25kg/2lb 12oz truckles

The texture of Wheems is crumbly and aerated with tiny holes, almost like a soufflé. At only a few days old, the cheese has a sharp lemon tang; after two weeks, however, it has developed a wonderfully rich, creamy taste with a strong suggestion of honey and only a faint hint of lemon. When toasted, it leaches fat, like other Jersey cheeses, but gains rather than loses flavour and has a pleasantly gritty, nutty feel. (See page 162 for a lemon tart recipe.)

The cheese is made without starter for the sake of organic purity; at the moment, the rennet is ordinary vegetarian, but Mike would be happier if they could find an alternative made from ingredients which he could trace to source. After rennet is added and the curd has set, it is cut into 1.5-cm/$^{1}/_{2}$-inch squares and left to stand for about two hours while the acidity rises; this is followed by gentle scalding, during which, instead of the usual stirring, it is broken by hand. It is then left to settle, drained, and hung up in a cloth overnight. In the morning, it is broken up by hand again, salted, and finally moulded and pressed. The usual maturing time is about two weeks.

Index

Cheeses

Organic cheeses are marked with an asterisk (*).

cows'

soft and fresh

Caboc (Highland Fine Cheeses), 246

Cornish Pepper, Herb and Garlic (Lynher), 113

*Crannog (Loch Arthur Creamery), 232

Elmhirst (Sharpham Creamery), 109

Galic (Highland Fine Cheeses), 246

Gruth Dhu (Highland Fine Cheeses), 246

Highland Crowdie, 245

Hramsa (Highland Fine Cheeses), 246

Jervaulx (Fortmayne Farm), 209

Seator's Orkney, 248

Wealden Round (Neal's Yard Creamery), 175

Wester Lawrenceton Fresh Cheeses, 242

Yorvik (Fortmayne Farm), 209

mould-ripened

Bath Soft (Park Farm), 76

Belle d'Ecosse (Easter Weens), 229

Bonchester (Easter Weens), 227–8

Cooleeney, 122

Finn (Neal's Yard Creamery), 175

Kelston Park (Park Farm), 77

*Pencarreg, 158

St Killian (Carrigbyrne Farmhouse), 121

Sharpham, 108

Somerset Brie (Lubborn Cheese), 93–4

Somerset Camembert (Lubborn Cheese), 95

Teviotdale (Easter Weens), 229

York (Park Farm), 77

semi-soft

Make Me Rich (Northumberland), 223

Waterloo (Village Maid), 29

Wester Lawrenceton Sweet-milk, 243

semi-hard

Avalon (R. A. Duckett), 79

Beamish (Swaledale), 217

Caerphilly (Teifi), 157

Carron Lodge Lancashire, 200

Caws Cenarth, 165

Caws Mamgu (Caws Cenarth), 165

Cotherstone, 219

Devon Garland (Peverstone), 97

Doddington (North Doddington Farm), 224

Duckett's Caerphilly, 78–9

Duckett's Smoked Caerphilly 80

Gorwydd Caerphilly, 161–2

Hereford Hop (Malvern), 168

Hunting Pink (Peverstone), 97

King Richard III Wensleydale (Fortmayne), 208

Kirkham's Lancashire, 196

Knightswood (Peverstone), 96–7

Llangloffan Coloured Cheshire, 154

St Cuthbert's Cave (North Doddington), 225

St Laudus (Menallack Farm), 115

Sandham's Lancashire, 197–8

Swaledale Cows, 216–17

Tiskey Meadow (Peverstone), 97

Wedmore (R. A. Duckett), 80

*Wheems, 252

White Wensleydale, 205

hard

Appleby's Cheshire, 179

Appleby's Double Gloucester, 180

*Ashdown Foresters (Sussex High Weald), 45

Berwick Edge (North Doddington Farm), 225

Coolea, 143

Coquetdale (Northumberland), 222

Cornish Yarg (Lynher Dairies), 113

Desmond (West Cork), 137

Double Berkeley (Charles Martell), 66

Double Worcester (Ansteys of Worcester), 171

Dunlop, 239

Gabriel (West Cork), 136–7

Harefield (Smart's), 63

Hereford Hop (Charles Martell), 64–5

Isle of Mull, 240–1

Keen's Cheddar, 91

Lincolnshire Poacher, 193

Llanboidy, 150–1

Llangloffan, 152

*Loch Arthur Organic Farmhouse Cheese, 230–1

Menallack, 114

Montgomery's Cheddar, 88–9

Mrs Rhodes' Farmhouse Toaster, 200

Northumberland, 221

*Old Plaw Hatch Organic 40

Old Scotland, 35

Old Worcester White (Ansteys), 170

Olde Sussex (Mike Turner's Dairy), 53

*Penbryn, 149–50

Peverstone 'Tasty' Cheddar, 99

Quicke's Traditional Cheddar, 102

Quicke's Traditional Oak-smoked Cheddar, 103

Quicke's Traditional Red Leicester, 103

Recipes and Makers